DISCARD

warblers & woodpeckers

warblers & woodpeckers

a
father-son
big year of
birding

SNEED B. COLLARD III

**MOUNTAINEERS
BOOKS**

For Braden

MOUNTAINEERS BOOKS is the publishing division of The Mountaineers, an organization founded in 1906 and dedicated to the exploration, preservation, and enjoyment of outdoor and wilderness areas.

1001 SW Klickitat Way, Suite 201, Seattle, WA 98134
800.553.4453, www.mountaineersbooks.org

Printed in the United States of America
Distributed in the United Kingdom by Cordee, www.cordee.co.uk

21 20 19 18   1 2 3 4 5

Design and layout: Kate Basart/Union Pageworks

Library of Congress Cataloging-in-Publication Data
Names: Collard, Sneed B., author.
Title: Warblers and woodpeckers : a father-son big year of birding /
    Sneed B. Collard III.
Description: Seattle, WA : Mountaineers Books, [2018]
Identifiers: LCCN 2018020636| ISBN 9781680511369 (paperback) |
    ISBN 9781680511376 (ebook)
Subjects: LCSH: Bird watching—United States—Anecdotes. | Bird watchers—
    United States—Anecdotes. | Collard, Sneed B. | Fathers and sons—Anecdotes.
Classification: LCC QL677.5 .C62 2018 | DDC 598.072/3473—dc23
LC record available at https://lccn.loc.gov/2018020636

Mountaineers Books titles may be purchased for corporate, educational, or other promotional sales, and our authors are available for a wide range of events. For information on special discounts or booking an author, contact our customer service at 800-553-4453 or mbooks@mountaineersbooks.org.

♻ Printed on recycled paper

ISBN (hardcover): 978-1-68051-136-9
ISBN (ebook): 978-1-68051-137-6

contents

april 1, 2016, southeastern arizona

Braden and I pulled into a gas station at the western edge of Doug-las, Arizona. Across the street stood the county jail, surrounded by fifteen-foot fencing and spools of razor wire that glinted menacingly in the desert sun.

It was only noon, but my son and I had already driven 150 miles and spent two hours at one of the meccas of American birding, Ramsey Canyon, on the flanks of the Huachuca Mountains. Now we prepared to veer off the beaten path to a destination less known and perhaps considerably more dangerous. To ensure success we needed what every explorer since John Wesley Powell had required—a full tank of gas and a family-size bag of Doritos.

After gassing up and settling with the cashier, I consulted my iPhone for directions to the San Bernardino National Wildlife Ref-uge. The Google Maps app had improved considerably since the era of Powell, but as we wended our way through quiet neighborhoods, down Fifteenth Street, and east onto a road that abruptly shed its pavement outside of town, I couldn't help but wonder if it might be leading us astray. I grew even more anxious when I realized that our moth- and fly-spattered rental car was the only civilian vehicle on the road. The vehicles we did see? Green-and-white SUVs emblazoned with Homeland Security logos and the words "Border Patrol" in block green letters.

"What are all these Border Patrol people doing here?" Braden asked as yet another agent roared past us.

Living in Montana as we did, the political and social realities of the US–Mexico border rarely entered dinner conversation, and I debated how much to say about them.

"Well," I hedged, "they're here to stop people from sneaking across the border, either to work or bring drugs over."

Braden's brow furrowed. "Is it dangerous here?"

"Uh, not really. There are some problems, but they are mostly on the other side of the border." Not my best effort at reassurance—and a little fast and loose with the facts—but I quickly added, "With these Border Patrol agents, we'll be safe."

"Why do they stare at us whenever we pass?"

"Just looking to see if we might be mules or coyotes," I said.

"Huh?"

"Never mind. I'll tell you later."

We followed the winding dirt road for fifteen miles, often within a couple hundred yards of the low fence that marked the boundary between nations. At a Y in the road we angled left, and our anticipation began to build at what we might see.

Our destination, the San Bernardino National Wildlife Refuge, had been established to protect critically endangered freshwater fish species such as the Yaqui Topminnow and Yaqui Chub. Braden and I, though, had come in the hope that we might score some migrating waterfowl and one particular bird species that could only be found here and one or two other places in the Lower 48—the Green Kingfisher. With their stylish looks, giant bills, and dynamic personalities, kingfishers are some of our favorite birds, and the Green Kingfisher's rarity would make it an especially vaunted addition to a Big Year list we hoped would top 250 species by December 31.

"The entrance should be right up here," Braden said, studying the map on my phone.

"Look, there it is!" I exclaimed, preparing to swing right, into the refuge.

I braked and turned—only to narrowly avoid crashing into two locked gates brandishing a sign: Road Closed.

"What?" Braden shouted, outraged.

"You've got to be kidding," I said, slamming my hand on the steering wheel. "This is public land! This is a public refuge!"

I looked over at Braden, "Is it a holiday today?"

He shook his head. "I don't think so."

"Well, crap."

"Look, it says the refuge is open to foot traffic," Braden said, reading further. "We can walk in."

After backing away from the gate, I parked the car in an adjacent, empty parking area, and we tumbled out. Although a nearby sign and map indicated a hike of only a mile or so to the ponds and riverbed that might hold the Green Kingfisher, my enthusiasm for such a trek dipped firmly into the "reluctant" category. Staring across the flat, dry landscape bristling with cholla cactus and mesquite, I could feel serious heat building on the giant frying pan of a desert surrounding us, and I knew it would only grow more intense as the afternoon progressed.

"What do you think?" I asked Braden.

His slack body language reflected my own ambivalence, but he said, "We're here. We might as well try it."

I sighed but nodded. Braden didn't always push himself in situations like this one, and, although I didn't look forward to the hike, I appreciated that he was willing to go for it.

"Let's bring water," I told him.

As we readied our packs, I heard the low hum of insects in the surrounding desert but didn't pay it much attention. I shoved a bottle of water into my fanny pack, slathered some sunscreen on both of us, locked the car, and asked, "Ready?"

"Yeah," Braden said, and we stepped over a metal bar and through a fence into the refuge. The humming of insects grew louder, but I continued to pay it little notice. Looking at the large refuge sign across the entrance road, I said, "Buddy, go stand next to that sign so I can take a picture."

Braden took a couple of steps forward and halted. In a frightened voice, he asked, "What are all these bees doing here?"

"What?"

I glanced up from my camera and for the first time noticed dozens—make that *hundreds*—of bees surrounding us. Even though he had recently turned thirteen, Braden harbored a serious insect phobia. Usually, in the presence of a bee or moth or dragonfly, I calmly encouraged him to relax.

Now alarm bells rang in my head. Because I'd written several books on invasive species, two words flashed through my mind: killer bees!

Relying on my extensive knowledge of invasive species and my acute analytical and organizational skills, I quickly formulated a plan.

"Run!"

Like startled jackrabbits, Braden and I tore off down the dirt road. We covered two hundred yards, all the while expecting to feel stingers piercing our flesh. We kept running, glancing over our shoulders as the bees fell farther behind, and finally, when I could no longer hear buzzing in my ears or see insects on our trail, I slowed, panting. Braden stopped ahead of me.

"Are you all right?" I asked.

"What are they *doing* there?" Braden demanded. Though neither of us had gotten stung, I could see that he was shaken.

"I don't know."

Guilt swept through me. I'd anticipated a dozen kinds of problems we might encounter on this trip, but killer bees hadn't been one of them.

Great parenting, I told myself, *especially for a kid terrified of insects.*

Still, I tried to stay upbeat.

"We're all right now," I told Braden. "They didn't follow us. Take a deep breath and drink some water." I gave him a reassuring hug and waited until he'd calmed down before we continued marching down the hot, dusty road. We saw a Northern Harrier swoop over creosote plants a hundred yards away and glimpsed some other little birds flitting between the mesquite trees. Braden's mood began to recover, and I thought, *Maybe this is going to work out after all.*

And that's when the second swarm of bees surrounded us.

"Run!" I again shouted.

Again we hauled off down the road as fast as our boots could carry us. Again we escaped being stung, but this time tears filled Braden's eyes.

"I don't like this place!" he yelled, walking frantically in circles, even more agitated than before.

"I know," I told him, "but watch where you're stepping. There are probably rattlesnakes out here too."

Braden exploded. "Will you stop telling me about dangerous things? The drug dealers, the killer bees, the rattlesnakes! I want to get out of here!"

"I'm sorry, son. I agree. We should head back to the car."

Just then, an official refuge truck approached with two men in it. They pulled over to say hello, and I noticed that neither of them wore uniforms.

"Does this road ever open up?" I asked them.

"No, not since 9/11," one said.

"Homeland Security," the other one added.

"Well, do you think you could give us a ride down there?" I asked. "We've already run into two swarms of Africanized bees."

"No kidding? I wish we could, but it's the liability thing. We're just volunteers ourselves. But have a nice day."

Yeah, you too—and thanks for the help.

Frustrated and anxious, Braden and I started walking back to the car, keeping a sharp ear out for more buzzing sounds. Braden paused to study some rather drab, nondescript birds in a nearby creosote bush.

"Black-throated Sparrows!" he proclaimed.

"What? Really?" I asked. I had never heard of a Black-throated Sparrow, but it turned out to be a Life bird—or Lifer—for both of us, a species that we had never seen before and, as such, counted toward our Life lists and our Big Year lists. More important, these new birds helped take Braden's mind off the threats surrounding us.

Fortunately we didn't encounter any more marauding bee swarms, but about a quarter mile from the parking lot Braden suddenly halted and pointed at the road ahead.

"Daddy, look!" he hissed, lifting his camera.

I raised my binoculars. "What?" At first I didn't see it. Then a camouflaged shape about the size of a chicken emerged through the lenses.

"Greater Roadrunner!" Braden exclaimed.

I'd glimpsed a roadrunner earlier in the day, but this was Braden's first—and another Lifer. The bird gave us only a quick look before scurrying off into the creosote, but it was enough. A grin like a crescent moon spread across Braden's face, and he raised his hand for a high five.

I slapped his palm. "Does that make up for the killer bees?" I asked.

He took a few steps to think about it.

"Maybe," he said.

CHAPTER 2

blame owen wilson

The idea to do a Big Year had first entered our brains thanks to a movie my wife, Amy, had picked for us to watch a couple of years earlier. That movie, based on Mark Obmascik's entertaining book *The Big Year: A Tale of Man, Nature, and Fowl Obsession*, featured a trio of rabid birders in pursuit of the North American single-year species count record. Neither Braden nor I had read the book, but the film version starred three of our favorite actors—Owen Wilson, Jack Black, and Steve Martin—and we enjoyed it so much that we watched it two more times before returning it to Crazy Mike's Video down the street.

I'll admit that before seeing the movie Braden and I had never heard of a Big Year. That's not to say that we didn't take an interest in birds. Every year we gave money to the Audubon Society, and I'd written four children's books focusing on the wonder and diversity of bird life. For several years our family also had enjoyed watching and identifying birds that visited our backyard feeder: Black-capped Chickadees, Dark-eyed Juncos, and White-breasted Nuthatches, along with occasional more dazzling species such as Evening Grosbeaks, American Goldfinches, and once a Lazuli Bunting.

Still, it wasn't until we watched *The Big Year* that Braden—not quite eleven at the time—embraced birding for himself. With the closing credits still rolling, he turned to me and said, "Daddy, we should do a Big Year."

"Okay," I said.

It was a rash, impulsive response for a parent, but I appreciated my son's interest and wanted to encourage it. I also confess that I thought it unlikely we'd ever follow through with the enterprise. Amy and I had seen other interests migrate through our household—and keep going—and I figured we'd probably bird for a while and then move on to something else.

To my surprise, Braden stayed focused. Together we began visiting local nature areas, keeping bird journals and tallying species. That year Braden's interest benefited from two once-in-a-lifetime travel opportunities. In June, Amy's parents took him on a weeklong National Geographic cruise to the island of Svalbard, high in the Arctic Circle. He returned a transformed kid, gushing about kittiwakes, alcids, jaegers, Ivory Gulls, eider ducks, and other birds I'd only vaguely heard of.

Later in the year I had the opportunity to travel to Taiwan as a visiting author. I spent a delightful week with students and staff at the Taipei American School, and then Amy brought Braden and our eight-year-old daughter, Tessa, over to join me. After bicycling and eating our way through Taipei, we circumnavigated the island by train. Birding wasn't the focus of the trip, but Braden and I stayed alert to interesting avifauna and picked up our first bulbuls, wagtails, mynahs, and babblers.

Neither of these trips contributed to a Big Year, which considered species strictly from the official checklist of the American Birding Association (ABA) for the Lower 48, Alaska, and Canada. The trips *did* cement Braden's fascination with birds—a fascination that would only increase.

Braden and I wrapped up our first Big Year with a less-than-electrifying count of 120 or so bird species. The following year we decided to back away from simply tallying species and instead focus on improving our birding skills. I began trying to get a real handle on identifying ducks and local Montana songbirds. For Braden's birthday, Amy and I bought him the second edition of *The Sibley Guide to Birds*, and it became his regular bedtime reading.

When he entered sixth grade at Washington Middle School, Braden met an astonishing birder his own age. Nick Ramsey lived part-time with his mother in town but spent the balance of his time with his father on a private fifteen-thousand-acre wildlife reserve called MPG Ranch, just south of Missoula. Late in the spring, Nick invited Braden to MPG for a weekend of birding, and Braden came home with twenty or thirty new Lifers and a dozen stories to tell. More importantly, he had found a peer who shared his passion for birds.

The rest of the year Braden and Nick birded together whenever opportunities arose. One weekend I took them to a place I'd discovered while researching my book *Fire Birds: Valuing Natural Wildfires and Burned Forests*. In the Blue Mountain burn area outside of Missoula we hiked through the so-called "dead forest," racking up Hairy Woodpeckers, House Wrens, Western Tanagers, and both Western and Mountain Bluebirds. During a lull in the action, I said, "Let's stop and sit on this log for a while and see what shows up."

We broke out peanut butter sandwiches and stared up at a dazzling mountainside draped with lupine, paintbrush, and Arrowleaf Balsam Root.

Suddenly we heard a loud Velcro-like tearing sound behind us.

"Run!" Nick yelled.

We scrambled up the slope just as a thirty-foot dead larch tree crashed to the ground.

Wide-eyed, we gaped at each other.

"Did you see that?" Nick shouted.

"It almost fell on top of us!" Braden said.

The tree would have missed us by a good five or six feet, but who said birding couldn't offer an adrenaline rush?

Even though we weren't doing a Big Year, several more birding adventures awaited us over the next few months. I co-led Braden and his Boy Scout troop on a weeklong canoe trip on the Missouri, where each evening we witnessed armadas of Common Nighthawks soaring above the river. Braden, Nick, and I hit the bird ponds around Warm Springs, near Butte, where in one morning we tallied more than sixty species, including a Prairie Falcon and hundreds of

Yellow-rumped Warblers. Back in our own Missoula neighborhood, an explosion of Evening Grosbeaks descended on us, filling the cottonwood and pine trees for more than a week. Nick also took Braden back to MPG Ranch for another long, glorious weekend of birding.

As the months passed, Braden's voice grew deeper, and he began to shave. His interest in birds intensified. As our second year of birding wound down, he began telling me, *basso profundo*, "Daddy, I want to do another Big Year next year."

This time I gave more consideration to my response.

"Uh, I don't know, Buddy."

I welcomed the idea—at least in theory. What dad wouldn't want to spend a year outdoors with his kid, exploring the country, looking for wildlife? The reality was that I didn't feel up to the task. Despite my best efforts, my skill at identifying birds by sight still wobbled between poor and pathetic. Further handicapping me, I had lost much of the high range of my hearing and had suffered from tinnitus since my early twenties—a product of junior high school band, too many headphone sessions with the Rolling Stones, and a punishing scuba diving class in college. My impeded hearing robbed me of a vital tool for mastering bird identification: the ability to learn—and even detect—species by their songs.

On a more practical level, Amy and I didn't have the financial resources for an all-out assault on North America's bird species. Birding could be expensive—especially when you had to fly to different parts of the country to pursue your quarry. Finally, there was this little thing called work that I felt duty-bound to continue, both to pay the bills and fulfill my social contract with society.

Still, I thought, even if my hearing sucked and my skills were lagging, Braden was probably ready for a real Big Year. He knew birds well enough that we could figure out most of what we encountered. If we brought cameras along and took pictures to help us identify birds later, we might be able to bag 200 or even 250 species.

Also weighing favorably in the decision, several economical travel opportunities had emerged that might make a modest Big Year feasible. As usual, Braden and I would be traveling to Missouri in March, where I would speak at the Children's Literature Festival held at the University of Central Missouri in Warrensburg. Even more exciting, in April I would participate in an annual educational conference in Houston.

"Houston could be crazy for birding in April," I told Braden. "Tons of species should be migrating north from Central and South America. If we went a few days early, we might pick up a hundred birds there alone!"

Beyond that, we'd signed up Braden for weeklong Boy Scout trips to Puget Sound and Glacier National Park, and I felt sure we could probably find ways to visit one or two other regions of the country through my work—or my credit card limit. Even if we didn't, one more factor finally convinced me to jump on board.

Even though he still called me "Daddy," Braden was growing up.

With him about to turn thirteen, I wondered how much longer he would want to hang around with his dad.

I had no idea, but I did recognize that I couldn't afford to miss an opportunity that might never come again. Before making a final decision, I asked Amy what she thought.

"He would love it," she said.

"What about the cost?"

"We'll make it work," she said. "If this is important to you, you should do it. Besides, it will be more difficult to pull him out of school for birding once he's in high school."

My wife's support cinched it. If Braden wanted to do another Big Year, I was in.

arctic beginnings

January 2, 2016.

With the morning light still faint in the sky, I crept into Braden's room and shook his shoulder.

"C'mon, son. Let's see some birds."

Normally groggy in the morning, he popped up wide-eyed. "Are we going?"

There'd been some doubt about our official Big Year kickoff because of a possible snowstorm, but I grinned and said, "Yeah. Get dressed."

Thirty minutes later I backed our gnarly four-wheel-drive mini-van out of the driveway. The sky hung heavy and cold over the Missoula Valley, and the thermometer read seven degrees Fahrenheit, but our spirits soared. After months of anticipation, we had officially begun our quest to have our best birding year ever.

Like all other self-respecting birders, we had originally planned to begin our Big Year on January 1 but agreed to postpone our official start a day so that our family could participate in a YMCA New Year's Day mini-triathlon. That may have been a tactical mistake given that the thermometer dropped ten degrees that night. Still, we'd rolled the dice and were eager to take what we could get the next morning.

"How many species do you think we'll see today?" Braden asked as I navigated the minivan through Missoula's empty streets.

"A couple of hundred at least."

He threw me what I called "the adolescent look," an expression of barely contained intolerance of his father's juvenile sense of humor.

"Seriously, Daddy. How many?"

"Hmm. I'm guessing twenty-five," I said. "How about you?"

"Maybe twenty-eight."

We agreed to shoot for twenty-seven, and by the time we reached US Highway 93 at the south end of town we had picked up Black-billed Magpie, American Crow, and Rock Dove. Even better, we were heading to our favorite go-to birding spot, the Lee Metcalf National Wildlife Refuge near Stevensville. Secretly I thought we might crack thirty or thirty-five birds—if everything flew our way.

As always, on the way down 93, I marveled at Montana's scenery. To our west, the dramatic Bitterroot Range—the same mountains that had almost snuffed out Lewis and Clark—rose like a snow-capped fortress a hundred miles long. To the east, across the wide valley, the less ostentatious Sapphire Range framed the horizon. With views like this, we didn't really need birds, yet they were our purpose. As we continued south, however, only the occasional Common Raven seemed to defy the gloomy weather and play along with our plans.

At Florence, I turned left to pick up the Eastside Highway and expected to see a few birds as we crossed over the Bitterroot River.

"You see anything?" I asked as we rumbled across the bridge.

"Not even a duck."

"I guess the birds just hunker down when it's this cold," I mumbled.

It wasn't until we almost reached the refuge that we spotted our first real prize—a big hawk perched on a telephone pole.

"What is it?" Braden asked, peering out the window as we whizzed by. "Do you think it's a Rough-legged?"

"I don't know. Let me turn around."

I pulled off on a side road and pointed the car back toward the hawk. In this kind of cold, I especially appreciated the minivan's large, slanted front window. Although I owned an ancient 1986 Toyota 4Runner that Braden and I often used for birding around Missoula, it was a lot less reliable than the minivan and definitely not as roomy. Enjoying the comfort of the minivan's soft bucket seats, both Braden and I trained our binoculars on the impressive, stoic-looking raptor a hundred yards in front of us.

Braden consulted his copy of *Sibley*. "It's got a white head and brown streaks running down its breast," he said. "Dark belly too. It's not a Red-tailed. Definitely a Rough-legged."

Looking through my own ancient Golden handbook, *Birds of North America: A Guide to Field Identification*, I concurred. Then, suddenly, the hawk took off and swooped toward the field next to it.

"Look! It's going after something!" Braden exclaimed.

We saw movement as six or seven large, low shapes scattered across the frozen ground.

"Ring-necked Pheasants!" Braden shouted, staring through his binoculars.

We watched as the Rough-legged dive-bombed the pheasants, but the hawk was wasting calories. The game birds easily outmaneuvered the buteo, and it soon returned to another telephone pole perch. We cautiously drove toward it, and I risked frostbite to cinch the ID with a couple of photos. When we turned into Lee Metcalf a few minutes later, our Big Year count stood at six.

Even though I'd lived in Montana since 1996, I hadn't fully appreciated the magic of Lee Metcalf National Wildlife Refuge until Braden and I had seriously plunged into birding a couple of years earlier. For birders, the refuge offers several priceless features. It sprawls across a variety of distinct habitats including wetlands, riparian areas, and Ponderosa Pine forest, and a system of trails makes these areas accessible to almost anyone. The refuge's two most *important* features are that it is only forty-five minutes from our house and that waterfowl can find at least some open water at Lee Metcalf any time of the year.

That day the duck ponds greeted us with both good and bad news. The bad news was that our current cold spell had paved 90 percent of the ponds' surface with ice. The good news? The ice had forced the remaining ducks into small patches of open water close to the road, giving us a good chance to observe them.

As I was setting up my tripod and camera, my fingers throbbed from the cold, and every time I inhaled I could feel ice crystals cling to the insides of my nostrils. Even before I'd gotten everything secured, Braden began calling out species.

"Mallards. What are those things—oh, Green-winged Teals. Northern Pintail!"

With my camera, I focused on a second group of ducks over to the left. "Braden, is that a male goldeneye over there?"

Braden trained his binoculars that way. "Yep."

"Which one?"

"Common."

"Where are the Buffleheads?" I asked, continuing to search the pond through my camera.

"Don't know," Braden mumbled as he intently studied a group of Lesser Scaups.

The absence of Buffleheads rankled. We could usually find one here, and they were one of my favorite birds. Why? One simple reason: I could identify them.

Although Braden could absorb new bird identification details at rates rivaling a Pentagon supercomputer, I often joked that about the only thing I could tell for sure was the difference between a pigeon and a Bald Eagle—and only on a good day. Although I'd graduated with a marine biology degree and spent the last thirty years writing science and nature books for young people, my fifty-six-year-old brain struggled to distinguish species in the field. I hadn't tried to learn any birds at all until I'd been in my thirties, and details that I did pick up quickly seemed to migrate with the seasons. I had no solid theory about why this was so except for the general belief that it was easier for a younger brain to learn new things. In my twenties, I had learned taxonomic details of plants, marine invertebrates, and other organisms with relative ease but, alas, that no longer seemed to be the case.

To overcome this shortcoming, I schlepped along a camera everywhere I went. If neither Braden nor I could identify a bird on the spot, we could usually figure it out later by studying its enlarged image on a computer. Of course, some birders scorned this approach. Their attitude seemed to be, "If you aren't an expert, you shouldn't be out there birding at all." My response? "Get bent." The camera had proved a wonderful learning tool not only for me but also for

Braden, Nick, and other young birders I knew. And this year? Well, camera in tow, I was determined to make real progress improving my field identification skills.

With our bird count up to fifteen, we departed the duck ponds and headed to the forest and riparian areas of Lee Metcalf. Despite bagging a few ducks, Braden's face mirrored the somber skies overhead. The National Weather Service had called for clearing and sunshine by midday, but to our chagrin an inversion layer remained clamped like an iron lid over the Bitterroot Valley, keeping skies gray and temperatures at ten degrees.

"Which trail should we take?" Braden asked as we got out of the car.

"Let's go where we saw the Great Horned Owl last spring. Maybe we'll see one again."

We crossed a short bridge and turned left down the main trail. After a quarter mile I wondered why I felt so cold and realized I'd forgotten one of the clothing layers I'd intended to wear. Braden also began to complain about the subfreezing temperatures.

"Let's not go too far," he said.

"Where's your birding spirit?" I challenged. "It's our Big Year. We've got to sacrifice, right?"

Braden managed a smile, and we pressed onward. At an irrigation ditch, we spotted a flock of Mallards and Canada Geese, but in the forest not a feather fluttered. We reached a trail intersection.

"Which way?" Braden said.

To our left, I saw nothing. Straight ahead, however, I spotted a distant dark shape atop a snag next to the Bitterroot River.

"Hey, look. That might be worth investigating."

We tromped toward the mystery bird, and as we grew near, Braden asked, "What is it? Kestrel?"

We both pegged it as a raptor of some sort, but it lacked the thick body of a buteo. Like Braden, I was thinking falcon, but it looked too big to be a kestrel, and I didn't think a prairie or peregrine would be sitting next to the river like that.

"Accipiter?" I asked, thinking Cooper's Hawk.

Braden focused his binoculars. "Definitely not an accipiter."

That falcon feeling continued to stay with me, and I'm not sure why, but I finally asked, "Could it be a Merlin?"

I had never seen a Merlin but had heard a birding friend, the amazing photographer and writer Kate Davis, talk about them.

"Yeah," Braden said, nodding. "I'm thinking Merlin."

We hadn't brought *Sibley* from the minivan, but I did have my camera, and using Braden as a tripod I fired off a couple of confirmation photos. In the cold, the falcon had fluffed out its feathers like an unflappable puffball. Even with my camera shutter clicking away, the bird regarded us casually.

Leaving it in peace, we continued around the trail loop. Neither of us had ever seen the forest so dead. A Great Blue Heron did a flyover above the Canada Geese, but Braden and I shook our heads at how little bird activity surrounded us.

Finally we heard the faint *tap-tap-tap* of a woodpecker and, after ten minutes of craning our necks toward a stand of Ponderosa Pines, located a lone female Downy. As we hurried back to the car, I glanced down the main trail to see our presumed Merlin still sitting there, surveying its frigid domain.

Back in the minivan we used *Sibley* and our photos to confirm that our mystery falcon had indeed been a Merlin. Leaving Lee Metcalf, we also picked up Wild Turkey—the bird, not the booze—and then made our way back toward Highway 93. Even though the Merlin had made our excursion worth the effort, I could tell that we both felt underwhelmed by our species tally.

Braden slumped in his seat. "Are we going home?" he asked, his tone betraying a readiness to call it a day.

"Let's see if we can pick up Black-backeds," I told him. "Sound good?"

His voice brightened, and he sat up straighter. "Yeah!"

As we drove north to Lolo, Braden spotted a Northern Harrier, but with my eyes on the road, I missed it. At Lolo, though, we turned west up Highway 12. Our destination: a burn area along the side of the road about ten miles in.

While researching *Fire Birds*, I'd delved into the fascinating world of burned forests, thanks to University of Montana biologist Richard Hutto. An international expert in several ornithological areas, Dick is best known for introducing the world to an astonishing fact—that dozens of bird species prefer burned forests to all other habitats. The poster bird for burned forests is a remarkable species, the Black-backed Woodpecker.

Although more than one hundred bird species make serious use of burned forests, the Black-backed has evolved an exclusive relationship with them and is almost never found outside of newly charred tracts. Why? Because burned forests support thriving beetle grub populations, grubs that provide feasts for the Black-backed, Three-toed, and other woodpecker species.

As I was writing my book a forest fire burned through part of Lolo Valley, and when I visited the burn the following spring I was delighted to discover Black-backeds investigating the area. That had been two years ago. But I thought, *It's only been three years since the fire. Maybe we'll get lucky and spot one today!*

Ten miles in, I saw the white fence that served as a landmark for our destination. I flicked on my left turn signal as I began slowing the minivan, searching for the small pullout on the left side of the highway. Finally I spotted it—buried under a foot of snow. With a chrome-plated diesel pickup riding my ass, I made a split-second decision to turn and hope for the best. I twisted the wheel and plowed into the pullout, our van's low undercarriage scraping the snow's icy surface. We lurched to a stop.

This being Montana, I'd shelled out an extra three grand to buy the four-wheel-drive version of our minivan a year earlier, but I'd never tested it in snow this deep. Optimistically, I rammed the gearshift into reverse and the vehicle lurched backward a foot or two. Next I shoved it into drive and tried to turn it around, but the van's tires were built for the road and lacked serious traction. It wasn't long before I had them spinning uselessly. With effort, I managed to cajole the van sideways, parallel to the highway, but that's as far it would go. After a long minute of whining and growling, it refused to budge another inch.

I killed the engine.

"What's wrong?" Braden asked. "Are we okay?"

I sighed. "We're stuck."

He looked at me with alarm. During my childhood I'd broken down or got stuck in cars dozens of times with my dad, but I realized that this was the first time Braden had ever enjoyed such an experience. "What are we going to do?" he asked. "Should we call for help?"

I stared through the windshield at the forest in front of us. "Naw. We'll figure it out later. Let's go find some birds."

For the first time that day, blue sky shimmered above us, but in the shade of the burned forest, temperatures clung close to single digits. We slogged through the snow, trying to locate birds by sound, but a serious drawback to the location was that cars from nearby Highway 12 assaulted us with a steady stream of noise pollution—mostly from rigs pulling snowmobiles up to Lolo Pass.

After fifteen minutes Braden said, "I'm cold. Let's go back."

I pointed to a thick stand of larger trees. "Let's try over there."

We picked our way along Lolo Creek, its gentle splashing providing a nice contrast to the trucks roaring by on the highway, and as we approached the stand of trees we halted.

"Did you hear that?" Braden asked.

Even with my crummy hearing and the background noise from the road, I had heard something. "I think so," I told him.

We kept walking. At first the forest stayed silent, and I thought, *We must have imagined it.* Then we heard it again, louder this time.

Tap-tap-tap.

We hurried onward, scanning high in the trees. Soon we saw movement. First one bird, then several more. Two flew off across the highway, but two others stuck around.

"Are they Black-backeds?" Braden eagerly asked.

"I don't know." Through my zoom lens I located one of the birds and recognized the black-and-white coloring typical of most woodpeckers. Then I saw a broad white slash down its back.

"I think they're Hairies," I said.

Braden studied them. "Are you sure?"

"Yeah. The back of a Black-backed is almost solid black. Even a Three-toed has mostly black on its back."

Surprisingly, neither of us felt too disappointed. We reminded ourselves that any bird sighting—especially a woodpecker—is a fun bird sighting. Also, during our last visit here more than a year earlier, I had observed four juvenile Hairy Woodpeckers. Now I wondered, *Could these be the same birds?* I smiled at the thought.

After observing the Hairies for a few minutes, we trudged back to the minivan—still stuck in the snow.

"How are we going to get out?" Braden asked.

I had of course failed to bring a snow shovel or any other appropriate tool for such a situation. Rifling through the vehicle, the best

I could come up with was a windshield ice scraper. I shoved it into Braden's cold hands.

"Here. Start digging."

Kneeling down, we began to excavate a track in front and back of each of the tires—Braden with the scraper, me with my gloved hands. I didn't know if we could clear enough snow to let us escape, but I figured we might as well try before calling AAA.

We had been digging for only five minutes when the angels appeared—two young guys towing a snowmobile trailer. They pulled off on the other side of the highway and sauntered over. "You need help?"

I shook hands with them. "Yeah—thanks!"

A couple of pushes later, Braden and I were cruising back down the highway—my attitude toward snowmobilers permanently improved. Heading along Lolo Creek, Braden even added American Dipper to his list, and we rolled back into Missoula with a bird count of twenty-five for Braden and twenty-two for me.

Our Bird of the Day? Merlin.

The excursion hadn't quite lived up to our expectations, but we'd take it.

Our Big Year had officially begun.

CHAPTER 4

planning over owls

One problem with beginning a Big Year in Montana was that, well, we were in Montana. *In winter.* Sure, the season brought a handful of rare birding opportunities—Snow Buntings, Rough-legged Hawks, and possibly Gyrfalcons and Snowy and Great Gray Owls—but until reasonable weather returned, most of Montana's birds had wisely fled the state for Palm Springs or Orlando.

In anticipation of this, we had set up our bird feeder just before New Year's, after being forced to take it down the previous fall because of heavy black bear activity in our neighborhood. It took the local birds a full week to reacquire it, but on January 7 a bushel of Black-capped Chickadees, Mountain Chickadees, and Pygmy Nuthatches graced the view from our kitchen window. That same week I spotted White-breasted Nuthatches and Dark-eyed Juncos at another feeder just down the street.

Still, we had extra time on our hands and decided to devote some of it to closely observing available birds and learning more about them. The New Year's cold snap, for instance, impressed on both of us a rule perhaps obvious to more experienced birders: when it's gray and temperatures dip below twenty degrees, most birds like to stay in their holes, watch TV, and drink beer like the rest of us. We also were gaining a greater appreciation of which kinds of birds liked to forage together. I'd witnessed mixed flocks of birds in Costa Rica but had never appreciated that temperate birds could form mixed foraging flocks too. Watching the birds at our feeder, Braden and I became aware that a variety of species often teamed up, perhaps improving predator detection or their chances of finding important food caches.

When we weren't watching the local birds, we huddled together to study up on species we might see later and to refine our birding battle plans for the rest of the year. We joined the American Birding Association and ordered specialized birding guides for Texas and various regions we planned or hoped to visit. We quizzed each other on warblers, flycatchers, and ducks. We both read *Kingbird Highway: The Biggest Year in the Life of an Extreme Birder*, Kenn Kaufman's account of his own burgeoning passion for birds as a young man.

I also bought our airline tickets for Texas and Arizona.

Did I say Arizona?

By happy coincidence, just a few days into the new year, I received an email from my friends Bruce Weide and Pat Tucker. This year, they informed me, they had rented a ranch in southeastern Arizona for two weeks. What's more, Braden and I were invited!

When Braden got home from school that evening, I sat him down and told him the good news.

"It should be amazing birding—and in a brand-new ecosystem for us," I said. "The problem is that we can't afford to do this and take you back to the literature festival in Warrensburg. You can either do Texas and Missouri or Texas and Arizona. What do you think?"

It was an almost impossible decision for a twelve-year-old.

Braden had accompanied me to Missouri the previous three years and had formed bonds with many of the authors and illustrators who converged there. He often talked about them, and his somber expression told me that the thought of not seeing those people this year pulled at his heart. On the other hand, bird activity in March failed to justify Missouri's reputation as the Show Me State. Sure, we would see Northern Cardinals and a Blue Jay or two, but the pickings were slim.

Arizona would be a different story. The land of my own birth promised ornithological riches beyond our imagination: exotic hummingbirds, flycatchers, woodpeckers, raptors, buntings—maybe even a tropical trogon. If we really wanted to build a list, Arizona would supply the bricks.

"I don't know," Braden told me. "I really want to see everyone in Missouri again, but I don't want to miss Arizona. What do you think I should do?"

"Well," I said. "I'm not going to Arizona without you, but it's your choice."

"Do you think we'll ever get invited back to Missouri?"

"Probably, but we don't know when."

Braden let that grind around in his crop for a day, then came to a decision.

"Arizona," he told me.

"You're sure?" I asked, but the excitement on his face left no doubt.

"Yeah," he replied.

That night we confirmed dates with Bruce and Pat and forked over more of my hard-earned cash to Delta Airlines.

We spent the rest of the month dreaming about Arizona and Texas and picking up birds when they happened to present themselves. We located a Ferruginous Hawk and Northern Shrike out near Walmart. In the crackers and chips aisle of Costco, we ID'd the year's first House Sparrow. Near our house I spotted a pair of Pileated Woodpeckers working the dead cottonwoods above Rattlesnake Creek. As the month wound down, we also looked forward to a particularly special birding opportunity.

On the last Saturday of January we rose early. I burned some bacon and scrambled some eggs, and then we hurried down to a University of Montana parking lot to rendezvous for a rare field trip—to observe owls with legendary owl expert Denver Holt.

Denver founded the nonprofit Owl Research Institute, near Charlo, Montana, about an hour north of Missoula, more than twenty-five years earlier, and since that time he had been conducting extensive long-term population studies on several different owl species. When I moved to Montana, I had heard that Denver occasionally took groups of birders out to catch and band owls, but since

Braden had swooped into birding I hadn't heard of any trips—until this year.

Reading our local Audubon chapter newsletter I learned that, after a five-year hiatus, Denver had agreed to take local members out to catch and band owls. As thick curtains of snow began falling all across Missoula Valley, twenty of us caravanned out past Walmart to a dirt road running behind the Missoula airport. We parked our cars and began a slow trudge across ice-encrusted snow, post-holing down a small draw, up a hill, and along an irrigation ditch until we reached the opening of another scrubby canyon.

There, Denver's team had set up a pair of mist nets—nets made of filament so fine that birds cannot detect them. Before trying to drive owls into the nets, Denver gave us a briefing on the day's target, the Long-eared Owl.

"We've been studying and banding these owls for thirty-one years now," he told us. "We've banded more than nineteen hundred of them. The owls almost always nest in magpie nests," he said, pointing to a neat cluster of sticks perched above us. "When we first started coming here, we could catch ten, fifteen at a time. Now we catch far fewer."

Denver went on to explain that probably no more than six thousand Long-eared Owls live in the entire United States. Partners in Flight, a network of 150 organizations dedicated to land bird conservation, gives a slightly higher population estimate, but it rates the owl a worrisome thirteen out of twenty on its "species assessment" list.

"Populations go up and down from year to year," Denver elaborated, "but we believe the trend is downward, just like it is for the Short-eared Owl. We don't yet know why the populations are decreasing. Around here it could be habitat loss, but up in the Mission Valley, if anything, there is more protected owl habitat than there used to be, so we're still trying to figure out what's going on. That's why it's important to have these long-term studies. Owls are so difficult to locate and observe that unless you get out in the field on a regular basis, you're just not going to know how they're doing."

With that, Denver directed us to chill—literally—on a nearby frozen hillside while he and his team tried to catch owls. Fortunately the blizzard had abated and a bit of cold winter sun poked out. We watched a coyote and two Red-tailed Hawks in the fields below and kept our fingers crossed that we would get to see an owl. Finally Denver signaled for us to approach. We found him flanked by two women assistants each holding a spectacular, living, breathing Long-eared Owl.

Denver showed us the birds' incredible camouflage, specialized features that helped reduce noise while flying, and subtle coloration that indicated sex and maturity. The two he and his assistants had caught that morning were males, and one of them had been banded before. The owls patiently put up with us as Denver stretched out their wings, pointed to the disks around their eyes, and even pulled back their head feathers to show us their ear holes.

The owls kept their long "ears"—tufts, actually—bent back against their heads while Denver talked. "They're clearly stressed by us right now," Denver explained. "When I first started taking groups out, I got a ton of flak from people who didn't think I should be subjecting the owls to getting handled and exposed to groups of people. But you know what? It hasn't driven them away. If we came out here next week, we'd find these same owls still here. And the real benefit is that over the years, trips like these have helped turn hundreds of people into owl enthusiasts who support owl conservation and habitat protection. Now all kinds of people and groups do trips like these."

Denver finished his talk and then invited Braden and the only other young person in the group, a girl of about eight, to study the owls up close. A dozen cameras fired. Then it was time to let the banded owl go. As we all eagerly spread out to watch, the owl's handler released the bird. On silent wings it flew straight up the gully, beneath the canopy of scrubby trees.

We all thanked Denver, and then, while he and his team banded the other owl and packed up their gear, we began trudging back to our cars. For Braden and me it was a perfect way to cap off the month. Better yet, eleven months of birds and surprises awaited us.

JANUARY BIRD LIST

Sneed's List (37)	Braden's List (39)
Black-billed Magpie	Black-billed Magpie
American Crow	American Crow
Canada Goose	Canada Goose
Mallard	Mallard
Northern Pintail	Northern Pintail
Green-winged Teal	Green-winged Teal

Lesser Scaup	Lesser Scaup
Common Goldeneye	Common Goldeneye
Ring-necked Pheasant	Ring-necked Pheasant
Wild Turkey	Wild Turkey
Great Blue Heron	Great Blue Heron
Bald Eagle	Bald Eagle
Red-tailed Hawk	Red-tailed Hawk
Rough-legged Hawk	Rough-legged Hawk
American Coot	American Coot
Killdeer	Killdeer
Mourning Dove	Mourning Dove
Downy Woodpecker	Downy Woodpecker
Northern Flicker	Northern Flicker
Merlin	Merlin
Common Raven	Common Raven
Hairy Woodpecker	Northern Harrier
Black-capped Chickadee	Hairy Woodpecker
Mountain Chickadee	American Dipper
Pygmy Nuthatch	Black-capped Chickadee
Ferruginous Hawk	Mountain Chickadee
House Finch	Pygmy Nuthatch
House Sparrow	Ferruginous Hawk
Northern Shrike	House Finch
Rock Pigeon	House Sparrow
European Starling	Northern Shrike
Pileated Woodpecker	Rock Pigeon
Dark-eyed Junco	American Kestrel
Red-breasted Nuthatch	European Starling
White-breasted Nuthatch	Dark-eyed Junco
Brown Creeper	Red-breasted Nuthatch
Long-eared Owl	White-breasted Nuthatch
	Brown Creeper
	Long-eared Owl

CHAPTER 5

midwinter blahs

I'm going to zip through most of February and the first few weeks of March. I know, I know. This undoubtedly comes as a shock given Braden's and my optimism at the end of January, but the truth is that for the next six or seven weeks, birding generally sucked. Braden and I picked up only nine and thirteen species respectively in February, and not many more through the spring equinox. Our major highlight of these weeks wasn't birds but Braden's February birthday, when he struck terror into his parents' hearts by officially becoming a teenager.

One of our challenges during this time was that I was juggling four different writing projects, all of which devoured available birding time. At the beginning of the year, I had warned Braden that other than our longer out-of-state birding trips, I could set aside only one full day for birding each month. This year, bad weather often scuttled even this modest ambition.

In early February we managed to corral what we called "Los Tres Birditos"—Gray Jay, Steller's Jay, and Clark's Nutcracker—during

Braden's Boy Scout ski day near Philipsburg. We also nabbed a few new waterfowl on a return visit to Lee Metcalf. Later in the month, I flew to the Washington, DC, area for school visits and picked up half a dozen birds that counted toward my Big Year list.

"That's not fair," Braden complained when I called to tell him about it.

"I know," I told him, "but we're not competing against each other. I'm your teammate, right?"

"Yeah," he reluctantly admitted, "but I still wish I'd gotten to come with you."

"So do I, but I'll bet you pick up most of these birds when we go to Texas."

"I hope so."

In mid-March, our family drove across the state to Billings for the Montana State Spelling Bee. Braden had qualified for it by finishing third in Missoula County, but he seemed just as excited by our birding prospects as he was about the spelling competition. On the drive out, we picked up Snow Goose and Tundra Swan from the freeway, and on the day of the bee we woke up early to investigate Pictograph Caves State Park on the east side of town. The park turned out to be closed, but on the approach road we added Mountain Bluebird and Horned Lark to our Big Year lists.

Even with these finds, it was a dismal performance—all except for the spelling bee, where Braden tied for twelfth in the state.

Much more interesting than our personal birding woes was the weather. The year 2015 had been the warmest year ever recorded across the planet, and despite the self-serving histrionics of the Grand Old Climate Change Denying Party, 2016 was shaping up to be even warmer. In western Montana in February, El Niño raised temperatures a full five degrees above average. March also rolled in warm, and guess what?

The birds noticed.

When Tessa and I took a bike ride through our neighborhood on March 5, I was floored to see Red-winged Blackbirds in a patch of cattails—a full month ahead of schedule for that location. That afternoon Tessa ran inside shouting, "Daddy, I just saw a humming-bird!" Meanwhile, down at the MPG Ranch, Braden's friend Nick reported that Say's Phoebes, Tree Swallows, and Western Bluebirds had all begun to show up weeks ahead of time.

The extremely warm temperatures were undoubtedly bad news for the planet, including some species of birds. In 2015 thousands of murres and other seabirds had washed up dead along Alaska's coast—likely a result of disrupted food chains caused by warmer ocean temperatures. On the other hand, radical weather patterns also were famous for depositing rare, exotic migrants into the ABA countable area. They didn't help Braden and me with *our* Big Year lists, but they helped unleash a storm of furious, hard-core birder activity by people gunning for Neil Hayward's 2013 ABA Big Year record of 749 species. By mid-March, while I still struggled to tally my sixtieth bird for the year, the world's top birders had tracked down more than four hundred species—and they weren't slowing down.

Braden and I hadn't yet learned of this epic birding activity, but it wouldn't have made any difference if we had. As March drew to a close, we simply noted the warmer weather, put our pitiful winter bird counts behind us, and prepared for what we hoped would be a much more productive spring.

FEBRUARY BIRD LIST

Sneed's List (13)	Braden's List (9)
Gray Jay	Gray Jay
Steller's Jay	Steller's Jay
Clark's Nutcracker	Clark's Nutcracker
Pine Siskin	Pine Siskin
Common Merganser	Townsend's Solitaire
Belted Kingfisher	Common Merganser
Ring-billed Gull	Belted Kingfisher
Eastern Bluebird	Eurasian Collared-Dove
Northern Cardinal	Pileated Woodpecker
Black Vulture	
Northern Mockingbird	
Blue Jay	
American Robin	

CHAPTER 6

arizona bound

On March 30 I woke Braden before dawn. Trying not to disturb Amy and Tessa, we dressed, tossed our bags into my 4Runner and headed to the Missoula airport. As usual, I was impressed by how well Braden got himself together for an early flight. Then again, this was a trip we'd been looking forward to more than any other. A trip that in many ways would define our year of birding: our big trip to Arizona.

"How many new birds do you think we'll see?" Braden asked as we settled into our flight.

It wasn't the first time we'd considered the question, and the truth was that I hadn't a clue. In books such as *Kingbird Highway*, *The Big Year*, and *Wild America*, which I'd just started reading, it seemed commonplace for birders to rack up more than a hundred species in a day. Of course these were experts, people who didn't dismiss little brown birds as "LBBs" and who could tell the difference between a Swamp Sparrow and an immature White-crowned.

"How many do *you* think?" I asked Braden.

Like Amy, Braden tended to be cautious by nature, and I could almost hear the calculations clicking in his head. "Hmm," he said. "We'll be there a little before the main migration, but there will still be resident birds we've never seen. I'm going to guess thirty."

"*Thirty!*" I teased. "Where is your birder machismo? Your bravado? I'm going to guess fifty."

"You always guess too high," he said.

"It's called optimism," I said, and for this trip I had a feeling I might actually be underbidding. I kept such thoughts to myself, however, and as we rode the rental car shuttle from the Phoenix airport, we picked up our first new bird, Great-tailed Grackle, soon to be followed by a second, White-winged Dove. My son and I didn't fly all the way to Arizona to bird the 602 area code, though, so as soon as we loaded our considerable baggage into our rental car, we hit the interstate and headed south through saguaro country.

"Wow," Braden said, studying the cactus-studded landscape around us, "This isn't anything like what I'd thought. When you told me about Arizona, I thought it would just be flat and barren. This is cool."

I looked around and had to agree.

We stopped for lunch in Casa Grande, and thanks to an internet search picked a restaurant named BeDillon's—perhaps the only restaurant in town with wildlife habitat in its backyard. While we waited for our food, we stalked lizards and doves amid the cacti out back and picked up the trip's third Big Year bird: Curve-billed Thrasher. Although all three of our new birds were Lifers for Braden, I had probably seen these species before. Since I'd never bothered keeping a Life list until the past couple of years, however, I decided to consider them Lifers for me too—a practice I would continue going forward.

South of Casa Grande, we took a back road off the interstate toward Saguaro National Park. I picked up American Kestrel—a bird Braden already had—for my own Big Year list, and by two in the afternoon we were pulling into the Saguaro National Park western district visitor center, where our real birding began. As soon as we stepped out of the car, an all-star cast of desert birds swirled around us. They included Cactus Wrens, a Pyrrhuloxia, unknown hummingbirds, even a surprise flock of Yellow-rumped Warblers.

"Daddy, come on!" Braden impatiently shouted as I tried to get my tripod set up.

"Just calm down," I told him. "The birds aren't going anywhere."

Yeah, right. For a thirteen-year-old, this was like telling him to ignore the last slice of pizza at a birthday party. After all, he'd spent years looking forward to a trip like this. What if he missed all the birds because his bumbling father was too slow to get his ass in gear?

"Go!" I barked. "I'll catch up to you."

My own impatience stemmed from the fact that while zeroing in on a Cactus Wren I'd made a sickening discovery: my wonderful Canon 7D and 100–400 mm lens didn't appear to be focusing, especially at long ranges.

I'd suspected as much while packing a couple of days before but had been hoping I was wrong. No such luck.

My son had become engrossed in a flock of tiny birds about fifty feet away when I called out, "Braden, come here for a minute."

"What?" he shouted back. "I'm trying to photograph these warblers."

"I need your camera."

Reluctantly he stomped back over to the car. "Why?"

"Something's wrong with my camera."

"But we're missing all the birds!"

"I know," I said, feeling both his and my own frustration. "I can't help it."

For the next fifteen minutes, as steam poured out of Braden's ears, I swapped his camera equipment with mine, trying to figure out the problem. I couldn't. My camera refused to focus sharply.

It was a major setback. One of my primary goals for the trip had been to get good photos for a planned children's book on woodpeckers. Now, right at the beginning of the trip, it looked like I'd have to scrap that plan. I debated buying replacement equipment, but I doubted I'd be able to find a camera shop with the gear that I needed, even if I could afford it. *Maybe I can get it repaired*, I considered, but I abandoned that idea given how much we would be moving around in the next few days.

I tried to gulp down my disappointment, but fate mocked me. As Braden and I walked around the visitor center, a beautiful Gila Woodpecker flew directly overhead and landed on a nearby cactus.

Braden managed a poor shot of it from a distance, but I kicked myself. Why did my camera have to crap out on *this* of all trips?

The only good news was that Braden had started to relax as he realized that birds awaited us almost everywhere we looked. With plenty of daylight left, we decided to squeeze in the world-famous Arizona-Sonora Desert Museum just up the road. I'd visited there once years before, but I hadn't told Braden much about it. Once we got inside, he exclaimed, "This place is like a zoo!"

"Oh, didn't I tell you that?"

He punched me in the shoulder. "No!"

His spirits lifted even more as we began walking through the living wildlife exhibitions. We paused to watch the museum's resident mountain lion, javelinas, Mexican gray wolf, and sleeping coyote. I also seized a teachable moment and began instructing Braden on desert plants.

"After all," I told him, "a naturalist has to know plants too. Without plants, there aren't any animals."

"I guess," he conceded and then surprised me by quickly learning to identify creosote, ocotillo, cholla, brittlebrush, and other xerophytes along the paths.

As we were walking the Desert Loop Trail, we both spotted large birds to the south. I had left my malfunctioning camera—damn its soul—in the car, but I raised Braden's binoculars to my eyes.

"Those don't look like Turkey Vultures," I said. "Are they Red-taileds?"

More than most other bird groups, hawks befuddled me. Even within a species they showed huge variation in color, size, and markings depending on where they lived and how old they were. For this trip, I knew I'd be relying on Braden's exhaustive knowledge of *Sibley* to identify most of the raptors we saw.

Braden studied the birds through his camera for several seconds and then said, "I think they're Harris's Hawks."

"Really?"

As the hawks circled closer, Braden pointed out their defining features. Though they had appeared black from a distance, the hawks' overall dark-brown coloration resolved upon closer inspection. Unique, cinnamon-colored epaulettes graced the shoulders of each bird, while distinctive black-and-white tails flashed boldly in the afternoon sun. Three of the raptors flew together, performing complicated acrobatics over the museum, and, to our delight, one landed on a nearby saguaro.

"Now *that* is cool!" I said, taking the opportunity to try to memorize the hawks' handsome features.

We rounded out our visit by exploring the museum's hummingbird aviary and the walk-in aviary. The hummingbird exhibit proved particularly useful as we learned to identify Broad-billed and other species that would make regular appearances on the rest of the trip. At the walk-in aviary, Braden also picked up another Big Year bird. As we watched a poor roadrunner frantically trying to break out of the aviary, a Northern Cardinal—a bird I had tallied on my recent visit to the DC area—perched outside and peered in.

Ka-ching.

Before leaving the museum, we stopped by the gift shop to load up on souvenirs, including a large plush javelina that Braden couldn't live without. The thing was so cute I almost stole it for myself, and, as we drove down into Tucson to find our hotel, Javvy assumed his role as our official trip mascot. Despite my camera problems and moments of tension between Braden and me, the trip felt like it was coming together.

CHAPTER 7

a split decision

When we woke before six the next morning, we had a choice to make. My initial thoughts had been to hang around the saguaros for another day, figuring they would offer plenty of bird-on-cactus action. Braden had at first agreed, but to prepare for the trip we'd been reading Richard Cachor Taylor's *A Birder's Guide to Southeastern Arizona*, and its pages gave us a second, tantalizing possibility.

"Buddy, we face a difficult decision," I gravely informed Braden over breakfast.

"What is it?" he asked, managing to look concerned even with a quarter-pound chunk of waffle hanging from his mouth.

"Well, I know we were going to bird around here before heading east, but a place about an hour south of here sounds really good. It's called Madera Canyon, and the guide says it's often people's favorite Arizona birding spot—even better than Ramsey Canyon."

At this time of day, Braden's sleep-deprived teenaged brain managed only to respond, "What do you think?"

"Well, we squeezed in a lot of birding around here yesterday. I kind of feel like we should try this other place, at least so we know what it's like for future trips."

"Let's do that," Braden said.

Twenty minutes later, we were making our way south on I-19 toward Green Valley. It was an optimistic name for the town, especially given the Sierrita copper and gold mine rising like an industrial Death Star just to the west of the freeway. Nonetheless, we decided to pull off to try to find some wastewater treatment ponds supposedly favored by waterfowl. We didn't locate the ponds but instead discovered a pleasant, saguaro-lined neighborhood that offered glimpses of Gila Woodpeckers, White-winged Doves, and an assortment of other birds that fled before we managed to identify them. This detour, in turn, led us to Continental Drive and the road to Madera Canyon.

From the moment we stepped out of our car, Braden and I loved Madera.

"Daddy, Mexican Jays!" Braden shouted, bounding across the road to a group of oak trees.

"Really?" I asked, racing to catch up.

"And Acorn Woodpeckers!"

While Braden started firing off pictures, I enjoyed these handsome birds with my naked eye. I had to admit that both species surprised me. Glancing around, the whole *habitat* surprised me. Oak and sycamore woodlands were not what I usually thought of when it came to Arizona. This place reminded me much more of my backyard growing up in Southern California. I was especially tickled to find Acorn Woodpeckers here, a species I'd often watched defy utility crews by stashing thousands upon thousands of acorns in PG&E telephone poles.

I hurried back to our car to pay our day use fee, but as soon as I started filling out the form, Braden yelled, "Daddy! Come quick!"

"I can't!" I said, figuring he'd just seen something else we'd see a lot of, and I continued filling out the form.

"I mean it! Hurry!"

I didn't—and soon regretted it. By the time I paid our fee and joined Braden, he said, "Aw, you missed it. There were two Hepatic Tanagers right here."

"What?" I asked, staring frantically around. "Are you kidding?" "They just took off."

I swore under my breath. That would teach me to ignore Braden's exhortations.

We decided to head down the trail hugging Madera Creek, and were soon rewarded with glimpses of two species that would become trip favorites. Walking no more than a couple hundred yards, we saw the unmistakable form of a woodpecker land on a nearby oak tree. At first, I assumed it was another Acorn, but Braden exclaimed, "Arizona Woodpecker!"

My adrenaline surged. This was a bird we'd both been reading about, one I'd fervently hoped to see many times during our trip. "Yay!" I said, but the bird only gave us a glimpse before woodpeckering away. Five minutes later, we heard a beautiful high-pitched melody coming from the top branches of an overhead oak. I had no idea what it was, but Braden's dedicated study of *Sibley* once again paid off.

"I think it might be a Painted Redstart," he said, glassing the tree with his binoculars.

An elderly birder sauntered up to join us and introduced himself as Jim. Braden asked him, "Do you think it's a Painted Redstart?"

Jim also scoped the tree. "Yes. I think so."

He was from Portland, Oregon, and, like many other birders we would meet, he told us that Madera had become one of his favorite destinations. Together the three of us watched in wonder as the black, red, and white bird flitted from branch to branch, singing its frantic, high-energy song and raising its impressive bicolored tail-feathers, presumably to startle insects into revealing themselves.

Braden and I kept walking another quarter mile, spotting more Mexican Jays and—we thought—a Cooper's or Sharp-shinned shooting through the trees. As we'd already discovered, though, bird activity often seemed to occur in furious, fast-paced waves before fading to almost nothing. After a few more steps, I asked, "Do you want to head up to the lodge?"

Braden didn't hesitate. "Yeah. Let's go."

Santa Rita Lodge was one of several Madera Canyon hotspots, and there we discovered at least a dozen birders settled in to watch the feeder extravaganza. A flock of turkeys—the uncommon Gould's variety—hogged the stage, but those didn't interest us as much as the jays, woodpeckers, Lesser Goldfinches, Pine Siskins, Chipping Sparrows, Bridled Titmice, and, more than anything, the hummingbirds swarming the site. As an adolescent, Braden liked to assess the playing field before entering into a conversation with a stranger—except, I realized, when it came to birds. Surrounded by avian wonders and like-minded birders, he quickly struck up a conversation with Steve Kaye, a veteran birder, blogger, and photographer. Our newest acquaintance had trained his tripod-mounted camera on a feeder being visited by a pair of Magnificent Hummingbirds (renamed Rivoli's Hummingbird in 2017), and Braden wasted no time before asking him questions.

"Has anything rare shown up here?"

"Well, there was a Hepatic Tanager about forty-five minutes ago," Steve said, "and the occasional Bridled Titmouse."

"What about trogons?"

"None today. They usually don't come to feeders. Yesterday morning I saw one right near here, though."

Braden's eyes widened. "Really?"

"Yes. I've been staying here a few days, and yesterday I stepped out to my back porch to scan for birds on the feeders. I didn't see any and was about to head back inside, when movement caught the corner of my eye. A trogon had been sitting there the whole time! The bird was so near that when I raised my camera, I discovered it was too close to photograph. That was up there with my best bird experiences ever."

"That's so cool!"

Braden and Steve continued talking, each obviously enjoying the conversation. After a few minutes, Steve glanced over at me and said, "It looks like you've got the next Kenn Kaufman on your hands. Next he'll be hitchhiking across the country in search of birds."

I laughed. "Hitchhiking? I hope not," I said, but I was proud of how much Braden had learned and how he communicated and interacted with adult birders.

We stayed at the feeder for the next hour, eating our bagel lunch, chatting with Steve and other birders, and, when possible, taking photos. Before we left we also felt duty-bound to visit the little gift store at the lodge. That's where I discovered the answer to a question that had been nagging me: why did the lodge allow anyone to sit and bird here for free?

The answer: birders were cash cows.

Within minutes I blew seventy-five bucks on T-shirts, bird guides, and peanut butter cups. I also struck up a friendly conversation with one of the store's proprietors, Becky, who sounded interested in ordering some of my books for her shelves. I left the store feeling that heavenly endorphin rush that only comes from spending a wad of cash on fun stuff, and we headed to the car with a mixture of regret at departing such a beautiful birding spot and anticipation for our next destination.

We returned to Green Valley to refuel, grab a second lunch, and grocery shop. We needed the supplies because we were heading off to spend the next four days at a remote location with our friends Bruce Weide and Pat Tucker.

I had met Bruce shortly after moving to Missoula in 1996, when I joined a group of Montana children's book writers. In each other, Bruce and I quickly discovered kindred spirits. Like me, Bruce and his wife, Pat, had studied biology but had veered from their biologist paths when an orphaned wolf pup named Koani had landed in their lives. Bruce and Pat quickly realized that if they did not adopt a way of life that revolved around this new arrival, they would be forced to euthanize her. Fortunately they lived on thirty heavily wooded acres in the Bitterroot Valley, and after Koani came along they built a large, one-acre enclosure for her and dedicated themselves to her well-being, which included everything from walking her three or more hours a day to dumpster diving for fresh animal carcasses behind butcher shops.

Pat and Bruce decided to start a nonprofit group called Wild Sentry, and each year between 1991 and 2006, they traveled the country with Koani and her canine companion, an adorable mutt named Indie. They put on thousands of programs at schools, natural history museums, and community centers, educating kids and adults about wolves and their role in the environment. Each program climaxed with the appearance of Koani to a chorus of oohs, ahs, and applause.

After Koani passed away in 2007, Bruce and Pat found themselves with a sudden windfall of time. They bought two goats, Zack and Jesse, and started goat packing throughout the West. A few months before our trip to Arizona, Bruce had sent me the email notifying us that he, Pat, and the goats had rented a Forest Service cabin called Half Moon Ranch in the Dragoon Mountains, a couple hours east of Tucson. After visiting Madera Canyon, Braden and I reached the ranch in the late afternoon.

I half expected us to be the only people intrepid enough to travel all the way to southeastern Arizona for some free nature lodging and companionship. Instead we found the ranch parking lot packed with half a dozen cars and RVs. Like Koani, Indie had passed away, but Pat and Bruce had adopted two new dogs named Fay and Pita, and Pat and the dogs enthusiastically greeted us at the ranch house. Right away, Braden and I felt like we belonged. The ranch house had been deeded to the Forest Service by its previous owners, a bona fide Arizona ranching family, and the property sprawled across several acres in the shadows of Cochise Stronghold, the natural granite fortress where the eponymous Apache leader and his band had held out against white aggressors.

The looming oak- and juniper-covered Dragoons were stunning, but we soon discovered that Half Moon Ranch also would provide some of our best birding of the trip. Besides being located in excellent bird habitat, the property boasted a quarter-acre pond just behind the house that, in the heart of a desert, proved an irresistible magnet for an entire community of birds. Within moments of our arrival, Vermillion Flycatchers and Chipping Sparrows welcomed us, and it wasn't hard to predict that many more birds would make an appearance over the next few days.

Most of Pat and Bruce's other visitors were out hiking, so after unloading our gear into a bedroom set aside for us, Braden and I decided to take a short walk up a nearby draw. We saw nothing on our hike up, but as we reached the mouth of the draw, we were treated to another Painted Redstart, hummingbirds, and a tiny gray bird I was pretty sure I'd never seen before.

"What the heck is *that*?" I asked Braden, looking through my binoculars.

Braden didn't hesitate. "It's a Verdin!"

"A *what*-in?"

"A Verdin," Braden impatiently explained. "They're in with titmice and Bushtits. Do you see its yellow head?"

"Yeah," I said, enjoying the antics of the subtle, active little bird. It was Braden's twenty-sixth Big Year bird since arriving in Arizona, and my twenty-seventh, a rate of almost one new Big Year bird per hour!

That evening we ate dinner and enjoyed the company of Pat, Bruce, and their many guests. They hailed from every part of the West and included a fair number of naturalists and dedicated outdoor enthusiasts. Several began avid birding discussions with Braden, even consulting with him on interesting birds he or they had spotted. It was a wonderful way to wrap up the month, but we turned in early, and it was a good thing. Even though we didn't know it yet, the next day we would set off for one of the country's most legendary birding hotspots, a place that when mentioned in conversation sent even the most self-controlled, veteran birders drooling all over their L. L. Bean polyester vests.

MARCH BIRD LIST

Sneed's List (38)	Braden's List (41)
American Wigeon	Ring-billed Gull
Ring-necked Duck	American Wigeon
Bufflehead	Ring-necked Duck
Barrow's Goldeneye	Bufflehead
Hooded Merganser	Barrow's Goldeneye
Golden Eagle	Hooded Merganser
Red-winged Blackbird	Golden Eagle
Snow Goose	Red-winged Blackbird
Tundra Swan	Snow Goose
Horned Lark	Tundra Swan
Mountain Bluebird	Canvasback
Turkey Vulture	Horned Lark
Harris's Hawk	Mountain Bluebird
Eurasian Collared-Dove	Turkey Vulture
White-winged Dove	Harris's Hawk
Anna's Hummingbird	White-winged Dove
Gila Woodpecker	Anna's Hummingbird
American Kestrel	Gila Woodpecker
Cactus Wren	Cactus Wren
Curve-billed Thrasher	Curve-billed Thrasher
Yellow-rumped Warbler	Northern Mockingbird
Brewer's Sparrow	Yellow-rumped Warbler
Pyrrhuloxia	Brewer's Sparrow
Great-tailed Grackle	Northern Cardinal
Rivoli's Hummingbird	Pyrrhuloxia
Black-chinned Hummingbird	Great-tailed Grackle
Broad-billed Hummingbird	Rivoli's Hummingbird

Acorn Woodpecker

Arizona Woodpecker

Mexican Jay

Bridled Titmouse

Bewick's Wren

Townsend's Warbler

Painted Redstart

Chipping Sparrow

Lesser Goldfinch

Vermilion Flycatcher

Verdin

Black-chinned Hummingbird

Broad-billed Hummingbird

Acorn Woodpecker

Arizona Woodpecker

Mexican Jay

Bridled Titmouse

Bewick's Wren

Townsend's Warbler

Painted Redstart

Chipping Sparrow

Hepatic Tanager

Lesser Goldfinch

Vermilion Flycatcher

Verdin

CHAPTER 8

legal immigration

Our original plan for April 1 had been to hang with Bruce and Pat for a day before launching into birding side trips. One thing I cherished about travel, though, was the freedom to alter plans and scrap schedules as conditions changed and opportunities arose. To wit, Friday morning Braden and I both woke before dawn with an unexpected abundance of energy and figured we'd better take advantage of it. By the time the sun rose above the Chiricahuas, we had saddled up the car and were galloping toward one of America's most iconic birding locations: Ramsey Canyon.

Located on the northeastern edge of the Huachuca Mountains, Ramsey Canyon had earned a worldwide reputation as a birding Shangri-la. One reason is that many Mexican bird species have ranges that barely extend over the border into Arizona, and Ramsey Canyon proved an excellent place to see them. On any given spring day, a lucky visitor to Ramsey might be rewarded by a Greater Pewee, Hepatic Tanager, Northern Beardless-Tyrannulet, or Elegant Trogon.

Even more exciting for serious Big Year birders is that rare migrants also frequently show up at Ramsey. The American Birding Association rates birds on a scale of 1 to 6 based on how commonly they occur in the ABA region. The vast majority of species are categorized as Code 1 or 2—"regularly occurring North American avifauna." To have any shot at a respectable Big Year list, hard-core birders also have to scoop up significant numbers of Code 3, 4, and 5 rarities, and Ramsey is a good place to find them. (Code 6, by the way, is defined as "extinct or extirpated from the ABA Checklist Area, or all survivors are held in captivity.") Braden and I didn't even dream about aspiring to the ranks of the semiprofessional birders who chased down such species. Arriving at Ramsey, we expected mostly Code 1s, maybe some 2s, but if a Code 4 or 5 happened to show up, well, that would be dandy too.

We pulled into the tiny parking area at 7:59 a.m.—exactly one minute before the preserve opened. Neither of us had any idea what to expect, but as we got out of the car a Painted Redstart warbled enthusiastically in a tree above us.

Braden grinned. "Well, that's a good sign!"

I laughed and could feel my own excitement rise.

Ramsey Canyon Preserve had been purchased and created by the Nature Conservancy and to enter we had to walk through its main building, where an outdoorsy elderly woman greeted us.

"Where are you visiting from?" she asked.

"Montana," I answered.

"Oh, beautiful country up there. Well, you timed it just right, didn't you?"

I hesitated. "What do you mean?"

"Oh, you haven't heard? Yesterday, we had both Flame-colored Tanager and Tufted Flycatcher in the reserve."

Braden and I looked at each other.

I had never heard of either bird, and Braden looked only moderately more informed, but it didn't take a genius to guess that both species were rarities.

"Where do we go to see them?" Braden asked.

"Well," the woman said. "I think they were both at the upper end of the nature trail."

"C'mon, Daddy," Braden said, pulling on my sleeve. "Let's go."

I paid our entry fees and, after a quick stop at the restroom, off we went.

Immediately, Ramsey—like Madera—reminded me of the canyons I grew up exploring in Southern California. The species of oaks may have been different, but the towering sycamores, occasional manzanita, and smell of dry, dusty leaves all touched a familiar, spiritual place in me. We took a moment to examine the bird feeders behind the visitor center, but except for a single Broad-tailed hummer, the feeders hung deserted.

"Maybe it's too early," I told Braden.

He nodded, and we continued up the trail.

Unfortunately, it seemed that we might be too early for most of the birds at Ramsey. Already, I'd noticed that the birds of Arizona seemed to get up later than in Montana or California. As we hiked, we saw Mexican Jays and Acorn Woodpeckers, but even the woodpeckers exuded a *mañana* attitude, content to hang out on a high branch, sip their lattes, and soak up some early rays.

We made our way about half a mile to the top of the trail without seeing much and paused there to chat with other birders and see if any cool species would show up. The birders hailed from all over the world, and the foreign visitors especially scoured the canyon with intense, scrunched-up faces, as if their whole happiness depended on nailing down rarities. Others ambled along more casually. Clearly, birding Ramsey was old hat to them. I felt somewhere in between. I wanted to see birds but had lived long enough to realize that what I observed would largely be up to the birds, not me.

Despite my attempts at a more Zen-like attitude, by 9:00 a.m., our bird count languished, and I could feel disappointment creeping in. I could see it on Braden's face too.

Some world-class birding hotspot, I thought.

To make matters worse, two days of Mexican food had begun to roil my intestines.

"C'mon," I told Braden. "Let's head back to the car for something to eat and then try it again." (Read: *I need to get to the visitor center bathroom as soon as possible!*)

After a snack of peanut butter cups for Braden and Pepto-Bismol for me, I led Braden back up the nature trail, and finally, with the air warming, Ramsey Canyon's birds began living up to their reputations—at least partly. We picked up House Wren, Townsend's Solitaire, and Hutton's Vireo for our Big Year lists. Most exciting to me, we encountered a pair of Hepatic Tanagers—the Code 2 birds I'd missed in Madera Canyon the day before. The tanagers gave us and half a dozen other birders extensive, leisurely looks, and Braden and I even fired off some decent photos with his camera.

We continued to the top of the trail and again waited for the Flame-colored Tanager and Tufted Flycatcher, but perhaps the Nature Conservancy owed them money. For whatever reason, they failed to appear, so we began making our way back down the canyon. Near a small cabin along the trail, we did pick up a Code 2 Greater Pewee, one of dozens of birds whose ranges barely creep north across the US–Mexico border. A Painted Redstart put on a dazzling display in front of us—but then zoomed away before Braden could take a decent photograph.

"Argh!" Braden shouted. "He was so close! I am never lucky when it comes to taking pictures of birds."

I had often heard these kinds of frustrated remarks from Braden, and, as a parent, well, they bothered me. Though frequently afflicted by similar feelings, I had learned that success in life usually depended more on attitude than luck, so I felt duty-bound to try to correct this negativity.

"That's not true," I said. "You've taken a lot of really good photographs."

"It doesn't seem like it," he said. "Your photos are a lot better."

"Braden, *I have better equipment*. And besides, do you know how many lousy photos I take for every good one I get? You just have to keep at it."

He gave another exasperated sigh, clearly not convinced.

"Anyway," I continued, trying to direct his mind toward something else, "what do you think? Have we seen everything here? If we leave now, we could make it over to San Bernardino."

His blue eyes swept the canyon around us. "Yeah," he answered. "Let's go."

We continued clomping back down the trail, pleased with the birds we'd seen but overall a bit let down by such a highly esteemed place. It was kind of like going to the Café du Monde in New Orleans and not being able to order beignets or visiting the Vatican on the one day the Sistine Chapel happened to be closed for maintenance.

"Next time," I told Braden, "we should try to hike some of the canyons south of here. I'll bet we'd see just as many birds—maybe more."

Right then, we noticed five or six birders excitedly looking at something across the creek bed.

We hurried toward them, and as we arrived, a woman turned to us. "The Tufted Flycatcher!" she said.

"Where?" Braden asked.

"You can't see it right now," a man said, "but it's been landing on that branch over there."

I saw nothing, and that familiar fear of all birders pierced my chest: *I've missed it!*

Then another woman breathlessly said, "John's got it in the spotting scope!"

"I see it now," said Braden, looking through his binoculars. Following his gaze, I could just make out a small bird perched on a branch in full sunlight, fifty yards away.

I quickly took my turn at the spotting scope, and the distant creature metamorphosed into a full-sized sharp, crisp bird with stunning features. Shaped like other flycatchers but with a more prominent pointy crown, the flycatcher sported a rich brown head and back and a dazzling orange breast.

"Braden, quick. Take a look," I hissed. Braden lowered his binoculars and stepped up to the more powerful spotting scope.

"Wow!" he exclaimed.

As I mentioned, we had never even heard of Tufted Flycatchers until the preceding couple of hours but in that time had learned that they had been recorded fewer than a dozen times in the ABA region and had been assigned an elite Code 5 designation. This enhanced my excitement at seeing one, but it did not prevent me from pondering the absurdities of political borders and the insouciance with which animals treated them. Sure, the flycatcher was a Code 5 here, but a hundred miles to the south it might be as common as chickadees are in Montana.

Leaving Ramsey Canyon with eight Big Year birds, including five Lifers, we didn't realize that we were about to get a much more intimate look at borders—and their political and biological realities.

CHAPTER 9

homeland insecurity

Heading south from Ramsey Canyon, we munched on peanut butter sandwiches and dropped into a large valley as the road curved east.

"Look!" I told Braden. "That's Mexico right over there."

He looked up from *Sibley*. "Where?"

"Right there! Those mountains right over there are Mexico."

"That's *Mexico*?"

Both of us gazed in a kind of wonderment. It wasn't the first time I'd viewed our southern neighbor across the border, but this vista was certainly the most dramatic. Beautiful desert valleys and mysterious mountains shrouded in blue haze stood only a couple of miles away, but they might have been on the other side of the earth because of a simple line drawn by two nations.

I, of course, understood the need for the border—to control immigration, drug and human trafficking, and arms smuggling—but at the same time I felt how ridiculous it was too. Those mountains over there, the ones we could almost touch, undoubtedly harbored avian and cultural riches Braden and I could only imagine. Yet because of the border, poorly thought-out drug laws, our lack of investment in drug education, the violence that our policies and Mexican drug cartels had created, corruption in Mexico and in Washington, DC, and a hundred other things Braden and I had no control over, we could not safely go over there.

Before our trip I had toyed with the idea of bringing our passports and at least taking Braden across the border for a good Mexican meal, but a quick look at State Department statistics dissuaded me. Nogales, south of Tucson, had been listed as the nineteenth most violent city in Mexico. Agua Prieta, just across from Douglas, where we were heading, had been listed even higher, at seventeenth. I might have headed over on my own, but with my thirteen-year-old son? Not worth the risk.

Still, that didn't keep me from daydreaming about what that tantalizing terrain over there might be like.

After about an hour paralleling the border, we drove through the desert mining town of Bisbee. From there we pushed on to Douglas for gas and Doritos and finally out to the San Bernardino National Wildlife Refuge, where we confronted the two deadly swarms of killer bees described in chapter 1.

After surviving the would-be apian assassins and spotting the Black-chinned Sparrows and Greater Roadrunner, Braden and I walked back to where we'd left our car in the San Bernardino parking lot. It remained the only car anywhere in sight, which didn't surprise me. Between the closed access and the killer bees, this ranked as one of the most disappointing experiences I'd ever had on our nation's public lands.

Resigned to our unlucky afternoon, we loaded our gear into the backseat. As we prepared to head out, however, a Fish and Wildlife ranger arrived and rolled down his window to chat. I got the feeling that he rarely had the opportunity to talk with anyone out here, especially this time of year and about something other than law enforcement. He eagerly told us about the refuge, sharing information about the endangered fish species, the invasive bullfrogs (the volunteers we'd encountered earlier came out here to shoot them a couple times a week), and how the refuge had been closed since 9/11.

"That's a real bummer for people like us who drive way out here," I told him. "Could we ride in with you?"

"No," he said. "I would if I could, but I'm not allowed to."

Man, people sure are helpful around here! I thought. *I get it, though. My son and I do look like drug traffickers.*

"But what you can do," the ranger informed us, "is drive back down the road and park at Slaughter Ranch. From there it's a lot easier to walk into the refuge. They might not even charge you if you're just here to bird."

I thanked him, and as he rumbled down the road Braden and I climbed back into our car.

To our relief, Slaughter Ranch, also known as San Bernardino Ranch, proved more welcoming than the refuge. Following the short access road, we spotted two more roadrunners and then found ourselves pulling up to a park-like setting with arching oaks, elms, and sycamores surrounding a large artificial pond. We entered a small office, where a young woman greeted us and handed us a refuge brochure. When I asked about the entry fee, she said, "Oh, there's no charge if you're birding."

We began our visit by walking up to the large irrigation pond next to the ranch house. Designated a national historic landmark in 1964 and now a museum open to the public, the ranch had been owned by John Slaughter, famous for helping to establish law and order in the nearby town of Tombstone. Slaughter was a well-known figure on the Arizona frontier in the late nineteenth century and early twentieth century. He knew Wyatt Earp and Pancho Villa and did a lot of remarkable things in his life, including helping to track Geronimo. Local legend has it that one of Slaughter's employees built a house, dubbed "the Mormon House," straddling the US–Mexico frontier. This supposedly allowed him to legally keep two wives, one on each side of the border.

At the pond, Braden and I added Blue-winged and Cinnamon Teals to our Big Year lists, along with a Yellow Warbler in the trees surrounding it. Then we headed to the nearest small holding ponds—home to some of the refuge's critically endangered fish species. We were delighted to see Rough-winged and Tree Swallows zooming like fighter jets over the water. Then Braden flushed an American Bittern, which rose into the sky, casting us the evil eye for disturbing it. As we were leaving, I thought I glimpsed one of the endangered Yaqui River fishes rising to the murky surface, but that could have been, ahem, fishful thinking.

From there we set off to explore the more distant ponds we'd originally intended to see before we'd been ambushed by bees. The ponds were situated next to a dry arroyo called Black Draw, and that's where we hoped to find our primary target for the afternoon, the Green Kingfisher, and, if fortune really shined down on us, a Yellow-billed Cuckoo. Alas, the half-mile hike reminded me of Clint Eastwood's long march through the desert in *The Good, The Bad, and The Ugly*— hot, dry, and in this case, not worth the effort. At the ponds, we saw a couple of Vermillion Flycatchers, but that was about it.

We dragged our hot, tired, disappointed bodies back to the ranch, where we encountered the caretaker, Fred.

"Did you see the Green Kingfisher?" Fred asked.

"No. We were looking for it behind the big gravel mounds there."

"Oh," he said. "He hangs out about a hundred yards down the draw. I've been seeing him lately."

Uh, yeah, I thought. *That would have been nice to know before we trekked out there.*

Despite my grumpy state of mind, Fred proved to be a nice, friendly guy and a good conversationalist. I asked if they had any problems with the border right there.

"Yeah," he said. "Recently, they've been using the refuge to cross. Mostly mules carrying drugs. So far there hasn't been any violence. They show us their guns and we show 'em ours, and they usually back away. Me and my partner wear emergency beacons. If we press down on them and don't report in, the Border Patrol comes racing out here. Did you guys see the Great Horned Owl?"

"No. Where is it?" Braden asked, suddenly lifted out of his heat-induced torpor.

"Turn around."

We both did quick one-eighties to see, not fifty feet from us, a mother Great Horned Owl hunkered low in the fork of a cottonwood, incubating her eggs.

"She was here last year too," Fred told us as I fired off photos of this unexpected bonanza. "A big storm came up and blew the babies out of the tree, so we had to hand-raise them. When I'm doing my chores around the grounds, the owl often follows me around."

Braden and I grinned at each other. *Thank god for Fred!*

Before we left, I asked, "Hey, we were going to grab dinner in Douglas. What's the best Mexican restaurant there?"

"Just a minute," he said, ducking back into the office where we'd gotten the brochures earlier. He reemerged with a flyer for La Fiesta Café. "There are several good restaurants, but the rest are owned by the cartel."

"The cartel operates on both sides of the border?" I asked, astounded.

"Sure do," said Fred. "They've got relatives on both sides, but I don't like giving my money to them."

"We don't either," I told him. "Thanks."

And with that we headed back to Douglas for dinner and, with the sun sinking low over the Dragoons, our new home at Half Moon Ranch.

CHAPTER 10

cochise stronghold

Saturday, April 2, I woke relieved that for the first time in three days I wouldn't have to drive hundreds of miles. Instead the day promised to be one of relative rest, a chance to kick back, enjoy Bruce, Pat, and their dogs and goats, and maybe do a bit of hiking around the ranch. *Later,* I thought, *I might get really crazy and crack open a beer!*

Shuffling into the kitchen at about 7:00 a.m., I found that I had the house to myself. Since arriving at Half Moon Ranch two weeks before, Bruce and Pat had developed a ritual of climbing up to the bench of a nearby hillside to watch the rising sun light up the fabulous rocks of Cochise Stronghold. This morning, I realized that I'd already missed the sun's performance, but I didn't really mind. I proceeded with my plan to cook breakfast and started doing the prep work while I waited for the others to return.

After breakfast, most of us parked ourselves on the back porch for a couple of hours of reading and writing. Braden and I furiously tried to catch up on our journals and make sure our bird lists were accurate, but those darned birds kept interrupting! Every few minutes, a

Vermillion Flycatcher or flock of Cedar Waxwings or White-throated Swifts would swoop in, causing a stir that set us back five or ten minutes. While none of Bruce and Pat's guests seemed to embrace birding like we did, most harkened from outdoors or scientific backgrounds, and nearly everyone took an interest in new avian arrivals.

As I filled my journal pages with the events of Ramsey Canyon and Slaughter Ranch, I occasionally heard woodpecker drumming from the direction of a sycamore stand across the pond. I couldn't claim to identify one woodpecker drumming pattern from another, but this one did sound exotic to my Montana ears. When the next machine-gun burst rattled through the air, my self-restraint collapsed. "C'mon," I told Braden. "Let's go find out what the hell that is."

Grabbing binoculars and camera, we cut through a side gate and bushwhacked to the source of the drumming. Almost immediately we saw the familiar swoop of black-and-white wings as a woodpecker landed above us.

"What is it?" I asked, raising Braden's camera.

"Ladder-backed!" Braden exclaimed.

I got the camera lens focused and, sure enough, found myself looking at my first Ladder-backed Woodpecker. A few moments later, a second woodpecker joined the first.

Braden and I high-fived each other. LBWOs, as the American Ornithological Union dubbed them, aren't the most spectacular birds, with their fairly pedestrian black-and-white markings, but we'd never seen them before, and they ranked high on our list of trip priorities. We enjoyed watching the pair in the tree above us for a full ten minutes as they probed and pecked for food, and it was a good thing—these would be the only Ladder-backed Woodpeckers we would encounter during our trip and, for that matter, the entire year.

After lunch, we set out with Pat, Bruce, their dog Fay, Bruce's longtime friend Hans, and the two goats. Bruce had heard about a cave up a nearby draw and wanted to investigate. Bruce and Pat's one-eyed dog Pita lobbied to join us, but age had been catching up with him, so we locked him in the ranch house before heading out.

Like the hikes on preceding days, this one triggered wonderful childhood memories of scrambling through the backcountry of Southern California. We followed a thin trail through oak forest and then found ourselves climbing over large boulders and searching out trails through manzanita-filled scrub. I followed behind with Hans, Pat, and the goats while Braden and Bruce blazed the trail ahead.

Once again I took pleasure in seeing Braden conversing with adults, especially Bruce. Though they had never had their own kids, Bruce and Pat had a special way with them that was accepting, interested, and enthusiastic. At least once a year we tried to get together, and Bruce made a particular effort to pull Braden aside and show him things from his vast experience as a rock climber, backpacker, storyteller, and naturalist. Braden's age and adolescence didn't often allow him to acknowledge Amy and me as experts at much of anything, but that attitude didn't extend to Pat and Bruce. As we hiked, I could see my son closely questioning Bruce about something. I couldn't hear exactly what, but the way they kept glancing back down the trail, I surmised it had something to do with managing the goats.

After an hour of bushwhacking, we took a break at a small clearing.

"Do you think that's the cave up there?" Hans asked. Several hundred feet above the canyon, two black holes stared out from the rock wall.

"I don't know," said Bruce. "They said it was a circular entrance."

"Maybe it looks circular from a different angle," Hans suggested.

As we were discussing it, an intruder suddenly entered the clearing.

"Pita!" Pat yelled. "You numbskull! What are you doing here?"

Somehow Pita the arthritic one-eyed dog had managed to escape the ranch house and follow us up the canyon. It had taken a toll on him, too. Wobbly and chest heaving, Pita looked on the verge of collapse from his exertions, so Bruce filled his own hat with water and led him to a patch of shade.

My son walked over to join them. "Is he all right?" Concern filled Braden's voice.

"I think so," Bruce said. "We just have to let him rest for a while."

While Braden and Bruce worried over the dog, Pat looked at Pita with fond disgust. "What an idiot. He just doesn't know he can't do things like this anymore."

I could relate. As age crept up on me, I wondered if I'd be smart enough to recognize my own limitations. I hoped not. Pita set a good example for me. Like him, I planned to stay in denial for as long as possible.

While everyone else headed back down the canyon, I remained with Bruce and Pita. Twenty minutes later, Pita got to his feet and led us home as though nothing had happened.

That night Braden and I could already feel the sadness of a great trip drawing to a close.

"I'm going to miss Arizona," Braden said, looking through the photographs he had taken that day.

I knew my son well enough to know that he was referring not just to Arizona but also to Bruce, Pat, and the other people he'd gotten to know at the ranch. Even as a teenager, Braden formed attachments to people quickly—especially those who played a role in making his world a larger and richer place, whether that was introducing him to new ideas or helping him do things he hadn't yet imagined he could. This quality was one of many things I loved about my son, and I remembered being the same way at his age.

"Do you think we'll be able to come back here again?" Braden asked me.

I knew the answer he wanted to hear, but I always tried to be honest with him. I walked over to sit on the bed next to him and put my arm around his shoulders. "It's hard to say, Buddy. There's so many other places to see, and it's going to get harder as you get older. Maybe we can come back, though."

"I hope so," he said. "Maybe we could bring Mama and Tessa next time."

"That's a good idea," I said. "I'll bet they'd like it here."

We sat silently for a moment. Then Braden asked, "Where are we going tomorrow?"

We already had debated how to spend the next day—our last full day of birding before having to head back to Phoenix—but hadn't yet come to a decision. The town of Portal was one obvious option. Sitting on the far side of the Chiricahua Mountains, the tiny town was a famous birding destination, particularly for hummingbirds and the Elegant Trogons that nested up nearby South Fork Cave Creek. It was also a two-hour drive each way.

"I don't think I'm up for another four hours in a car," I told Braden. "But look, Chiricahua National Monument is just across the valley. It's supposed to have good birding too. Why don't we check that out instead?"

His shoulders slumped an inch at not giving Portal a try, but he gamely agreed. Then he insisted, "We have to go to Portal the next time."

"It's a deal," I said.

We were burning up the highway by seven the next morning. Our melancholy of the night before had been replaced by the excitement of seeing yet another totally new wild place and, we hoped, totally new wild birds. Driving directly into the rising sun, we sighted coyotes and roadrunners, the usual impressive display of hawks, and a new Life bird, the Scaled Quail. One bird we did *not* see was an Inca Dove, a bird that had eluded us the entire trip. We'd searched for them in Douglas, where they were supposed to be as common as creosote bushes, but they must have spotted us coming.

"Keep your eyes out," Braden instructed me. "This might be our last chance to see one."

Alas, we had not performed the correct sacrifices of birdseed and peanut butter cups, and Inca magic failed to bless us on the drive.

When we arrived at Chiricahua National Monument, we were only the second car in the visitor center parking lot. Although the center hadn't yet opened, a ranger spotted us from within and came out to greet us. As usual, my first question was where we should spend our time birding.

"Most people head up the trail right here," the ranger told us. "You're too early in the year for Mexican Chickadees, but up higher I thought I heard some warblers in the trees below the trail. You're also in luck today. The road to the top has been closed all season, but we decided to open it today for one day only."

"Terrific," I said, thinking, *San Bernardino could take customer service lessons from this place.*

Braden and I followed the ranger's advice and walked about a mile up the trail, but the birds seemed in no hurry to put in an appearance. At our turnaround spot, however, we discerned suspicious black shapes soaring high above the canyon.

I looked at them through my binoculars. "I think they're Andean Condors."

"Very funny," Braden said.

"Well, they're not Turkey Vultures," I said.

Braden focused his camera. "They're not Red-taileds either. Oh, did you see that?"

"Yeah!"

As one bird had circled, we both got a clear glimpse of black-and-white bands on its tail.

"I'm thinking Zone-tailed Hawk," Braden said.

"Sounds good to me."

On the hike back down, other birds began revealing themselves. We got a quick look at a Red-naped Sapsucker, a Lifer for me, and our best look yet at Arizona Woodpeckers. Using Braden's camera, I even snapped a decent photo of one—except for the branch cutting right in front of its head. Argh!

Back at the parking lot, it was a no-brainer to head to the top of the mountains, and the drive up impressed me as much as anything we'd seen on the trip. Hundreds of hoodoos and spires rose from the canyon walls around us, and at Massai Point we found interpretive signs that explained this fascinating geology. Twenty-seven million years earlier, the massive Turkey Creek Volcano had erupted just to the south of us. One thousand times more powerful than the eruption of Mount St. Helens, Turkey Creek had deposited one hundred cubic miles of ash and other material onto the surrounding landscape. Over time, the ash had compacted together and then begun to erode into the stunning complex of pillars and spires that dominated the monument.

Braden and I didn't know if we'd find anything bird-wise at the summit, but we followed the little nature trail and quickly scored another Lifer for me—Black-throated Gray Warbler—along with a Spotted Towhee and a beautiful Blue-gray Gnatcatcher. Venturing down the nearby Echo Canyon Grotto trail, we also found Ruby-crowned Kinglets and Violet-Green Swallows. Scrabbling among the towering hoodoos and through narrow rock clefts made me feel like the Humphrey Bogart character in *Treasure of the Sierra Madre* and, more importantly, gave Braden his first intimate taste of the canyon landscape that has made the Southwest so famous.

After driving back to the visitor center, we made a feeble attempt to explore the seldom-used downstream trail, but five days of hiking and travel finally began to catch up with us. After only a quarter mile, we decided to turn around—but not before seeing another Black-throated Gray Warbler and our last Painted Redstart of the trip.

It was a nice good-bye gift from this part of southern Arizona.

CHAPTER 11

gas station birding

By the time I finished shaving the next morning, Braden had already joined the rest of the crew to enjoy a final sunrise on Cochise Stronghold. I did some packing, then went out to find them. After we watched dawn's spectacular orange flames burn down the rocks, Braden and I returned to the house to clean our room and finish loading the car. Our stuffed mascot, Javvy, assumed his place on the front dashboard; then we gave Bruce and Pat big hugs and said a reluctant good-bye to Half Moon Ranch.

My thought had been to stop in Benson for breakfast, but Braden and I felt impatient to make tracks, so we raced to Tucson and carbo-loaded at a Denny's there. Our return flight didn't depart Phoenix until 6:30 p.m., giving us almost a full bonus day to bird, and we decided to kick it off with another session at Saguaro National Park. Our car's gas needle was diving toward empty, so before heading to the park I pulled into a gas station.

"Braden," I said, pointing to a gravel and scrub patch behind the gas station, "a real birder would go check out that vacant lot for new species."

He punched me on the shoulder. "Then why aren't you doing it?"

"Someone has to do the dirty work," I told him.

He scoffed but headed toward the back of the station while I swiped my credit card, selected my grade, and began filling the tank. As I sucked heavenly smelling hydrocarbons into my nostrils, I happened to glance toward the chain-link fence that separated the station's property from the vacant lot. I couldn't see Braden but did a double take at a surprising shape poking along our side of the fence—a roadrunner!

Leaving the pump to gurgle and chug, I grabbed Braden's camera and made my way over to the bird as stealthily as possible. It saw me coming and jumped the fence, but it didn't go far, and I was able to capture several crisp images as it glanced back at me with haughty suspicion. As I lowered the camera, Braden rushed up to me. "Daddy, hurry!"

"Braden, there was a roadrunner right here! It's gone, though."

"Daddy, come here! Quick!"

I'd learned my lesson with the Hepatic Tanagers and hurried after Braden to the corner of the fence.

"Look, do you see it?" he asked, pointing at a couple of Palo Verde trees. "White-crowned Sparrow. And over there is a Vermillion Flycatcher!"

"I see them!"

"There was a flock of Verdins over there too," Braden added.

We both laughed with delight. Who knew that one of Arizona's birding hot spots could be found behind a gas station?

At the Saguaro National Park western district visitor center, our luck continued with an amazing view of a Gila Woodpecker feeding on saguaro fruit. Braden even snapped a decent photo of it. Since getting good Gila photos had been one of my goals for the trip, we began searching for others, and it didn't take us long to locate an active nesting hole in a huge, gnarled saguaro. The woodpeckers, however, knew squat about proper lighting and kept landing on the shady side of the cactus.

Win some, lose some.

Even after a quick stop at the Arizona-Sonora Desert Museum, we arrived back in Phoenix with plenty of time to bird. From a previous trip, I had remembered seeing ducks in the pond in front of the Phoenix Zoo, so we decided to give that a try.

No ducks.

"Let's try the botanical gardens next door," I suggested.

Ten minutes later we were walking across the parking lot to the front entrance. We didn't have time to go in, but I recalled that the Desert Botanical Garden was a wonderful wildlife habitat, and, sure enough, in a mesquite tree next to the parking lot we saw an Anna's Hummingbird. Then, in the same tree, Braden spotted a Black-tailed Gnatcatcher, our last Big Year bird of the trip.

"Wow," I said. "Can you believe that? Let's go celebrate."

And we did—with a Mexican lunch at a restaurant on East Indian School Road. It wasn't the best meal we'd ever eaten, but neither Braden nor I cared.

I raised my plastic cup of root beer. "Here's to an awesome expedition—sixty-three Big Year birds in one trip!"

Braden clinked his Coke against my root beer, and we both took a sip.

"And remind me again, what did you guess before the trip?" I teased him. "Thirty?"

"Well, I didn't know," he defended himself. "I didn't think we'd see that many! Besides, you guessed low too!"

"Well, yes," I grudgingly admitted, "but not by as much."

We both took another sip.

"So," Braden said, setting his glass down. "It's time to decide on Bird of the Trip."

"That's going to be a tough one," I said. "Let's list the candidates. Gila Woodpecker's got to be on there. Arizona Woodpecker too. Ladder-backed?"

Braden shook his head. "Nah. We only saw them once, and they were kind of plain-looking. Vermillion Flycatcher has to be a possibility."

"Definitely."

"Mexican Jays and Magnificent Hummingbirds?"

"Maybe. And don't forget Greater Roadrunners."

"Yeah," Braden said.

Braden and I kicked it around for another couple of minutes, but despite all the excellent choices and arguments for each bird, our ultimate choice had never been in doubt.

Painted Redstart.

"We saw it every day," Braden summarized. "It was beautiful and had a great song. Besides, it was just so *cool*."

"I agree. Painted Redstart. Bird of the Trip."

We again clinked our cups to finalize the decision.

After another long swig, Braden said, "Thanks for bringing me to Arizona."

"Of course," I said.

houston or bust

Back at home, the next week proved every bit as frantic as I'd anticipated. During the course of just a few days, I had to prepare for and
present a talk at the Montana Library Association conference. I had
to get my car tuned up and my hair cut. I had to pack for Braden's
and my combined birding and work trip to Texas. Most urgently, I
had to find a way to get my camera and zoom lens repaired.

At the suggestion of my photographer friend Paul Queneau, I
joined the Canon Professional Services program, which rushed
repairs and offered loaner equipment. I FedEx'd my camera and
lens, but I was concerned about the camera body, which I had bought
used. Even if I got it repaired, it might give me further headaches
later on. In light of that—and the growing importance of obtaining
good photos for my science and nature books—I decided to splurge
on a brand-new camera body, Canon's 7D Mark II, along with a 1.4X
extender to let me zoom in even closer to my bird subjects.

Remarkably, both the new and repaired camera equipment
arrived on my doorstep with two days to spare, and I managed

to accomplish all of my other tasks. Even better, I squeezed in a daddy-daughter date with Tessa, pulling her out of school an hour early to go see *Zootopia*.

Ten days after returning from Arizona, Braden and I were again sitting on an airplane, this time heading for America's city of cement, Houston.

"Do you think we'll see a lot of birds?" Braden wondered out loud. After the incredible time we'd spent in Arizona, his voice betrayed a lack of enthusiasm for the Lone Star State.

"I think so," I said. "But I really don't know."

"I wish we could go to Brownsville," he lamented.

"Me too. But there's so much to see around Houston. I think it's smarter if we just stay there, don't you?"

He nodded. "Probably."

One of the difficult parts of planning this trip had been how to allocate our time. We had only four days to bird and at first thought that would be adequate to hit most of the Texas coast. The more we started checking out good birding spots online and in Mel Cooksey and Ron Weeks's excellent *A Birder's Guide to the Texas Coast*, the more we restricted our geographical ambitions. Nonetheless, I decided to let Braden pick our birding locations, and he'd figured out a promising itinerary for us.

"So, what's your official prediction for how many Big Year birds we'll see?" he asked me as a Delta flight attendant handed him a bag of peanuts.

"What's yours?" I countered.

"I'm going to say forty."

"That's all?" I asked. It was more than he'd predicted for Arizona but still pretty pessimistic considering he'd never birded the South, and new Life birds could be perched on every tree branch. "Well, I'm going to say fifty-five," I countered. "But I wouldn't be surprised if we got more."

"I hope so," he said.

We landed at George Bush Intercontinental Airport just before midnight and caught a cab to a nearby hotel. The next morning I left Braden to sleep in, shuttled to the rental car facility, and picked up our wheels. By ten we were heading to our first Texas birding spot, a place Braden had chosen called the Jesse H. Jones Park and Nature Center.

To reach the park, we drove through a suburban neighborhood only a few miles from the airport. We spotted our trip's first year bird, Great Egret, in a pond, but I was dismayed to see a brand-new subdivision going up right next to the park. As legendary as Houston's unfettered growth had become, it appeared to show no signs of slowing down.

Still, Jesse Jones served as an oasis amid the sprawl, and at the visitor center bird feeder we made our first truly exciting discovery: Indigo Bunting, a bird that only rarely reached Montana and one we'd never seen. The park's resident naturalist recommended we continue our visit by exploring the Cypress Boardwalk Trail a mile or so farther into the park, and we took her advice—only to be ambushed by squadrons of mosquitoes.

"What are they doing here?" Braden demanded, vainly swatting at his face and back.

"Welcome to the South."

Mosquitoes weren't killer bees, but they forced us into a hasty retreat to the car for bug spray. Slathered in repellent, we regrouped for a counterattack and stormed the boardwalk a second time.

We quickly observed an abundance of cardinals, blue jays, and doves, along with an exciting Lifer for Braden: Red-bellied Woodpecker. As we picked our way through a bottomlands area full of cypress trees, I halted and hissed, "Braden, come quick!"

On a cypress knee only twenty yards distant, a yellow bird flitted and poked for food. I didn't know what it was but guessed it belonged to the group of birds I most wanted to see and learn about on this trip—warblers. Braden confirmed it.

"Prothonotary Warbler!" he said, quickly raising his camera to his eye.

Barely as long as an index card, the warbler was one of the prettiest birds I'd ever seen. Its head and breast feathers shone a vibrant yellow that provided a shocking contrast to its black, unadorned eyes. Its wings were mantled in soft gray, and a greenish cast covered its back. We watched the lovely little bird, enchanted not only by its beauty but also by the fact that it really existed. During the week before our Houston trip, Braden and I had quizzed each other nightly on warbler identification and read about the birds' epic voyages across the Gulf of Mexico. To read about them and actually see one, though . . . well, it was the difference between reading about Texas barbecue and sinking your teeth into a steaming pulled pork sandwich.

Ten minutes later, I spotted a shape that got my adrenaline flowing even more. It perched on a dead snag overlooking a large swath of forest and—as usual—Braden beat me to the identification.

"Red-headed Woodpecker!" he shouted just as I got the bird into focus.

Now I was really feeling it. Not to be confused with the Red-bellied Woodpecker or the Red-cockaded Woodpecker, the Red-headed was a species I had longed to see since first becoming interested in woodpeckers almost four years earlier. Looking at it through my camera, I had to admit that it was even more impressive than I'd imagined, with its startling white rump and a head that looked dipped in bright red paint. We tried moving closer to the bird, but its perch rose from an impenetrable tangle of growth, so we reluctantly moved on. The woodpeckers weren't finished with us. Looping around a different trail closer to the visitor's center, a large bird flew across our path and landed on the trunk of a snag fifty yards away.

"Pileated," said Braden.

I focused my camera but was getting fed-up with my son beating me to the punch.

"I don't think so," I spat back. "I'm pretty sure that's an Ivory-billed."

Ivory-billed Woodpeckers, of course, are a species that most scientists consider extinct, and our chances of seeing one in the suburbs of Houston, hovered just below zero.

Braden socked me on the shoulder. "You're an Ivory-billed," he told me.

"So is that," I responded, refusing to give in.

My son didn't bother to respond.

Before leaving Jesse Jones we picked up Carolina Chickadee, then celebrated the morning with lunch at Mo's BBQ just up the road. When they learned we were from Montana, Mo's staff rolled out the red carpet and made sure we enjoyed our first taste of Texas—complete with a stuffed spud the size of an ostrich egg.

"Man, this is the best baked potato I've ever had," said Braden, excavating it like he was a backhoe. I only plowed halfway through my own mound of food but sucked down two glasses of iced tea in preparation for a busy afternoon.

From Mo's we headed toward the next birding location Braden had selected, W. G. Jones State Forest.

I didn't know why Braden had picked W. G. Jones, but I didn't really care. I simply reveled in the fact that he had picked out a place without consulting with me. Call it pride in watching my son learn to do things for himself or sloth on my part, I was happy to, for once, just follow directions.

Google Maps, though, obviously needed a birder on staff, because it guided us to the middle of a suburban neighborhood with nary a walking trail in sight. I pulled over next to a couple washing their SUV, and when I told them what we were looking for, they laughed and pointed us in the right direction. Five minutes later we stumbled into the forest headquarters, and there, looking over some informational displays, I finally gleaned what made this forest so special.

"Braden, did you know this is a place for Red-cockaded Woodpeckers?" I asked him, surprised.

"Well, duh. I told you that. That's why I picked it out."

"Huh," I grunted. "Must have missed that."

"You miss a lot of things," Braden ribbed me.

Fact was, I couldn't have been more thrilled. Unlike the unfortunate Ivory-billed, the Red-cockaded Woodpecker remained very much extant. Its populations were struggling, however, and it didn't take a genius to understand why. As we walked out into the nearby woods, we saw yet another sprawling Houston subdivision hemming in the reserve, and that was a problem—especially for the Red-cockaded.

The Red-cockaded specializes on longleaf pine forests, a habitat that once dominated ninety million acres of the South. In the last two centuries, loggers, agricultural interests, and urban sprawl have waged a relentless campaign against these beautiful forests, with devastating consequences. From a population of 1 to 1.6 million *groups* of birds, Red-cockaded Woodpecker numbers have fallen to about 6,100 groups today.

Fortunately the birds were officially protected under the Endangered Species Act of 1973, and, since then, federal and state agencies have made dedicated efforts to safeguard and improve scarce Red-cockaded habitat—including this postage stamp forest we were standing in.

"So, where are the birds?" I asked. In a cordoned-off area, biologists had painted green bands around the trunks of half a dozen trees that the birds used for nesting and roosting. Red-cockaded

Woodpeckers share some similarity to Acorn Woodpeckers in that they are known to live in family groups and cooperate raising their young. That's why biologists and government agencies count them in groups instead of as individuals.

Unfortunately, we had arrived at a lousy time of day to see the birds. The woman at the forest headquarters had told us that the best time was first thing in the morning, and we were hitting the forest at 3:00 p.m., when even the most active birds usually settle down for a siesta. We walked about half a mile without seeing any woodpeckers, but on our way back to the car, we encountered another man with binoculars.

"See any woodpeckers?" he asked.

"No, not yet," I told him.

"But we saw a Prothonotary Warbler over in Jesse Jones Park," Braden volunteered.

The man introduced himself as Ted Wolff from Chicago, and Braden and I shook hands with him. I explained that we were on the first day of our first Texas birding expedition.

"We're doing a Big Year," Braden elaborated. "We're up to 130 species."

"Not bad." Ted nodded. "I did a Big Year a few years back."

"Really? How many species did you get?"

"I got 503—more than 300 of them in Illinois."

Braden looked suitably impressed. "We're going to High Island tomorrow," he said. "Have you ever been there?"

"I stopped by there Monday," Ted told us. "But it had been about thirty years before that. I'm heading there again tomorrow to see what I can pick up."

Before we parted company, Ted asked, "Say, do you want to swap phone numbers in case we see something?"

"Good idea," I told him, whipping out my cell phone.

Even though we'd been skunked in the first Red-cockaded nesting area, our Red-cockaded map showed another nesting area right across from the headquarters where we'd parked. To reach it we would have to brave one of the most terrifying four-lane highways I'd ever seen. Looking at the onslaught of cars rushing in both directions, I debated crossing the highway on foot and prudently decided against it. Even in our car, it took me ten minutes to find an opening in the traffic and elevated my blood pressure to levels that threatened to give me a stroke.

Relieved to have survived, we climbed out of our car and hiked down another trail through widely spaced longleaf pines. I spotted a Red-headed Woodpecker relaxing on a branch, and another cluster of marked trees, but Red-cockaded Woodpeckers continued to elude us.

Turning down another path, Braden halted.

"Wait. Do you hear that?"

I listened but detected only the usual ringing in my ears. "No. What was it?"

"Tapping."

We walked a few more yards and Braden whispered, "There it is again."

I still didn't hear it, but moments later, we saw a swooping flash of black and white above us.

"There it is!" Braden exclaimed.

We trained our optics on the high branch of a pine tree, and, sure enough, discerned the unique white face and black-and-white barring that could only belong to a Red-cockaded Woodpecker. A second bird flew onto a nearby branch.

After firing off a couple of blurry photographs, I quickly telephoned Ted Wolff.

"Ted, we're looking at a pair right now!"

I could hear labored panting through the phone. "I'm on my way," he huffed.

Of course, just as Ted arrived, the woodpeckers disappeared. Ted waved his hand dismissively.

"It's always like that," he said.

We kept walking together and saw a hawk dive into a dramatic stoop after some unseen prey. I also saw my first-ever Tufted Titmice—adorable little gray birds that sported jaunty caps—drinking from a puddle. By this time, the sun had started to sink, and I could feel late afternoon creeping into the air. As we were about to bid Ted a second farewell, however, Braden shouted, "There they are!"

This time we all got good looks at the woodpeckers, and Ted's face stretched into a smile.

"That was worth it," he proclaimed.

For Braden and me, the birding day hadn't quite ended. As we made our way through Houston's heavy traffic toward our hotel in the tiny town of Winnie, I observed something flying over the freeway—something my mind at first refused to accept.

"Braden!" I hollered, pointing out the front window. "Look at that!"

What I was staring at looked kind of like an egret, but with one important difference—it was pink!

Just as my brain was rejecting the idea that it might be a flamingo, Braden exclaimed, "Roseate Spoonbill!"

I was too busy watching the highway to make out the spoon at the end of the bird's bill, but knew that this was the only explanation because nothing else in the region even remotely resembled the bizarre beast we were looking at.

"Can you believe that?" Braden said, slapping my palm.

"Wow. I didn't think we'd see one just flying over the road, did you?"

"No. A definite Bird of the Day, Daddy."

"Yeah. No question."

Which was saying a lot considering the day of birding we'd just had. What neither of us knew was that our day offered only the barest hint of what lay in store.

CHAPTER 13

high adventure at high island

It's fair to say that, even though I didn't yet know it, the next two days would fundamentally change my understanding of birds and birding. The reason? We were about to visit a second mecca of American birding, one that eclipsed even the reputation of Ramsey Canyon—High Island.

Those who have watched *The Big Year* will remember High Island as the site of the famous "fallout" scene in which a giant storm concentrates migrating birds into a tiny area, giving birders an opportunity to rack up more than a hundred species in a matter of hours. Believe it or not, this really does happen. Usually species making the six-hundred-mile journey across the Gulf of Mexico to the United States accomplish the task in a brisk eighteen hours or so. Faced with stiff headwinds and driving rain, however, the trip can become a harrowing, life-threatening experience for many migrants. If they do manage to reach the Gulf Coast, they desperately seek the first refuge they come to, and for many that is High Island.

Biologists refer to High Island as a "migrant trap." The top of an immense underground salt dome, it pokes a mere thirty-three feet above the surrounding coastal marshes. That is enough to support a wooded patch of plants that birds need for food and shelter. Although High Island is not the only migrant trap along the Gulf Coast, it is undoubtedly the most famous. Once a site of oil exploration, it was recognized as an important bird haven by local birders in the 1940s, and in 1981 the Houston Audubon Society (HAS) purchased a four-acre wooded tract—"Boy Scout Woods"—that would become the core of a vital refuge. Since then the group has expanded and improved the site to accommodate the birds and the more than thirty thousand birders who visit each year, mostly in spring.

Even though we weren't experiencing fallout conditions, Ted had warned us to arrive at High Island early, as the parking lot filled up fast. Braden and I were on the road by 7:20 a.m. and within a couple of miles realized what a different habitat we were about to encounter. From the pine and oak woods around Winnie, the road transitioned into flat fields and wetlands as far as we could see. It didn't take long for us to add to our Big Year list. Braden called out Black-bellied Whistling-Ducks, and I spotted Cattle Egrets. Then a large bird launched itself from a telephone pole.

Braden and I looked at each other and simultaneously shouted, "Caracara!"

Members of the falcon family, caracaras are large, handsome birds of prey with chunky bills. Strictly New World birds—meaning they are only found in the Americas—about a dozen species live in Central and South America. Only one, the Crested Caracara, extends its range up into the United States, principally in Texas, Arizona, and Florida. Known for its striking white head, black cap, and vivid orange and blue beak, it was a bird I had hoped to show Braden but wondered if I'd have a chance, given its usual haunts. Seeing one right off the bat was a good sign that the birding gods were with us, particularly since it turned out to be our only caracara of the trip. Fifteen minutes later, still giddy from the caracara, we crossed a large bridge over the Intracoastal Waterway, and the giant water tower of High Island came into view.

True to Ted's predictions, High Island's main parking lot had already filled by the time Braden and I arrived. Fortunately plenty of street parking remained, and within minutes we found ourselves standing at the entrance to Boy Scout Woods. As a youth, Braden got in for free, but I shelled out twenty dollars for a colorful round patch that would allow me a year's entrance to the sanctuary.

Following Ted's advice, Braden and I made a beeline toward Prothonotary Pond, where we joined a dozen other birders poised with cameras and binoculars.

"Any action?" I asked a woman standing nearby.

"There's a Prothonotary Warbler over there," she said.

"Of course there is," I said, figuring that Houston Audubon probably hired at least one of the birds to remain here all day long.

"There's also a Black-and-White Warbler," she said, pointing into a tree about thirty feet away.

That got my attention. The Black-and-White was one of the warblers I had most hoped to see—once again because it was one of the few I thought I'd be able to identify. Braden and I got fleeting looks at it, and also saw our first Scarlet Tanager, Little Blue Heron, and another warbler, a Northern Waterthrush. As I tried to relocate the Black-and-White, I heard Braden asking someone a birding question and turned to discover Ted Wolff standing next to me.

"Oh, I didn't see you there," I said. "I was so busy looking at the birds."

We both laughed, and I asked him where we ought to go next.

"I was just telling Braden, you should definitely go over to Smith Oaks," he said. "Besides the rookery there, you might catch a lot of warblers."

"Sounds like a plan."

First, we had more of Boy Scout Woods to explore. We made our way to the boardwalk overlooking the marsh, but the winds were gusting so hard that we saw only a Green Heron and more whistling ducks. Walking back through the woods, we got a great look at our first Ruby-throated Hummingbird and, in the tree next to it, a White-eyed Vireo. One of our favorite finds of the day, however, sat perched in a mulberry tree right outside the main entrance: a male Rose-breasted Grosbeak.

Rose-breasted Grosbeaks are handsome birds, and the males have black heads, black-and-white wings, and a white belly topped by a startling pink bib. While eastern birders might not give the bird a second glance, to our Montana eyes it seemed no less exotic than a Scarlet Macaw or the Roseate Spoonbill we'd seen the night before. Braden and I hurried to take photos, but the magnificent creature wasn't going anywhere. Exhausted from its journey across the Gulf, the grosbeak had found the perfect perch, with plenty of food within a beak's reach. At least twenty birders uttered oohs and ahs, clicking camera shutters and talking excitedly below it, but the bird remained completely unperturbed by the hubbub it had created.

"The refuge is definitely paying that grosbeak to sit there," I told Braden. "I wonder if these birds get union wages?"

"Daddy," he groaned, giving me another sock in the shoulder.

To reach Smith Oaks, we had to wind our way through the actual town of High Island. About four hundred people live there, supported mostly, I'm guessing, by the influx of birders and beachgoers streaming through their community. There didn't appear to be any restaurants in town, but I noted a sign outside a church for a barbecue at noon—information I tucked away for later.

We had no trouble finding a parking spot at Smith Oaks and right away discovered a woman sitting at a picnic table, carefully watching a Black-throated Green Warbler perched in a tree. The Black-throated Green was my favorite warbler so far, not because it sported the most impressive colors but because it was the most cooperative. Warblers, I was learning, are not couch potato birds. They are adrenaline-driven dynamos, constantly flitting and pecking and poking—their evident strategy for finding food. Any warbler found sitting still for even a few moments was one that we had to take full photographic advantage of, and Braden and I spent several minutes with the Black-throated Green before moving on to the real draw of Smith Oaks—a tiny island called the Rookery.

Making our way down the main trail, we heard the Rookery before we saw it, and Braden eagerly trotted ahead of me to discover hundreds of garish Roseate Spoonbills and Neotropic Cormorants cackling and squabbling as if they were at a giant tailgate party. I caught up to him and we both stood there, entranced by the scene in front of us. Every bird seemed to be doing something interesting. Some sat on nests. Others preened. Many were locked in struggles over a favorite branch or poop-splattered patch of ground.

Thoroughly captivated, Braden said, "I could watch this all day."

As we studied the two dominant species, we occasionally saw other birds on the island or in nearby reed beds: Common and Purple Gallinules, Blue-winged Teal, Pied-billed Grebe, American Coot, and a solitary White Ibis pretending to be a spoonbill.

Our new friend Ted joined us. "You should follow some of the trails here too," he said. "I saw a lot of warblers a few days ago. Here, I'll show you."

Through our various exchanges of the previous twenty-four hours, Braden and I had learned more about Ted and his birding background. It turned out that Ted had begun to bird in college but had let his avian interests fall by the wayside upon entering the working world. After spending thirty-five years working too hard to build his landscape architecture business, he had decided that he wanted to do something besides work for the rest of his life. Since then he had resumed birding with a vengeance.

We followed him past the Rookery and down to a low trail that ran along a pond, but we saw only a few shorebirds.

"When I visited this pond thirty years ago," Ted told us, "it was totally clogged with invasive trees. Since then they've done a lot of work to restore it."

Chalk another one up to conservation and forward-thinking people, I thought.

The warblers were visiting other hangouts that day, and we didn't see a single one on the walk back to the parking area. Once there, though, a flock of songbirds zoomed above our heads and landed in a nearby tree.

"Cedar Waxwings!" I exclaimed.

A skinny, tense woman rushed up to me. She carried what looked like a field artillery piece or perhaps a rocket launcher, but it turned out to be a tripod-mounted camera with an intimidating 500 mm lens.

"Did you say Cedar Waxwings?" she demanded in a thick New York accent.

The woman's aggressiveness and evident lack of manners made me instantly dislike her, but I pointed to the tree. "Right over there."

Without bothering to thank me, she rushed forward, prepared to do battle.

It was lunchtime, and over Braden's objections I drove back to the church to queue up for a barbecue plate.

"Man, it's lucky they were doing this *today*," I told Braden. "I don't know where else we could have found lunch."

A pair of birders in front of us turned around. "Oh, this is no accident," they explained. "They put this on for the birders every spring. I think it keeps the church funded for the rest of the year!"

The food was good too. Braden and I took our plates out to the front porch and sat down to devour our beef, potato salad, and baked beans and wash it down with iced tea.

I belched. "That's what I'm talking about. This'll keep us going all afternoon. How you doing, Buddy?"

Braden set aside his mostly finished plate. "A little tired, but good."

I could see that, like me, my son could have used a nap back at our hotel but was determined to press on. "You're doing great," I told him. He put his head on my shoulder, and I gave him a quick back rub.

After lunch, we visited another patch of High Island forest called Hooks Woods. We saw no birds, but at a drip—a small fountain that provides birds with freshwater—we encountered the woman with the tripod-mounted camera. I started asking her about her equipment and discovered that, once engaged in conversation, she was quite friendly. She showed Braden and me terrific warbler photos she'd taken the previous day.

"Wow," I said, staring at a photo of a Black-and-White. "Where did you take this?"

"At Sabine Woods," she told me. "You and your son should go there. The birds are much more cooperative than here on High Island."

We thanked her and returned to Boy Scout Woods, where the male Rose-breasted Grosbeak still held court in his mulberry throne across from the main entrance.

We had no time to continue admiring him. Next to the grosbeak, cars were queuing up for one of the highlights of the day, an event that Braden and I didn't want to miss.

Among the many wonderful things about High Island is the fact that Houston Audubon provides morning, afternoon, and evening bird tours—for free! A company called Tropical Birding leads the tours, and the afternoon's offering focused on a group of birds that Braden and I still had a lot to learn about, shorebirds. About twenty vehicles caravanned from Fifth Street and turned south down to the gulf. As we reached Highway 87, I saw angry brown waves almost lapping up onto the road and could feel stiff gusts buffeting the car.

Wow, I thought. *It wouldn't take much more for the ocean to roll right over this entire area*—an observation that would acquire special relevance two days later.

We paralleled the shore for about eight miles before pulling in at a place called Rollover Pass, which featured an expanse of shoreline and shallow flats. The Tropical Birding guys set up spotting scopes, and within minutes we found ourselves studying Marbled Godwits, Dunlins, Black-bellied Plovers, Ruddy Turnstones, and at least six different species of terns. I was grateful to have the Tropical Birding guides along because, as challenging as I found warblers, shorebirds threatened to permanently short-circuit my brain. I glommed onto an expert named Wes Homoya, who patiently explained the more obvious differences between species, but even with his help I made little headway in identifying the shorebirds in front of me. While I struggled, Braden quickly mastered the differences between the tern species, making me feel the ossification of my brain cells even more.

At one point, looking through his binoculars, Braden exclaimed, "Daddy! American Avocets!"

I looked up from a spotting scope. "Really?"

"Right out there!"

I quickly located one and grinned.

"Nemesis bird!" Braden said, and I high-fived him. It was a bird he'd missed repeatedly in the past two years, and it seemed fitting that he would bag it here in this world-famous birding location.

From Rollover Pass, the Tropical Birding guides led us another sixteen miles west, passing through scattered beach communities until we turned down Rettilion Road, where we breathlessly paused to watch a Barn Owl take a dump from its owl house. At low tide or under calmer conditions, we could have driven along the beach to the Houston Audubon Society's Bolivar Flats Shorebird Sanctuary, but with the surf up, our group settled for birding near the beach parking area. There we picked up Sanderlings, Piping and Semipalmated Plovers, and Short-billed Dowitchers.

The highlight was the sheer abundance of American Avocets. While we'd spotted perhaps twenty at Rollover Pass, a flock of at least a hundred hung out here. Braden and I soaked up the view, watching these graceful orange, black, and white creatures as they hunkered down in the breeze. Every once in a while a birder or car would get too close, and the birds would lift up and fly forty or fifty yards. Then, as a group, they would alight back onto the sand—so gently I wondered if they even left footprints.

We watched the shorebirds for half an hour. Then I slipped Wes some beer money for his help and patience, and Braden and I headed back up the Bolivar Peninsula, spent but thrilled by the day's experiences.

"So," Braden asked as we drove along the coast. "Bird of the Day?"

"Oh, man, that's going to be tough," I told him. "Let's review the possibilities."

"Rose-breasted Grosbeak."

"Yeah, definitely a candidate. Black-and-White Warbler?"

"Well, we didn't really get a great look at that. Little Blue Heron?"

"Maybe. Black-throated Green Warbler?"

"Yeah. I'd say that's a possibility. How about Purple Gallinule?"

I scoffed. "They're like floating chickens."

"*Daddy!* They're not like floating chickens!" Braden exclaimed, unable to stifle a laugh.

I grinned. "Okay, what else?"

"Definitely American Avocets," Braden said.

"Caracara?"

"That seems like so long ago."

"Yeah, I know. So what's it going to be?"

"It's your day to choose," Braden told me.

I sighed. "Okay. I guess I'm going to have to go with—Rose-breasted Grosbeak. It was such a cool bird, and it gave us such a great look all day long, even if Houston Audubon did pay it to sit out there."

Braden punched me a final time but concurred. "I agree. It's definitely Bird of the Day."

Before we returned to Winnie to catch up on our journals, delete terrible photos, and hit the sack early, we took one last swing along Fifth Street, across from Boy Scout Woods. The Rose-breasted Grosbeak had finally departed, but as we approached some bottlebrush bushes we were rewarded with Orchard Orioles and Tennessee Warblers. While I got out to take photos, Braden wandered to a neighboring lot but came rushing back, a huge smile plastered across his face.

"You have to come! You're not going to believe this!"

I trotted after him to discover that there, in a tree, sat two Inca Doves—the species that had repeatedly outwitted us in Arizona only two weeks before. To be honest, the birds did not stun us with their magnificence. They looked just like any other gray dove except for the scaly appearance of their feathers. Braden and I didn't care. Finding one felt like an important accomplishment, and for the twentieth time that day we high-fived.

The doves stamped an exclamation point onto the end of our most amazing day of birding ever.

CHAPTER 14

meta-birding

Our plan for the next day had been to take the Bolivar ferry to Galveston. That night, however, we decided to save Galveston for another trip and instead use the following day to further explore the area around Winnie. We hadn't even touched Anahuac National Wildlife Refuge, and, though we'd seen a few warblers, Braden and I hungered for more.

"That woman with the big camera really liked Sabine Woods," I said to Braden. "What if we hit Sabine in the morning and head to Anahuac for the afternoon?"

"I wish we could go farther down the coast," he said.

"Me too. There's just so many birds to see right here, though. Don't you think we should see them?"

"Yeah," he acknowledged. "But next time we have to go to Brownsville."

The next morning, after grazing on the hotel breakfast buffet, we followed Highway 73 to Port Arthur, affectionately known as the Land of Many Oil Refineries.

Everyone who drives a car should visit Port Arthur and Sabine Pass to learn what our collective thirst for fossil fuels does to the environment. With wall-to-wall refineries, liquefied natural gas terminals, and offshore drilling barges, the place offers an end-of-the-world Mad Max landscape complete with pipes belching flames, stadium-sized storage containers, and hundreds of inebriating carcinogens wafting through the air.

"Why do they do this?" Braden asked, aghast at the industrial nightmare surrounding us.

"They do this because we all drive cars," I told him. "The only way to get rid of this is to get rid of gasoline-powered automobiles and fossil fuels."

"We should do that," he said.

"No argument here," I said, punching the accelerator of our supercharged six-cylinder rental car.

We were so impressed by the scale of the petroleum operations that at one point I pulled over to take a picture with my cell phone. I couldn't have been out of our car for ten seconds when a security detail in a black truck pulled up behind us. I didn't linger to learn what the men wanted. Instead I hopped back into the driver's seat and calmly continued south, watching in my rearview mirror as the petroleum police tailed us until we'd left the property.

Remarkably, in a water-filled ditch right next to one of the petrochemical installations, we tallied a new Big Year bird, Yellow-crowned Night-Heron. Just what it was doing in a ditch next to an oil refinery mystified us, but we were glad to add it to our Big Year lists.

We located Sabine Woods without any trouble and arrived early enough to park outside the main entrance. Like Hooks Woods at High Island, Sabine Woods is owned and managed by the Texas Ornithological Society and is another prominent migrant trap. Before a succession of hurricanes had washed it away, a road connected High Island with Sabine Woods, making it a must-bird destination. Now Sabine required an hour-long detour inland, rendering it less visited than its much more famous neighbor—bad news for birders but better for birds wanting to rest with minimal disturbance.

At Sabine, for the first time, Braden and I began to master the art of "meta-birding." Ted had explained it to us the previous day.

"Instead of looking for the birds," he said, "you look for the birders to see what they're looking at."

For warblers, this proved an especially effective strategy. Difficult to see in the best of circumstances, these small flighty birds could easily escape detection—unless, that is, dozens of eyes hunted them. Our first warbler of the day was another Black-throated Green that Braden spotted just off the path, but only a hundred yards later, we noticed a trio of birders staring up into a canopy of oaks. We hurried to join them.

"What do you see?" Braden eagerly asked.

A woman pointed. "There's a Black-and-White Warbler up there. We also just saw a Blue-winged and a Bay-breasted."

"Really?" I asked, desperately searching with my camera.

Over the next few minutes, we spotted all three birds, and watched the antics of an American Redstart—a Lifer for me.

Those first observations set the stage for the next couple of hours at Sabine. A dozen clusters of birders roamed the woods, spotting birds and helping others do the same. We had met a number of these birders the day before during the shorebird field trip, and our team effort produced almost a dozen warblers, including Ovenbird, Hooded, Northern Waterthrush, Prothonotary, and Worm-eating. The woods also held a who's who of tanagers, buntings, thrushes, and our first Eastern Kingbirds of the year.

After more than an hour, I plopped down on a bench to rest and noted with delight that a plaque read "In Honor of Sandy Komito."

"Look, Braden," I said. "Sandy Komito."

Sandy Komito was one of the prominent birders featured in the book *The Big Year* and had set an ABA Big Year record in 1998 with 745 species. Seeing his name here on the bench helped put in perspective what Braden and I were doing. *Wow,* I thought. *If Sandy has birded here, I'll bet almost every other major birder in the country has too.* It gave me a feeling of legacy, not so much for myself but for Braden. I didn't know if he would continue to pursue his birding passion, but it was plain to see that he could one day join the ranks of America's finest birders if he desired.

Not that Amy and I were pushing either of our kids toward a particular path in life. Instead we had been exposing them to as many experiences and perspectives as possible. An outstanding pianist and violinist in addition to being a social worker, Amy made sure the kids received solid music educations. With my science back-ground and love of travel and writing, I tried to introduce them to nature, other cultures, and history. The strategy seemed to be work-ing, as both kids had discovered subjects that ignited their passions. Tessa had developed a love of guitar, soccer, writing, astronomy, and Asian cultures. Braden had become an excellent writer and piano player, but at this point it was mostly all about the birds. And that was just fine with Amy and me. Sitting on Sandy Komito's bench, I experienced one of those rare moments of parental peace that comes from believing that maybe, just maybe, everything is going to work out fine.

I looked over at my son sitting next to me. "Ready to keep birding?"

He hoisted himself to his feet. "Yeah."

We continued wandering the woods. Every time we thought about heading back to the car, we spotted a new group of birders watching something rare and amazing.

Finally, after two hours, we decided to take a last look at one of the drips.

"Then we're leaving for sure," I told Braden.

Suddenly, behind us, we heard a familiar voice. "Hey, it's my Mon-tana friends!"

We spun around to find the woman with the big camera approach-ing us.

"You came!" she happily exclaimed.

We grinned. "Well, you made it sound so good."

"Have you seen anything?"

Braden rattled off our birds for the morning and then darted off for more meta-birding. Meanwhile, I showed our new acquaintance where the Prothonotary Warbler was hanging out, and we both took great photos of it. Finally, hungry and sort of ready to move on, I collected Braden, said goodbye to some of our new birder friends, and headed back toward Winnie. As we passed the oil refineries, the same Yellow-crowned Night-Heron waved to us—or maybe it was trying to flag a ride to escape the industrial wasteland of Port Arthur.

To reach our afternoon destination, we had to pass back through the town of Winnie, and here I must insert a warning to travelers. If you're staying around Winnie, Texas, *bring your own food.*

Denny's topped the list of local restaurants, but we'd already eaten there twice, so as we zipped back through town we settled for McDonald's to provide our basic caloric needs. That accomplished, we drove for thirty minutes through flat fields and wetlands to reach our next birding location, Anahuac National Wildlife Refuge.

After consulting with the resident naturalist, we took a short walk along a nature trail and then drove around the Shoveler Pond loop. With winds continuing to sweep the area, it was nice to do some car birding for a change, and on the loop we picked up half a dozen new Big Year birds, including a pair of Black-necked Stilts preening next to an eight-foot alligator that posed like a B-movie prop.

Our most exciting find of the afternoon occurred on the short drive between the loop and the Skillern Tract. We were cruising along at fifty miles per hour, when Braden suddenly hollered, "Daddy! Turn back! Scissor-tailed Flycatcher!"

For some reason my brain translated these words into an image of a Swallow-tailed Kite—probably because I'd seen photos of the kite but never the flycatcher. In any case, as we retraced our route I kept staring at the sky, expecting to see the fluttering image of a raptor waiting to pounce on an unsuspecting mouse or vole.

Braden, though, kept pointing to the fence next to the road.

"It's coming right up. Slow down!"

When I finally spotted the bird, I realized my mistake.

"Oh my god, *that's* a Scissor-tail?"

"Yeah, stop so I can take a picture."

Quickly calculating the angle, approach, and magnetic declination of our trajectory, I said, "No. He'll fly if I stop. I'm going to drive past him and then come back slowly. Roll down your window and get your camera ready, okay?"

"Got it," Braden confirmed.

I drove two hundred yards past the bird and then, checking for traffic, pulled another one-eighty.

"Okay," I said. "Here goes."

I slowed our car, letting Braden take a couple of shots while we were still moving, then pulled to a stop not ten yards from the flycatcher.

The bird didn't budge.

"He's incredible!" I whispered, slowly raising my own camera to try for some photos.

The flycatcher cooperated beautifully, and I just stared at it, amazed.

"I don't think I've ever even seen a picture of one," I told Braden.

With a beautiful white head and breast, pinkish-orange belly, and vivid red epaulettes, the bird was handsome even without its incredible tail. But that tail! It seemed to extend a good foot beyond the flycatcher's rump, making the bird appear like a mythical beast. As we watched, it took off from its post, darted to the ground, and flew up onto another post fifty feet away. We followed, mesmerized.

"That's one of the birds I most wanted to see on this trip," said Braden.

"I can see why. I thought you were talking about a Swallow-tailed Kite."

Braden looked at me with derision. "Really? That's what you thought? They are nothing alike."

I shrugged, defenseless. "They both have the word 'tailed' in them."

Braden didn't bother responding to that. Instead he said, "Bird of the Day."

"No doubt about it," I agreed.

The afternoon still had a couple more prizes to offer. At the Skillern Tract we headed out onto the boardwalk. Braden walked ahead, eager to get a closer look at some spoonbills on the horizon while I walked more slowly, glancing off to the sides. As I crossed a narrow, tangled waterway, my patience paid off when I surprised a tiny bird with a vivid yellow breast, black mask, and white band above the eye. It was one of the warblers I had been desperately trying to learn for the past week!

"Braden!" I called. "Hurry!"

He ran back to me. "What is it?"

"Down there. Yellow-throated—I mean Common Yellowthroat!"

At first Braden didn't see it. Then he spotted the bird—right before it dived deeper into a thicket.

We high-fived. "Our twelfth warbler for the day!"

"Even dozen."

On our way out of the Skillern Tract I also spotted a venomous cottonmouth snake curled up in some reeds, and we encountered a slider, a kind of water turtle, walking across the trail. Back out on the main road, we turned off onto one more birding spot that might hold potential—French Road. We drove by a second Scissor-tailed Flycatcher, and then I noticed a familiar shape in the middle of the road. I slowed and stopped.

"What is it?" Braden asked.

"I think it's another cottonmouth," I told him.

We got out of the car and approached. Sure enough, the snake's thick body and diamond-shaped head gave it away. When we violated its comfort zone, it opened its mouth, revealing its impressive fangs and cottony palate.

"Be careful," Braden warned me, hanging back.

I stayed ten feet away, close enough to get good photos without risking a trip to the emergency room. With that, we climbed back into our car. We were tired, hungry, and thrilled by another unbelievable day of birding. We also looked forward to one last day with the birds of High Island.

"If a storm comes in, we might even get some bird fallout conditions," I told Braden, glancing up at the gray sky.

I should have kept my mouth shut.

CHAPTER 15

unprecedented historical weather event

Since we had arrived in Texas, weather reports had predicted storms every day of our visit. We'd managed to dodge them so far, but finally, on our last day to bird, I awoke to the kind of downpour I had been expecting—and fearing—all along. After pulling on my sweatpants, I opened the drapes just in time to see a spectacular flash of lightning illuminate a grim charcoal sky. The resultant blast of thunder unleashed a fresh torrent of water that was rapidly turning the parking lot below into an inland sea.

I stared at the tempest, unsure what to do. The prospects for birding wavered between doubtful and "are you kidding me?" But I wasn't ready to throw in the towel.

Opting to let Braden sleep, I shaved and dressed, then went downstairs to try to assemble breakfast from the pickings left behind by a plague of early birders. By the time I returned, Braden had begun to stir.

I handed him a bagel. "It's really coming down out there."

He sat up and yawned. "Can we still bird?"

"I'm not sure, but get dressed, okay?"

He grunted gamely, and by nine thirty we had finished packing our stuff, checked out of the hotel, and optimistically pointed our car back toward High Island. Three to four inches of water covered the road, and I cranked the wipers to high, but they couldn't keep up with the deluge cascading down the windshield.

"Holy crap!" I exclaimed, keeping the car at twenty-five miles per hour, and a mile or so south of Winnie the reality of the situation finally soaked into my brain. I pulled the car under the eaves of a church and turned off the motor.

"What are you doing?" Braden asked, alarmed.

A fresh bolt of lightning shattered the sky.

I looked out at the storm. "Uh, Son, I don't think we're going to High Island today."

"What? Why not?" Braden stared at me, perplexed. Even living in Montana he'd never experienced this kind of violent weather—or the hazards it presented.

"The weather report this morning said eight to twelve inches of water have fallen in the past twelve hours," I explained, "and the road between here and High Island barely pokes up above sea level. My guess is that it will soon be flooded—if it's not already."

"Can't we at least try it?" His tone implied that I was giving up too easily.

I reluctantly shook my head. My wife considers me a risk-taker, and by some standards maybe I am. A big part of me wanted to go for it and try to reach High Island. Then again, one advantage to living fifty-six years is that I experienced at least occasional episodes of common sense.

"We'd need a boat," I told Braden. "I'm not even sure we can make it back to Houston."

Disappointment crossed my son's face, but I could see him begin to grasp the gravity of the situation.

"Let's try to stop somewhere on the way back," I suggested. "Just off the interstate, okay?"

"Sounds good."

What I didn't tell Braden was that I was almost as worried about the conditions on I-10 as I was about the road to High Island.

Fortunately the interstate didn't turn out to be nearly as terrifying as I'd anticipated. Traffic was light, the road seemed to drain well, and most people—even those driving testosterone-filled four-wheel-drive pickup trucks—kept their speed under fifty-five miles per hour.

While I kept my eyes on the road, Braden scoured both our Texas birding guide and a birding map we'd bought at Anahuac the day before. After discussing our options, we decided to make a seven- or eight-mile detour to the Trinity National Wildlife Refuge. It didn't top the list of the region's birding hotspots, but *A Birder's Guide to the Texas Coast* mentioned a dozen or so species that could be found there, and we had plenty of time to check it out. Unfortunately, when we arrived we found the main parking area deserted of people and birds and, with the rain pounding like a steel drum band against our hood and rooftop, we didn't even get out of the car. One small consolation was that on the way back to the freeway, we spotted a group of White Ibis and Little Blue Herons at the edge of a field. We stopped to watch them and take a few blurry photos from the car. Then we headed toward Houston.

I have to admit that a small part of me welcomed getting washed out. I'd been anxious about setting up my booth for the conference at the convention center, and I felt better about navigating Houston's downtown streets at mid-morning rather than at rush hour as we'd planned. As Braden used Google Maps to guide us toward the city center, we learned that authorities had closed the interchange from I-10 to I-45 due to the storm. Fortunately we were able to reach our exit and, after only a few wrong turns, located the George R. Brown Convention Center loading area.

The convention center stood as empty as the streets downtown, and it was only later that we learned that Houston's mayor had urged everyone to stay home that day. I felt like writing the mayor a personal thank-you note because, perhaps partly due to his actions, Braden and I were able to quickly schlep my books, banner, and author propaganda inside, do a little setting up, and make it out of there in under an hour.

By this time my stomach rumbled, and I really wanted to take Braden to Pappasito's, a local Tex-Mex chain I'd enjoyed on previous visits. With my phone, I located one a couple miles away, and we navigated the city streets toward it—only to find it closed. Just across the street, however, I spotted another restaurant. We drove over to it, and a man in a suit rushed up to our car.

"You come to eat?" he asked through my rolled-down window.

"Yes, sir," I said.

"Well, I've got the bar open, but I can't serve you any food."

"What's going on?" I asked.

He pointed at the sky. "It's the flooding. The buses aren't running, and my employees are having trouble getting downtown. Some are on their way."

"How long will it be?"

"I can't tell you," he said.

Only then did it begin to dawn on me just how severely the storm had slammed the region. *After all,* I thought, *if a storm can stop the flow of Tex-Mex food in Texas, it has to pack a pretty major punch.*

I looked over at Braden. "We might not have any better luck anywhere else. How about if we just wait in the car here and see what happens?"

He shrugged. "Okay."

While I stared out at the rain, I let Braden use my phone to play a video game—Angry Birds, of course—and after fifteen minutes I noticed a couple of employees slip through the restaurant's side door.

I gave Braden a nudge. "C'mon, let's go in."

To my surprise, the manager seated us. "We can make you enchiladas," he told us. "Will that work for you?"

"Guacamole?" I asked.

He smiled. "Sure."

"Sounds great," I told him, relieved that Braden and I would get a decent meal. It was too. The enchiladas were tasty and the guac fresh. Braden even ordered a Shirley Temple to celebrate while I gave a big tip to the staff for making sure we didn't go hungry.

As we munched on the last of our tortilla chips, only one question remained: where could we possibly bird that afternoon?

Braden flipped through *A Birder's Guide to the Texas Coast.*

"How about Katy Prairie?" he asked.

"Oh, yeah. I've heard of that," I said. "Someone told me it's really good."

Google informed us that it was closed.

"Okay, let's try the Houston Arboretum," I said. I had been there before and enjoyed it, and it seemed like a good bet on this sort of day. Even better, it was nearby.

"Sounds good," Braden replied.

Back in our car, we crawled Houston's streets and a short stretch of interstate toward the arboretum—only to discover that it too had closed and that floodwaters were creeping up the adjacent parkway.

"Geez," I muttered. "Have you ever seen anything like this?"

Flipping through the book, Braden said, "How about Bear Creek Pioneers Park? It's supposed to have Barred Owls, Acadian Fly-catchers, and a bunch of warblers."

"Worth a try," I said, navigating our way east on I-10. Twenty minutes later, I pulled off on Exit 751 and turned north toward the park. We crossed a canal raging with brown floodwater and debris, but we were on a thruway so I had every reason to believe we'd be okay. Half a mile farther, though, traffic slowed and began making its way into deeper water covering the road. I squinted through the windshield.

"Braden, are those cars making it through or are they turning around?"

Braden also peered ahead. "I can't tell."

Then I noticed that the water wasn't just covering the road—it was rushing across it like a mountain stream.

"Holy crap!" I said for the fourth or fifth time that day. I checked for cars behind me and pulled a fast U-turn.

"What are you doing?" Braden demanded. "Why are you turning around?"

"Look at the water on the road," I told him. "See how fast it's moving? Another few inches and we'd be in serious trouble."

My heart raced like a high-speed metronome. Houston wasn't just getting a little rain. It was getting hammered, and we were in the middle of it! I later learned that some parts of the city received fifteen inches of rain, most of it in a ten-hour period. That rainfall alone might not be catastrophic, but Houston sits barely above sea level and has more concrete than perhaps any other large US city. With a shortage of drainage ponds, the water spontaneously forms lakes and rivers such as those that Braden and I were encountering.

Still, like the defenders at the Alamo, neither of us was ready to wave the white flag. In a last desperate plea, Braden said, "Let's just try Jesse Jones Park near the airport."

"Okay," I said, "but that's the last place. This is a historic storm. If we can't get into the park, we're going to our hotel."

"Gotcha."

We drove the forty minutes north, staying on major roads and avoiding any more lakes and rivers in our path. Finally we pulled into the neighborhood that led to Jesse Jones Park, and guess what? The park was closed.

"Oh, man. They could at least let us walk in," I complained.

That's when we noticed something. The parking lot where we'd parked only three days before? It had become a lake three to six feet deep!

I shook my head. "Unbelievable."

A man in a nearby parked car noticed us and rolled down his window. "You trying to see the horses?" he asked.

"Uh, no," I said. "What horses?"

"Just up the creek, people were trying to save about 150 horses that got trapped. A lot of them were swimming and ended up here."

"You're kidding."

"No. People are really upset about it. Apparently, this isn't the first time this has happened, and the owners knew about the problem. They let it happen all over again."

I later learned that there had been about a hundred horses, and, thanks to the efforts of Samaritans, most had been saved.

We didn't get into the park, but about this time I noticed the rain easing. We also spotted three Red-headed Woodpeckers bickering outside the park entrance. The woodpeckers gave me an idea.

"C'mon," I told Braden. "Let's take a walk around the neighborhood. Who knows? If there are birds in the park, there might be more of them outside of it too."

Braden looked doubtful, but he strapped on his camera and binoculars, and we set off along a side street paralleling the fence and boundary of the park. A few cars drove slowly past, their drivers casting curious glances at the two nuts staring at trees and telephone poles through binoculars. After about three blocks, we came to a vacant lot abutting the park, and there, from a fifty-yard distance, we spotted a flash of blue.

"Indigo Bunting?" I asked.

Braden took a photograph. "Yeah."

"Nice," I said, glad that we saw at least one cool bird before calling it quits.

I walked deeper into the vacant lot, but Braden stood staring at the photo he'd just taken.

I turned back to him. "What're you doing?"

"Daddy," Braden said. "I don't think that's an Indigo Bunting."

"What is it?"

Braden studied the photograph. "It's—yeah: Blue Grosbeak!"

"You're kidding!"

"No! Look!" He showed me the photo on his camera's LCD screen.

"All right!" I said. "Amazing!"

We caught a few more glimpses of the grosbeak before heading back to the car. As we drove to our hotel, we high-fived each other one last time.

"Blue Grosbeak!" Braden shouted.

"That makes the day worthwhile, doesn't it?"

Braden nodded. "I'm so glad we saw it."

Though our only new bird for the day, the grosbeak was Braden's eighty-sixth Big Year bird and seventy-eighth Life bird of the trip. It was my eighty-third Big Year bird and seventy-fifth Life bird. With the day that we'd just experienced, I felt sure it was a bird we would remember for a long, long time.

CHAPTER 16

terror at 31,000 feet

Despite the storm, Braden's flight left on schedule the next morning. When it was time for him to board, he gave me a vigorous hug, and I tousled his unkempt hair.

"Have fun on the flight back, okay?" I told him.

"I will," he promised, but his somber voice betrayed sadness that our adventure had come to an end.

I smiled, trying to stay upbeat, but watching his plane pull back from the gate left a lump in my throat. Even though I knew I'd be seeing my son again in four days, his departure conjured up faded movie reels of farewells to my own father.

My parents divorced when I was eight years old, and a few months later my dad moved across the country, first to Massachusetts, then to Pensacola, Florida, where he took up duties as an assistant biology professor at the University of West Florida. My parents' custody agreement gave me six weeks with my father in the summer and one week at Christmas, but my mom usually allowed us to swap the Christmas week for an extra two weeks in the summer. While it seemed a good trade on paper, it also meant that I had only one brief window in which to spend time with my father every year.

Like Braden and me, my dad and I shared a deep bond, and those summers had been the highlights of my young existence. During our eight short weeks together, my dad and I spent countless hours fishing, searching for snakes and turtles, and staying up late to play cribbage while watching Johnny Carson on *The Tonight Show*. Even when my dad was working, I relished going to the university with him and hanging out in his lab with his graduate students. When that got old, I slipped over to the campus library and spent hours devouring books that my dad recommended. These tomes usually reflected peace-loving Buddhist philosophies and included *The Godfather*, *Exodus*, *Jaws*, *On the Beach*, and *All Quiet on the Western Front*. As an adolescent, I loved them.

Looming over each summer, however, was the painful reality that in a few weeks my father would put me on a plane back to California. Our tearful good-byes took a heavy toll. Although I never wished for my parents to get back together, almost fifty years later I still wondered if they understood what they'd put me through.

If there was an upside to all of this, it was that it made me determined to make the most out of every moment my kids and I got to spend together—even if it meant pulling the kids out of school or stressing the family budget. Because of my past, I understood the importance of taking Tessa on a father-daughter trip to New York or California, not to mention the Big Year adventures Braden and I were having. Watching Braden's plane taxi out onto the tarmac, I wished we could keep on birding Texas for another week or two.

But the bills still had to be paid, so, after watching his plane disappear I took a deep breath and headed back into Houston to try to bolster my career.

The conference was a bust.

There was a time when, at a big event such as this, I could sell a lot of books and, more important, line up invitations for paid author visits to schools and other conferences. Over the next three days, I not only failed to get a single bite for future engagements, I sold barely enough books to cover one night of my hotel stay.

Part of that undoubtedly had to do with the storm, but I also could write a Shakespearean tragedy about other factors, including big publishers, cash-starved school districts, and overbearing, ideological politicians determined to send education staggering back into the Dark Ages. Such a saga, however, would only raise my blood pressure and cause me to weep into my keyboard, short-circuiting my computer and ending my writing career once and for all. Rather than go through that, I'll just say that I did enjoy a few choice conversations with librarians and visiting some old friends who were also attending the event. Otherwise I felt hugely relieved when the conference came to a close and I could think about heading home.

After packing up my booth, I drove directly to the airport, boarded a plane, and settled into my seat for the two-hour connecting flight to Salt Lake City. As the plane lifted gently into the sky, I put the conference behind me, closed my eyes, and let my mind drift over our wonderful Texas birding experiences.

Then, an hour into the flight, I sat bolt upright.

Oh, my god, I thought. *I couldn't have done that!*

A steel blade sliced through my heart, and I quickly reached under my seat and jumped up to check the overhead rack.

This can't be true! my mind screamed. But it was.

I had left my camera bag sitting in the airport terminal.

Sweat broke out on my forehead, and I flushed with panic as the repercussions of my carelessness began to sink in. It was bad enough that I had left four thousand dollars' worth of camera equipment sitting in the airport. Worse was the fact that the camera held every one of the pictures I had taken on the trip!

As I struggled for composure, my brain raced through possible outcomes of this disaster:

- Someone would find my bag and turn it in to lost and found.

- The Transportation Security Administration would identify my bag as a suspicious package, call in the bomb disposal unit, and gleefully take my camera to the nearest vacant lot to blow it up.

- Someone would grab the case, and I'd never see my camera again.

Frankly, I considered the first option to be the most likely. Yeah, I know a lot of people lie, cheat, and steal, but I basically retain a positive outlook about most people's honesty and integrity. Still, this was not the time to take chances.

Deciding on a course of action, I rushed up to the first-class cabin, seized the chief steward by the lapels, and screamed, "I left my camera bag in the airport, and it has my entire life on it! You have to do something now or my brain is going to explode all over your first-class passengers!"

At least that's what I wanted to do. What I actually did was go to the steward and explain the situation to her.

"What are my options?" I asked, forcing myself to keep breathing.

She regarded me with empathy. "As soon as we land in Salt Lake City, go to Delta customer service and tell them what happened, and they'll contact the terminal. Maybe someone has turned it in already."

"Okay," I said, without feeling any better. "Thanks."

As soon as I returned to my seat, I got a better idea. As a different steward passed, I stopped him, explained my dilemma, and asked, "Can the pilot radio Houston to see if the bag's still there?"

"I don't know," he said. "But I'll try."

Now, it is truly out of my hands, I thought. In an attempt to get my mind off the camera, I conversed with a passenger next to me, a charming Indian man who worked in the Bay Area and told me all about his home country. Fifteen minutes later, the chief steward handed me a printout from the cockpit. It read:

UPLINK.MSG

** NO ACK REQUIRED **

WOW. THIS NEVER HAPPENS. MARY FROM IAH OPS WENT UP
TO THE AREA AND SHE DID FIND THE CAMERA BAG WITH THE
NAME COLLARD . . . A SUPV IS TAKING IT TO DELTA BAGGAGE
SERVICE. PLEASE HAVE PASSENGER COLLARD CALL.

I almost bear-hugged the steward. I'd had my beefs with Delta over the years, but this pretty much squared us forever.

CHAPTER 17

upping expectations

My camera bag arrived via FedEx three days later. However, with April winding down and our two biggest birding trips behind us, Braden's and my birding expectations dropped like the Dow Jones after Apple missed its earnings projections. What made the outlook unusually bleak was that I had only eight days to prepare for my last author school visit trip of the season, and I doubted that Braden and I would be able to squeeze in any serious birding during that time.

I was forgetting one important fact: it was spring!

A couple of days after returning from Texas, I took Tessa on a walk through what we called the Brown neighborhood. Located next to our own housing tract, the buildings of the Brown neighborhood were painted a uniform dung color. The neighborhood was home to retirees who maintained a strict "keep out" policy for interlopers. Over the years, I'd cultivated a perverse joy in flaunting this restriction. After all, many of the Brown neighborhood's residents walked through our neighborhood. *If they're going to do that*, I told myself, *I darned well am going to walk through their neighborhood.*

The Brown neighborhood was a tranquil place, with pleasant paths, sweeping lawns, and meandering waterways—just right for counting down the days before you die. Like many such artificial landscapes, it was basically a biological desert. Deer and crows lived there, along with a few robins and a pair of Mallards in the largest pond, but what could have been great bird habitat had been so manicured, mowed, and sprayed that I rarely saw any unusual animals within its boundaries.

I figured today with Tessa would prove no exception. We walked our usual route, and as we approached the large pond we startled a pair of ducks. My first thought was, *There are those Mallards again.*

As the ducks flapped past us, I did a double take—specifically at the ducks' heads.

"Tessa!" I exclaimed. "Those are Wood Ducks!"

Tessa wasn't passionate about birds, but she took an interest in all aspects of nature and good-naturedly tolerated Braden's and my birding obsession. She stopped to appreciate the ducks—even if they happened to be birds.

"Those are Wood Ducks?" she asked. "They're really pretty. Have you ever seen one before?"

"Only once. Twenty-five years ago."

I was so excited that Tessa and I hurried home to tell Braden. He was crestfallen.

"Wood Ducks?" he moaned. "Really? I've *never* gotten a good look at Wood Ducks."

"I'm sorry," I told him. "We'll see more for sure."

Then I had a better thought. "Hey, c'mon. Let's jump in the car. Maybe they're still there."

His face brightened like the sunrise over Cochise Stronghold. "Really?"

We hurried back—in my car this time—and again disregarded the Brown neighborhood's "trespassers will be shot on sight" policy. We parked near steps that led to a path that would take us around to the pond.

"Be quiet and stay alert," I whispered, binoculars at the ready. "The Wood Ducks seem especially flighty."

As we walked down the steps, Braden suddenly crouched and said, "There they are!"

Fifty yards away, in the grass bordering an irrigation canal, sat not one pair of Wood Ducks but two! One pair immediately fled, but we settled in to observe the other pair for a good fifteen minutes as they bobbed for insects. With their orange bills and patterned faces, they reminded me of an exquisitely painted African mask, and I loved watching how they behaved, methodically trying to flush any little arthropod morsel from the vegetation.

"Wow, Wood Ducks!" Braden exclaimed as we walked back to the car. "Thanks for taking me to look at them."

"Are you kidding?" I said. "That was awesome."

April hadn't finished with us either. Acting on a tip from the husband of Tessa's third-grade teacher, Braden and I spent a morning in a patch of riparian woodland watching baby Great Horned Owls and while there discovered our first nest of Pileated Woodpeckers. The next day, Braden spotted an Osprey—the first of the year—in Greenough Park, while at our bird feeder I saw the year's first American Goldfinch.

As the last couple of days of the month trickled away, my Big Year total stood at 209, while Braden's inched ahead to 213. Having surpassed the double century mark, Braden and I faced a crisis.

"You know," I told him. "I'm thinking our Big Year goal of 250 isn't ambitious enough."

"I agree," he said.

"What do you think it should be? Three hundred fifty? Four hundred?"

"Four hundred? Really, Daddy?" His voice oozed with adolescent derision. "We don't have any big trips left," he reminded me, "and there's no way we'll pick up two hundred more birds in Montana. I say we shoot for three hundred."

I pondered that for a moment and let out an exaggerated sigh. "Okay. Three hundred it is."

On the face of it, it seemed like a reasonable number—but only if we maintained at least a modest momentum. Would we? Could we? Were there enough birds left in Montana to reach that goal?

We were going to find out.

APRIL BIRD LIST

Sneed's List (121)	Braden's List (124)
Loggerhead Shrike	Loggerhead Shrike
Gambel's Quail	Gambel's Quail
Broad-tailed Hummingbird	Broad-tailed Hummingbird

Tufted Flycatcher	Tufted Flycatcher
Greater Pewee	Greater Pewee
Hutton's Vireo	Hutton's Vireo
House Wren	House Wren
Townsend's Solitaire	Blue-winged Teal
Hepatic Tanager	Cinnamon Teal
Blue-winged Teal	American Bittern
Cinnamon Teal	Greater Roadrunner
American Bittern	Great Horned Owl
Greater Roadrunner	Northern Rough-winged Swallow
Great Horned Owl	Tree Swallow
Northern Rough-winged Swallow	Lucy's Warbler
Tree Swallow	Yellow Warbler
Lucy's Warbler	Black-throated Sparrow
Yellow Warbler	Canyon Towhee
Black-throated Sparrow	White-throated Swift
Canyon Towhee	Ladder-backed Woodpecker
White-throated Swift	Say's Phoebe
Ladder-backed Woodpecker	Blue-gray Gnatcatcher
Say's Phoebe	Ruby-crowned Kinglet
Blue-gray Gnatcatcher	Cedar Waxwing
Ruby-crowned Kinglet	Phainopepla
Cedar Waxwing	Scaled Quail
Phainopepla	Swainson's Hawk
Scaled Quail	Zone-tailed Hawk
Swainson's Hawk	Red-naped Sapsucker
Zone-tailed Hawk	Violet-green Swallow
Red-naped Sapsucker	American Robin
Violet-green Swallow	Black-throated Gray Warbler
Black-throated Gray Warbler	Spotted Towhee
Spotted Towhee	White-crowned Sparrow
White-crowned Sparrow	Black-tailed Gnatcatcher
Black-tailed Gnatcatcher	Roseate Spoonbill
Roseate Spoonbill	Barn Swallow
Barn Swallow	Great Egret
Great Egret	Red-headed Woodpecker
Red-headed Woodpecker	Red-bellied Woodpecker
Red-bellied Woodpecker	Blue Jay
Carolina Chickadee	Carolina Chickadee
Tufted Titmouse	Tufted Titmouse
Carolina Wren	Carolina Wren
Prothonotary Warbler	Prothonotary Warbler
Indigo Bunting	Indigo Bunting
Common Grackle	Common Grackle

Red-cockaded Woodpecker	Black Vulture
Black-bellied Whistling-Duck	Red-cockaded Woodpecker
Pied-billed Grebe	Eastern Bluebird
Neotropic Cormorant	Black-bellied Whistling-Duck
Double-crested Cormorant	Pied-billed Grebe
Snowy Egret	Neotropic Cormorant
Little Blue Heron	Double-crested Cormorant
Tricolored Heron	Snowy Egret
Cattle Egret	Little Blue Heron
Green Heron	Tricolored Heron
White Ibis	Cattle Egret
Purple Gallinule	Green Heron
Common Gallinule	White Ibis
Inca Dove	Purple Gallinule
Chimney Swift	Common Gallinule
Ruby-throated Hummingbird	Inca Dove
Crested Caracara	Chimney Swift
White-eyed Vireo	Ruby-throated Hummingbird
Gray-cheeked Thrush	Crested Caracara
Northern Waterthrush	White-eyed Vireo
Black-and-white Warbler	Gray-cheeked Thrush
Tennessee Warbler	Northern Waterthrush
Summer Tanager	Black-and-white Warbler
Scarlet Tanager	Tennessee Warbler
Rose-breasted Grosbeak	Summer Tanager
Orchard Oriole	Scarlet Tanager
Brown Pelican	Rose-breasted Grosbeak
American Avocet	Orchard Oriole
Black-bellied Plover	Brown Pelican
Semipalmated Plover	American Avocet
Piping Plover	Black-bellied Plover
Marbled Godwit	Semipalmated Plover
Ruddy Turnstone	Piping Plover
Sanderling	Marbled Godwit
Dunlin	Ruddy Turnstone
Western Sandpiper	Sanderling
Short-billed Dowitcher	Dunlin
Willet	Western Sandpiper
Laughing Gull	Short-billed Dowitcher
Least Tern	Willet
Black Tern	Laughing Gull
Common Tern	Least Tern
Forster's Tern	Black Tern
Royal Tern	Common Tern

Sandwich Tern	Forster's Tern
Barn Owl	Royal Tern
Yellow-crowned Night-Heron	Sandwich Tern
Eastern Wood-Pewee	Barn Owl
Eastern Kingbird	Yellow-crowned Night-Heron
Yellow-throated Vireo	Eastern Wood-Pewee
Red-eyed Vireo	Eastern Kingbird
Swainson's Thrush	Yellow-throated Vireo
Wood Thrush	Red-eyed Vireo
Gray Catbird	Swainson's Thrush
Brown Thrasher	Wood Thrush
Ovenbird	Gray Catbird
Worm-eating Warbler	Brown Thrasher
Blue-winged Warbler	Ovenbird
Hooded Warbler	Worm-eating Warbler
American Redstart	Blue-winged Warbler
Bay-breasted Warbler	Hooded Warbler
Blackburnian Warbler	American Redstart
Black-throated Green Warbler	Bay-breasted Warbler
Mottled Duck	Blackburnian Warbler
White-faced Ibis	Black-throated Green Warbler
Black-necked Stilt	Mottled Duck
Whimbrel	White-faced Ibis
Solitary Sandpiper	Black-necked Stilt
Scissor-tailed Flycatcher	Whimbrel
Common Yellowthroat	Solitary Sandpiper
Boat-tailed Grackle	Scissor-tailed Flycatcher
Blue Grosbeak	Common Yellowthroat
Wood Duck	Boat-tailed Grackle
American Goldfinch	Blue Grosbeak
	Song Sparrow
	Wood Duck
	Osprey

CHAPTER 18

the big weekend, day 1

As May began, a seemingly insurmountable number of projects and deadlines loomed over me. I had to

- finish writing and designing a book on snowshoe hares and climate change
- complete a hundred or so pages of a textbook for teachers
- prepare a weeklong writing camp for disadvantaged youth in eastern Montana
- organize the annual bicycle trip for forty-five Boy Scouts, siblings, and parents of Braden's troop
- fix our irrigation system and plant the vegetable garden
- attend to what seemed like dozens of band concerts, soccer games, fund-raisers, work crews, and other kid-related activities.

Not content with this load, I also accepted a job writing two nonfiction books for an online educational company in a desperate attempt to replenish our bank account after Arizona and Texas.

Predictably the birds demonstrated a total disdain for my work-load and kept taunting Braden and me with their presence. Before I could begin tackling my to-do list, I had to dash out to Red Lodge and Billings for three days of school visits, and on the drive I picked up my first Osprey of the year—and my second, and third, and tenth—along with Western Meadowlarks and Yellow-headed Blackbirds, three of which flew across I-90 in front of me. In Billings I spent a hot after-noon hiking along the Yellowstone River, where I spotted the year's first California Gulls and a surprising flock of thirty American Avo-cets. The next morning I headed out to Pictograph Cave State Park, where I observed a trio of American Kestrels thrusting and parrying along the rimrock, and had up-close-and-personal time with a group of very vocal Canyon Wrens, a prized addition to my Big Year and Life lists.

Meanwhile, thanks to Amy, the birds continued to bother Braden too.

While I'd started pursuing one-on-one trips with the kids pretty much from the time they could crawl, Amy had mainly limited her-self to taking them to her parents' house in Portland, Oregon. This year, she decided it was time to broaden her horizons. Over the weekend of May 20, she and Braden flew to Seattle to stay with our friends Steve and Carol and go see Billy Joel at Safeco Field. Despite the huge crowds and an endless search for dinner, Bill Joe did not disappoint. Even better, Steve, Carol, and their daughter Jasmine indulged Braden's birding passions by taking him birding not once but twice. He picked up eight new Big Year birds, including one that struck me with envy, Wilson's Warbler.

Even with these unexpected listing opportunities, Braden and I agreed that our May totals looked pathetic considering the time of year and the waves of migrants streaming across the continent. As the month coasted toward a close, I'd notched only nine new birds for May, while Braden had scored about twice that. It was time, we decided, to mount a last-ditch effort to save the month—and our self-respect.

On the afternoon of Friday, May 27, Nick Ramsey waited for us at the gate of MPG Ranch—our first stop in an ambitious effort to see as many birds as possible around the Missoula area over the next day and a half. I think I was more pumped than either of the boys.

Despite good intentions, this was the first time we'd gotten to bird with Nick all year, and I knew I would learn a lot from him. Even more exciting, this would be my first time visiting MPG.

The history of the ranch intrigued me. In several stages, beginning in 2009, the fifteen-thousand-acre property had been purchased by a conservation-minded philanthropist. The land had suffered from more than a century of cattle grazing, but the new owner harbored a vision of restoring the ecological integrity of the ranch and turning it into a center for scientific research. I'd first heard of MPG from Dick Hutto, the ornithologist I featured in *Fire Birds*, but the ranch had kept popping up in conversations with other biologists and writers. After Braden and Nick began forming a friendship through birding, I discovered a most unlikely coincidence: Nick's father, Phil Ramsey, managed the entire property!

MPG extended for four miles along the Bitterroot River and reached all the way up and over the first ridgeline of the Sapphire Mountains. As soon as Nick climbed into our minivan, I began peppering him with questions:

"What are you planting there?"

"That fence will keep deer out?"

"Why isn't leafy spurge growing here?"

Nick patiently fielded everything I threw at him, but he and Braden made sure I kept returning to our primary focus: birds.

As we'd prepared for the weekend, Braden had asked me, "So what should our goal be for the weekend?"

I zipped my camera into its carrying case and looked over at him. "I'm thinking sixty total species, including ones we've already seen this year. What about you?"

Braden was filling water bottles at our sink. "I'm thinking sixty-five," he said—the first time he'd ever guessed higher than I had.

"The thing is," I continued, "we have to add at least twenty new birds. By now most of the birds are almost finished raising their young, and, once they do, they're going to be quieter and more difficult to find. This could be our best chance to find a lot of them for our Big Year list. Do you think we can get that many?"

Even since Texas I had noticed Braden's increased confidence in his bird-finding abilities. Now he considered my question and matter-of-factly answered, "I think so."

Our weekend started out well. Just driving down to MPG, Braden and I ID'd twenty species, including one new Big Year bird, Lewis's Woodpecker. Minutes after picking up Nick, he called out a Lifer for me—Vesper Sparrow.

For the next two hours, Nick guided us to the ranch's birding hotspots. With Nick's help, Braden and I tallied seven more Big Year birds, including at least five more Lifers for me—Bullock's Oriole, Rock Wren, Spotted Sandpiper, Savannah Sparrow, and Western Kingbird. Even more fun than checking off birds was seeing the ranch for the first time and hearing Nick and Braden banter. At one point they began talking about the four-letter bird codes that are used by many bird banders and scientists.

"I've got a WEKI on the telephone pole over by the barn," Nick said, raising his binoculars.

"WEKI?" Braden asked, raising his eyebrows.

"Western Kingbird," Nick said as if the answer were obvious, then explained. "Each bird has a four-letter alpha code, usually made up from the first two letters of the bird's first name and the first two letters of its last name. Of course there are exceptions."

"Like what?"

"Well, Barred Owl and Barn Owl. Both would be BAOW, and no one would be able to tell the difference, so they get the codes BDOW and BNOW respectively. Oh, there's a SAPH on the tractor."

"Say's Phoebe?" Braden asked.

"Yeah, you're getting it."

As Braden and Nick continued to talk about and identify birds, not a little competitiveness emerged between the two. As good a birder as Braden was becoming, Nick had developed an amazing gestalt. With even the smallest glimpse of a bird fleeing over the horizon, he'd shout out "Bullock's" or "Lazuli"! The hilarious thing was that he often botched his first ID. Birds got him so excited that he'd just blurt out the first thing that flashed through his brain. He almost always quickly corrected himself, but one reason he and Braden made such a good team is that my son insisted on pinning down the IDs for himself. Together the two boys almost always came up with the right identification, and I relied on that heavily, especially when it came to the sparrows, wrens, and other little brown birds we encountered.

When it looked like we'd spotted everything we were going to, we headed over to the main ranch house, where Nick's father, Phil, and his girlfriend, Amy, greeted us. Phil handed me a beer and we stood around a crackling campfire getting to know each other while watching the sun sink behind the Bitterroot Mountains. Like me, Phil had majored in biology but, unlike me, had continued on for his PhD. He had located MPG for his employer and set in motion the master plan of restoring the property and turning it into a research center. I learned that, like Braden, Nick was only the latest naturalist in his family. As I watched Nick, his sister Maggie, and Braden race around the barn playing hide-and-seek, I felt glad that all three of them could grow up in such a spectacular and interesting environment, one that could nurture a special passion such as birding.

After a filling meal of barbecue and one of the best rhubarb pies I've ever eaten, Braden, Nick, and I again piled into our minivan and drove up into the hills to look for Common Poorwills. I would have settled for an owl—any owl—but the birds shunned us. *You've seen enough for one day*, I could hear them thinking.

No matter. A full day of birding lay ahead. Nick guided us to our bivouac for the night—a cool little glass observatory that Nick and his dad dubbed the Duck Majal. We spread our sleeping bags, and, with Venus and Jupiter blazing brightly in the night sky, quickly lost consciousness. Our Big Weekend had just begun, and our species count already stood at forty-six.

CHAPTER 19

the big weekend, day 2

Our plan had been to get up early Saturday and continue birding MPG before going to the Lee Metcalf National Wildlife Refuge for the afternoon. Nick had shown us so many birds the previous evening, however, that the next day we all agreed to head straight for Lee Metcalf. As we left MPG we were treated to half a dozen Lewis's Woodpeckers sitting on fence posts. I slowed the minivan to a crawl so that Braden and Nick could take photos, but the birds were camera shy, keeping just a fence post or two ahead of us. After three or four failed attempts to photograph one, I declared, "Daylight's a-wasting!" and hit the accelerator.

To have a successful weekend, we had to score big at Lee Metcalf, and we had to score especially big on waterfowl. As we pulled up to the duck ponds, we saw with dismay that only a few of the dappled varmints dotted the water. Scanning through binoculars, Braden and Nick called out American Wigeon, Gadwall, Redhead, Northern Shoveler, and Pied-billed Grebe—most of which already occupied our Big Year lists. Even worse, only one or two of each species graced the ponds.

"Where are all the ducks?" I lamented. "I was counting on at least a Bufflehead!"

In the cattails, we could hear other birds clamoring for attention, so we walked over to investigate.

"Look!" Braden exclaimed, "Common Yellowthroat!"

"Where?" I demanded, desperately searching for the bird I had only glimpsed in Texas.

"He dove back into the reeds," Nick informed me.

"Of course he did," I grumbled, but within moments, the yellowthroat popped back up. Now all of us could bask in the warbler's full glory as he perched atop his cattail shouting, "Wichita! Wichita! Wichita!"

At least that's what Braden said it sounded like, and I had to agree. The best part of the yellowthroat's performance was that he perched in full sunlight only thirty feet away, and at least two or three other males answered—obviously staking out territories and trying to outmuscle others in the competition for females.

After a full half hour enjoying the warblers and some equally enthusiastic Yellow-headed Blackbirds, the boys and I continued our quest. Acting on a tip from another birder, we walked a forest loop to find a mother Great-horned Owl and two of her giant, fuzzy fledglings. Along the way we picked up another dozen species, including Pileated Woodpecker, Hermit's and Swainson's Thrushes, and a bird I was especially glad to rack up for the year, California Quail.

This last one is a surprise for birders from outside of Montana, but a population had been introduced into the Bitterroot in the last couple of decades, and the quail not only survived, they thrived. The gray, roundish, medium-sized birds reminded me of schoolmarms bobbing and glancing nervously around them. As much as I despised the introduction of nonnative species, I had a hard time conjuring any real resentment toward this handsome pair of game birds eyeing us from a fallen log. Maybe it was because of my California roots, but I just smiled, took a photo, and added them to our list.

Back in the parking lot, an older man approached us. "See anything good today?"

Braden and Nick rattled off a half-dozen species.

"How about you?" I asked the man.

He told us that he lived nearby and came to the refuge on a regular basis. "Was hoping to see more ducks," he said, "but the numbers are low."

"Yeah," I commiserated. "What's going on?"

Neither of us knew. Then he asked, "So where are you going next?"

"We want to get Bobolinks," Nick told him. "Down on Burnt Fork Road."

"Oh? I often see them up Bass Creek."

"If we went there," Nick lobbied, "we could get Chestnut-backed Chickadees too. I've seen them in the parking lot."

It was an easy decision. We all shook hands with the man and clambered back into the car.

"Oh," the man called back to me as I turned the ignition key. "As you're driving out, look for Wilson's Snipe. I've been seeing one on a fence post."

The Wilson's was a no-show, but the man's advice on the Bobolinks proved spot-on. I have to confess that I had no idea what a Bobolink looked like. An image of some kind of grouse scurried about my brain, but as we turned off Highway 93 and headed up Bass Creek Road, Nick and Braden educated me.

"They're in with blackbirds," Braden explained, flashing me the page in *Sibley*.

"You only find them in irrigated fields with tall grass," Nick added.

We passed a couple of cow pastures without a sighting. Then, as we drove by a wetter field with taller vegetation, Braden shouted, "There's one!"

I pulled over in front of a farm, and we hurried across the road.

The birds were at least a football field's distance away, but we managed good views through our binoculars. The Bobos didn't quite outclass the Common Yellowthroats, but I loved the dazzling white flash of their backs when they took their quick, low flights, their bellies brushing the tall grass before they dropped back to the ground and out of sight.

As we watched, the owner of the fields pulled up in his truck and asked, "What's all the excitement?"

"We're watching Bobolinks," I said.

"What are they?" he asked.

"Birds," I told him, a little smugly. "Do you see them here a lot?"

He smiled and gave me a friendly ribbing over my mispronunciation. "Well, I don't see *Bo*-bolinks, but I see plenty of *Bob*-olinks. In fact, just down the road, a lawyer from the city bought a place. He says he sees more Bobolinks here than anywhere he's ever been."

I thanked the man for letting us watch his birds, and then we headed on up to Bass Creek, where a half-hour hike netted us Western Tanager, Red-naped Sapsucker, and Steller's Jay. As I scanned the trees for a warbler, Braden shouted, "Daddy! American Dipper!"

I rushed over but was too late.

"He's gone," Nick said.

I moaned. "Again?" It was probably the tenth dipper I'd missed this year.

"This is getting ridiculous," I told the boys. "This thing has officially become a nemesis bird."

The good news was that it was barely noon, and we were still way ahead of schedule.

"Where to now?" Braden asked.

"I'm thinking Lolo Burn," I said. "Maybe we can score a Black-backed Woodpecker."

"I hope so," said Nick. Amazingly, for a kid who had seen more than 260 birds in Montana alone, the Black-backed had escaped his Life list—despite half a dozen attempts to find one. Braden and I, of course, were also eager to see one because a) it was a woodpecker and therefore way cool, and b) it would make an elite addition to our Big Year list. Still, as we headed north on 93 and turned west toward Lolo Pass, I harbored doubts.

"Did you see one when you came this winter?" Nick asked.

"No," Braden confessed. "And we got stuck in the snow."

"Well at least that won't happen today," Nick quipped.

I laughed, and a few minutes later I spotted the white fence across from the pullout. Another car occupied the parking space, but I had just enough room to wedge the minivan in next to it. The boys leaped out and almost immediately called, "Woodpecker!"

As they hurried toward the trees to find it, I also climbed out and recognized a familiar figure walking toward me.

"You looking for the Black-backed?" he called to the boys. "It's right over there. A nice male."

"Dick!" I said. "Good to see you." I walked over to shake his hand.

As I've mentioned, Dick Hutto was the subject of my book *Fire Birds*, but to me he was much more than that. In many ways he had turned me into a serious birder. About four years earlier he'd helped stoke my enthusiasm by taking me birding in my first burn area. In the process he'd shown me my first Black-backed Woodpecker and opened my eyes to the amazing bird life not only in burns but almost everywhere I looked. It's not an exaggeration to say that writing *Fire Birds* and birding with Dick had given me the foundation to be able to bird with Braden.

Together we followed the boys over to a large Ponderosa Pine and, sure enough, found a gorgeous male Black-backed, complete with vivid yellow crown, drilling for beetle grubs like his life depended on it—which it did.

"Life bird!" Nick exulted, high-fiving Braden and snapping off several quick confirmation photos.

Only then did it occur to any of us that introductions might be in order. "Dick," I said, "I don't think you've met my son Braden. And this is Nick Ramsey."

"Oh, yes," Dick said, shaking both of their hands. Speaking to Nick, he said, "I think I met you down at MPG once or twice, and I see your posts on eBird."

"I'm going to go get my tripod," I told them and headed toward the car.

By the time I returned, Dick had wandered off with Braden and Nick to look for songbirds, leaving me with the Black-backed Woodpecker. It was the first male I'd ever gotten close to, and I took about fifty photos before I finally convinced myself that I'd covered him.

After folding up my tripod, I joined Dick and the boys hot on the trail of MacGillivray's Warblers. Like Common Yellowthroats, MacGillivray's Warblers are less than eager to be seen. Dick had an amazing ear for birdcalls and identified sounds all around us, including several of the warblers, but I only got the briefest glimpse of one. Still, with Dick's confirmation, it was enough to check off—another Life bird for Braden and me.

The boys and I returned to Missoula for a leisurely lunch at HuHot Mongolian Grill. It was two thirty, and I could sense my body's "low fuel" light flashing. If we'd been in Arizona or Texas I would have just plowed ahead, but the siren calls for a nap were hard to resist this close to home.

"I'm good for one more place," I told the boys. "Where should it be?"

Nick and Braden looked at each other and nodded. "Greenough, definitely."

Greenough Park stretched along Rattlesnake Creek only a mile or two from our house, and before embracing birding I had walked through the park hundreds of times with my late Border collie, Mattie. I had never done any serious birding there, but when I had ridden through on my bike a couple of weeks earlier I'd heard dozens of spring birdcalls emanating from the cottonwoods, willows, and pines along the creek. I'd guessed that warblers had been making them, but that day the boys and I had a more ambitious target: Black-headed Grosbeaks.

"I saw them there last week," Nick told us. "They should still be around."

We parked the car and began walking the two-mile loop around Greenough. Like me, Braden began showing the strain of the day. He huffed and grumbled when he failed to see a Yellow Warbler in some willows.

"It's just like always. I look, and the bird is gone!" he groused.

"No, it isn't," I tried to soothe him. "You see lots of birds. A lot more than I do."

"It doesn't seem like it."

"Well, keep a good attitude," I told him. "If you stop looking, you're not going to see anything."

As usual he failed to venerate my sage advice, but also as usual he attempted to buck up.

He was right, though. Besides a half-dozen furtive Yellow Warblers, we didn't see a lot at first. I missed yet another American Dipper, and Nick thought he might have heard a Bullock's Oriole, but the park was as dead as a movie theater on a Tuesday afternoon.

As we reached the bridge at the top of the loop, however, the boys halted. "Over there!" Braden shouted.

My eyes snapped toward a feeder behind a house fifty yards away—just in time to see a winged shape disappear toward some trees.

"Black-headed Grosbeak!" Nick exclaimed.

"Are you sure?" I said, wishing for a better look.

"Absolutely," said Braden. "I got a great look at it."

Always upbeat—at least when it came to birds—Nick said, "Let's just wait. Maybe it'll come back."

We perched on the rail of the bridge, and I scanned the creek in vain for dippers. The grosbeak didn't come back either, so we decided to move on. As we walked a few steps forward, though, the female Black-headed suddenly appeared. The whole time we'd been waiting, she had been happily stuffing herself on sunflower seeds on the *other* side of the feeder! After taking ID photos, we continued our loop. We finally got a great look at a Yellow Warbler, followed by a perfectly perched Cedar Waxwing. We also saw our first Hairy Woodpecker for the day, but by this time I felt like Forrest Gump after he'd run across the continent three or four times.

"I'm tired," I told the boys. "Let's go back to the lower bridge. I saw some poop on a couple of rocks in the creek, and I just want to wait to see if an American Dipper shows up."

We didn't have to wait. As we followed a side trail in search of warblers, a small gray bird suddenly streaked past, skimming the water's surface.

"Dipper!" I rejoiced. "Finally!"

There wasn't just one bird but two, and they landed on a rock only fifty feet downstream.

"Okay," I said, after watching the dippers bob up and down on their rock. "Now we can go home."

That night at our house we tabulated our total, which came in at seventy-five for the day, one better than Braden's and my best day ever, in Texas. Overall, our Big Weekend count had climbed to an astonishing eighty-nine species.

Braden voiced what we were all thinking. "If we go to Seeley Lake tomorrow," he said, "we could crack a hundred species for the weekend."

All along I had made it clear to the boys that if they wanted to bird on Sunday, they were on their own. After the incredible success we'd already had, however, the thought of reaching one hundred birds for the weekend dangled like a big chocolate bar in front of me. Still, I hesitated. "I don't know, guys. I really should get some work done. Let's just see how we feel in the morning, okay?"

I could tell that both Braden and Nick wanted to push it, but they also knew how lucky they'd been to spend the day and the previous afternoon birding. While I went through my camera deleting bad photos, Nick spent the rest of the evening showing Braden how to set up an account on eBird, the amazing online tool that Dick Hutto had alluded to. Created by Cornell University's Lab of Ornithology, eBird allows birders to record and share their bird sightings, learn about birding hotspots, and much more. Braden and Nick spent at least a couple of hours posting our weekend results and exploring various birding hotspots listed on the site. Finally, around 11:00 p.m., I called lights out.

CHAPTER 20

the big weekend, bonus day

Despite getting only six hours of sleep, I woke the next morning feeling energized. Work, I decided, could wait. I wanted to break one hundred birds for the weekend with the boys! Still, it was only 6:00 a.m., and I figured two teenagers could use another hour's sleep, so I decided to use the time to get ready and, most importantly, try to figure out what was going on with my camera.

The night before, after Braden and Nick had finished with eBird, I downloaded my photos from the previous couple of days onto my computer and found that I hadn't taken a single decent shot. Come to think of it, I hadn't been bowled over by my photos from Texas either. I'd put the Texas performance down to poor lighting, but now I suspected that something else was going on. I felt especially disheartened by my yellowthroat and Black-backed photos from the day before. The photography conditions had been perfect, but all my photos looked slightly blurry, and many were washed out.

I didn't understand it. I'd bought a new camera body. I'd sent in my telephoto lens for repair. I'd bought a 1.4X extender, transforming the lens from a 100–400 mm to a muscular 140–560, but still my photos looked mediocre, even worse than they had a couple of years ago when I owned less impressive equipment.

"What is going on?" I grumbled.

I decided that at some point I really needed to take a wildlife photography course, if only to learn how to properly use my complicated camera. For the time being, I came up with a couple of things that might make a difference. The first thing I did was remove the UV filter on the lens in case it was leading to the washed-out look.

Second, I decided to remove the 1.4X extender. Even if I lost some range, the extender made it more difficult to hold the camera steady, particularly without a tripod. I also reasoned that since zoom lenses were already less sharp than fixed lenses, it was possible the extender just added one more level of blurriness to my photos.

I didn't know if either of these actions would help, but at least they wouldn't make my pictures any worse.

At seven, I went into the boys' room, yanked up the blinds, and said, "So, are you guys ready to go birding?"

Nick and Braden sat up, rubbing their eyes, and responded with determination more than enthusiasm. "Yeah."

We'd spent most of the previous two days birding southern and central Missoula County. On this day we headed toward its northeastern outpost: Seeley Lake. Dominated by spectacular, forested mountains and a string of idyllic lakes, the Seeley-Swan corridor abuts the Bob Marshall Wilderness area, one of the most wild and stunning tracts of land in the Lower 48. The boys and I harbored no aspirations of venturing into the Bob itself, but that doesn't mean we weren't on a mission.

Most people view birders as mellow nature lovers out to enjoy the outdoors in a state of tranquility. Birders I've met often conceal an opposite persona. What non-birders rarely witness is the ambitious, competitive, even aggressive side of birders that can emerge under extreme birding conditions or when specific targets have been set. With a goal of one hundred weekend species firmly in our sights, it was this almost militaristic side of birding that surfaced in Braden, Nick, and me that morning.

We drove to the trailhead for the Clearwater River Canoe Trail at the upper end of Seeley Lake, arriving there at zero nine hundred hours. Like Army Rangers carrying M27 automatic rifles and ammo belts, we leaped out of the minivan with binoculars and cameras slung across our shoulders and marched down to patrol the thick willows lakeside. Before even reaching the water's edge, the boys started calling out species.

"Yellow Warbler!"

"Tree Swallow!"

"American Redstart!"

"Redstart? Really?" I asked, hurrying to join them. The only American Redstart I'd ever seen had been in Texas a few weeks before. Not only had I never seen one in Montana, it had been a sore point that none of us had spotted one the previous afternoon in Greenough Park—a known redstart pickup area.

As I looked up into the upper branches of a tall willow, I saw the distinctive orange-and-black markings that could only belong to this sought-after bird.

"All *right!*" I shouted.

There wasn't just one redstart, either. For the next forty-five minutes we chased redstarts and Yellow Warblers in and out of the brush next to the parking area. I snapped off a few photos and checked to see if they were worth keeping, and to my amazement they appeared sharp and crisp on the camera screen. *I guess taking off the UV filter and extender was a good move,* I rejoiced.

Heartened by this news, I pried the boys away from the parking area, and we double-timed up the trail along the river running into Seeley Lake. Although we encountered the worst mosquitoes since Texas, we continued to make delectable discoveries. At a well-placed bird blind we watched two more male Common Yellowthroats. Just beyond that, Braden and Nick identified a couple of Northern Waterthrushes, a Fox Sparrow, Ruby-crowned Kinglets, and Pine Siskins. We also heard a Common Loon but couldn't catch a glimpse of it.

"That's okay," Nick told us. "They'll be at Placid Lake."

We returned to the minivan, quickly ate peanut butter sandwiches, and then headed to the other large lake in the area. We stopped at the main campground and talked to a woman working at the booth.

"Hi there," I said. "We're looking for loons. Can you recommend the best spot?"

The woman directed us to a small parking area a couple of miles up the lakeshore, but the loons hadn't gotten the message to meet us there. What we did find were dozens of off-road vehicles, motorboats, and jet-skis roaring around and across the lake.

"Why would you come out to this beautiful spot to thrash around on your gas-powered vehicles when you can enjoy just as much noise and craziness back in the city?" I said to the boys.

It was a rhetorical question. Even at Braden's age I had never fathomed this concept of "escaping town" only to make your camping experience as crazy, hectic, and noisy as your everyday life. Yet, more than ever, that was what millions of Americans considered to be the perfect vacation.

Maybe I'm just not a good American.

One thing was for sure. The noise and chaos of Placid Lake did not lend itself to loons, who prefer quiet, calm conditions.

Undaunted, we slowly circumnavigated the lake, looking for loons and a second sought-after species, Williamson's Sapsucker, which Nick had once spotted in this area. Braden and I had only ever seen one Williamson's—a drab female from a distance—and were eager for a better study of this seemingly elusive species. We spied three elegant Sandhill Cranes stalking each other across a meadow, and then Nick cried out, "Williamson's!" We all tumbled out of the car in time to glimpse the fleeting shape of a woodpecker. We followed it for a couple of hundred yards but couldn't relocate the bird.

"Knowing you, it was probably a Mourning Dove," Braden teased as we walked back to the minivan.

"No, it was definitely a woodpecker, but, yeah," Nick admitted, "it was probably a Hairy or something."

Frustratingly, our Big Weekend list stood at ninety-nine birds.

"We need one more bird," I told the boys as we continued driving.

"Stop here," Braden said. "I want to see if I can hear loons down on the lake."

I pulled over and Braden got out. As he scoured the lake with his binoculars, suddenly a medium-sized brown shape whizzed by our windshield and down the slope. My first thought was "robin," but I quickly rejected that possibility. The bird looked more like a diminutive base jumper wearing a glider suit.

"Nick, did you see that?" I shouted.

He had. "Ruffed Grouse!"

We yelled out the window to Braden, and he came running over.

"Ruffed Grouse!" Nick told him.

Braden's face fell. "I missed another bird?"

Before Braden could give full vent to his frustration, Nick said, "No. He's right down there. Just run down the hill through the brush and you'll flush him."

We watched as Braden made his way down the hillside. We didn't see him flush the bird, but five minutes later, he returned looking less crestfallen.

"Did you see it?" Nick asked.

He nodded. "I didn't get a picture, but I got it."

"Bird number one hundred!" I exulted.

The grouse wasn't our last Big Weekend score. We checked the southern end of Placid Lake for loons and again came up empty, but a Common Merganser zoomed across the lake, bringing our Big Weekend total to a whopping 101 species. For me, thirty-nine of those were Big Year birds, and twenty-one were also Lifers. Since Braden had birded MPG earlier in the year, his totals came in lower—thirty-four Big Year birds and fourteen Lifers.

Any way we looked at it, it had been an epic effort. It was the first time Braden and I had really gone all out to see how many birds we could find around our home territory. We'd had a terrific time, and it had given us invaluable knowledge about which birds live in Montana—and where and when. I finished the weekend with a much better grasp of our local fauna and a better appreciation of what an incredible place Montana is for birds. It was an added bonus that we'd blasted past our estimates for how many birds we'd see over the weekend—and moved considerably closer to our amended Big Year goal of three hundred species.

As we made our final notes for May, Braden's Big Year count stood at 255 birds, and mine was an even 250. The fact that we'd added so many Big Year birds over the weekend also compelled us make another irresponsibly rash decision: to increase our Big Year goal once again, from 300 to 350 species. Braden and I both knew this was pushing our luck, but Big Year fever had infected us and would not let go.

MAY BIRD LIST

Sneed's List (41)	Braden's List (41)
Cliff Swallow	Rufous Hummingbird
Canyon Wren	Western Bluebird
Western Kingbird	American Goldfinch
Rock Wren	Glaucous-winged Gull
Vesper Sparrow	Chestnut-backed Chickadee
Lazuli Bunting	Bushtit
Bullock's Oriole	Wilson's Warbler
Spotted Sandpiper	Western Kingbird
Lewis's Woodpecker	Rock Wren
Western Wood-Pewee	Vesper Sparrow
Western Meadowlark	Lazuli Bunting
Brewer's Blackbird	Bullock's Oriole
Brown-headed Cowbird	Spotted Sandpiper
Gadwall	Lewis's Woodpecker
Northern Shoveler	Western Wood-Pewee
Redhead	Western Meadowlark
California Quail	Brewer's Blackbird
Northern Harrier	Brown-headed Cowbird
Sandhill Crane	Gadwall
Vaux's Swift	Northern Shoveler
Bank Swallow	Redhead
Marsh Wren	California Quail
Hermit Thrush	Sandhill Crane
Yellow-headed Blackbird	Vaux's Swift
American Dipper	Bank Swallow
Western Tanager	Cliff Swallow
Bobolink	Marsh Wren
Black-backed Woodpecker	Hermit Thrush
Dusky Flycatcher	Yellow-headed Blackbird
Western Bluebird	Western Tanager
MacGillivray's Warbler	Bobolink
Black-headed Grosbeak	Black-backed Woodpecker
Osprey	Dusky Flycatcher
Sharp-shinned Hawk	MacGillivray's Warbler
Willow Flycatcher	Black-headed Grosbeak
Warbling Vireo	Sharp-shinned Hawk
Fox Sparrow	Willow Flycatcher
Rufous Hummingbird	Warbling Vireo
Song Sparrow	Fox Sparrow
Ruffed Grouse	Ruffed Grouse
Red-necked Grebe	Red-necked Grebe

the big lead-up

On June 1 I spent most of the day trying to round up medical forms, youth protection training forms, and other paperwork related to the upcoming Boy Scout bike trip that I was in charge of. Between those tasks I made phone calls to the bus company that would be transporting us, and to various other entities to make sure that the bike trip didn't wind up as the worst disaster since the US occupation of Iraq.

"Remind me not to do this ever again," I told Amy, shuffling through the stack of paperwork in front of me.

"What, you don't want to plan another Boy Scout trip?"

"Well," I grumbled. "Not this year."

Even with this workload, however, I had trouble excising birding from my brain—especially coming off our Big Weekend success. By the time Braden came home from school that afternoon I'd filled my gullet with Boy Scout bureaucracy. "You want to go on a short ride to shake out the bikes?" I asked him.

I could almost see the birding possibilities sweep across his irises. "Sure!"

"I'll bring the binoculars."

Over the past decade, the kids and I had worn grooves in a three-and-a-half-mile loop around Rattlesnake Canyon, the little valley where we live. The route took us past Rattlesnake School, across Rattlesnake Creek, past a community farm, up over a couple of hills, and down to a second bike bridge that recrossed the creek. It was a perfect circuit for injecting oxygen back into the bloodstream, but in the past year I'd also begun to recognize what an amazing variety of bird habitats it traversed.

That day, as we headed up the hills, Braden and I spotted flickers, robins, and Vesper Sparrows on fence posts next to some horse pastures. Coasting down the other side, we passed Red-winged Blackbirds buzzing in a small patch of cattails—the same early arrivals Tessa and I had noted in March. Past the upper bridge we took our mandatory rest next to the creek, and even before we lowered our bikes to the ground, Braden asked, "Did you hear that?"

I pulled the binoculars out of my pannier. "Yeah, I did. What do you think it was?"

"Well," he said, "it could be a Western Tanager, but it's probably another annoying robin."

"A robin that's smoked a pack of cigarettes," I asserted.

Through the binoculars, I saw nothing at first. Then—"Western Tanager!" I shouted, focusing on the bird.

"Give me the binoculars!" Braden demanded.

"Hold on! Hold on!"

We spent the next ten minutes watching the spectacular little bird, which belted out loud territorial calls from the tops of three different pine trees. A few minutes later we spotted a Yellow Warbler diving into a bush, and when we arrived home half an hour later, we completed our "yellow bird trifecta" with an American Goldfinch at our backyard feeder.

"Nice way to start out the month, huh?" I asked.

"Yeah," Braden said. "I feel like we're getting to know our neighborhood birds better, don't you?"

"Yeah, I do," I said, surprising myself.

Compared to Nick and Braden, my mind still acquired birding knowledge at a glacial pace. But slowly, ever so slowly, I was making progress. That seemed important because in three weeks our entire family would be watching birds—and a whole lot more—in a place I had never expected to see.

My mother-in-law, Carol, had first raised the possibility of a Galápagos Islands trip two years before. Much like my father-son and father-daughter trips, Amy's parents had been taking the kids on solo adventures since they were young, planning trips with Braden and Tessa on alternate years.

Shortly after taking Braden to Svalbard in the Arctic Circle, Carol had announced their next plan for Braden: a weeklong adventure cruise to the Galápagos. Normally I try to keep my mouth shut around my in-laws, but when they'd said Galápagos, Amy and I practically burst out as one, "We want to go!"

Carol and Walter had looked distinctly disconcerted that they might have to take Braden's parents along on the trip—not to mention pay for it—but Amy and I maintained a united front. Whenever the Galápagos came up, we made it clear that we wanted to be included. I'm not sure what made my in-laws relent. It may have been the understanding that Amy and I could have said no to the whole enterprise. Braden, after all, was our son, and it was up to us whether he went. A more likely explanation is that Carol and Walter are generous people. I think they just came around to the realization that taking our entire family would be a nice thing to do.

Even so, in the months leading to our departure, I'd kept myself in self-protective denial, thinking the trip might not happen. Growing up in a family of biologists, I had elevated the Galápagos to an almost mystical place in my pantheon of scientific destinations. Though neither of my parents had ever made it there, the islands were, after all, the "birthplace of evolution" and home to a fantastic menagerie of unique critters. I had dreamed of visiting the Galápagos for decades, but it was a bit like dreaming of going to outer space—conceivable, yeah, but highly improbable.

Now, only two weeks before we were due to fly to Portland to join Walter and Carol, the reality began to sink in. I began figuring out what gear to bring and took the kids to the YMCA pool to practice their snorkeling skills. Braden and I spent twenty or thirty minutes a night flipping through Galápagos guidebooks, memorizing the features of Nazca Boobies and Flightless Cormorants and calculating our odds of seeing them. I showed Tessa how to use her new camera, and she practiced by taking pictures of Amy and me at our most embarrassing moments.

In doing all this, something remarkable happened. Despite a heavy workload and mile-long to-do list, I began to get excited.

And as if that wasn't enough, plenty of pre-Galápagos birding adventures awaited us.

On a glorious Saturday in early June, several Boy Scout leaders and I pulled off the Boy Scout bike trip with no fatalities, a result I considered an unmitigated success. Our excursion took us on one of the most spectacular routes I have ever ridden, a stretch of the Milwaukee Road rail line that crosses the Montana–Idaho border. Dubbed the Hiawatha Trail, the ride begins with a transit of a 1.66-mile-long pitch-black tunnel. Having survived that, riders descend through nine more tunnels and across seven dizzying trestles, covering a total of fifteen miles. During the ride I couldn't focus on birds—I was too busy making sure scouts didn't nosedive off hundred-foot-high railroad trestles—but Braden spotted a Nashville Warbler along the trail, a Lifer for him and a major coup.

As I wrapped up a couple of big writing projects, I also decided to work in outings to see especially hard-to-find birds. When we'd encountered Dick Hutto during our Big Weekend, he had mentioned finding the nest of a Williamson's Sapsucker—a species Braden and I had searched for several times without success. A week later Dick graciously took us up to Blue Mountain Recreation Area just a short drive southwest of Missoula, and here we found the Williamson's nest and got stunning views of the parents bringing back beaks full of ants for their babies. The male especially was more dazzling than I had imagined. Its black body was detailed with bold white racing stripes on its head and wings, while its belly blazed yellow. Near the nest we also located nesting Hairies, flickers, and Lewis's Woodpeckers.

The Lewis's Woodpecker nest intrigued Dick. His own research had shown how important burn areas were to birds, but he had assumed that most of a burn's positive effects occurred in the first few years.

"For the first ten years after the burn," Dick said, "I never saw Lewis's up here. Now they're in here every time I come up."

"Why do you think that is?" I asked.

"I think it's because the wood of the dead trees is finally getting soft and cruddy enough for them to carve out holes. Lewis's are some of the weakest woodpeckers when it comes to drilling out holes, but now the trees might be just right for them. It makes me think that burned forests aren't just important right after a burn. They may help a whole succession of bird species for decades, maybe longer."

A few days later, stoked about photographing the Williamson's and Lewis's, I returned to our neighborhood Pileated nest. Although I had snapped reasonable photos of the adults, that had been *before* figuring out my camera problems. Now, leaving my UV filter and 1.4X extender behind, I returned to the nest for some ultra-crisp shots.

When I arrived, the nest looked deserted.

Shoot, I thought, *the young have already fledged.* That bummed me out because I didn't know when I might ever find another good Pileated opportunity. Trying to stay hopeful, I set up my camera and tripod and waited.

I sat for twenty minutes, enduring the scrutiny of passing drivers, bicyclists, and dog-walkers who all probably pegged me as an axe-murderer or meth dealer. During that time I located a Pygmy Nuthatch nest in the tree next to the Pileated nest, but didn't see or hear the slightest sign of the woodpeckers. Then I glanced up to see a pencil-thin stick protruding from the nest hole. At first I thought I was imagining it, but I jumped up to look through my camera's viewfinder and saw—a beak!

A moment later, a young Pileated Woodpecker cautiously peeked out into the bright sunlight. I fired off a few shots, but the fun had just begun. Soon a second baby also stuck its head out of the hole. Then one of the parents returned for a quick feeding frenzy. Twenty minutes later the other returned. I furiously pressed the shutter button, taking dozens of pictures.

The next day, with woodpeckers on the brain, Braden and I again rendezvoused with Dick—this time at a place called Pattee Canyon. Our goal? A Three-toed Woodpecker nest that Dick had discovered. Once again Braden and I saw the woodpeckers, but we also nabbed great looks at MacGillivray's Warblers right near the parking lot. We were so excited that, after grabbing Egg McMuffins in town, we headed straight for Lee Metcalf to get better photos of Common Yellowthroats too.

The result of our efforts is that we got terrific, sharp photos of four species of woodpeckers—photos I would need if I ever wanted to get my woodpecker book published. As I was looking over the

Pileated shots, I also made a startling discovery. In my photos of a parent feeding its young I spotted not just two woodpecker babies but three! I posted the image on Facebook, and a woman I know from the US Fish and Wildlife Service's National Wildlife Refuge System emailed to ask if she could repost it to their Facebook page. She also tweeted one of Braden's Common Yellowthroat photos from Lee Metcalf.

It was a great lead-up to what promised to be one of the most unforgettable experiences of our lives.

CHAPTER 22

layover birding

In planning our Galápagos adventure, we had decided to schedule two two-night layovers en route to Ecuador. The first, in Portland, was to pick up Amy's parents and nail down preparations for the trip. The second, in Miami, would give Amy's folks a chance to rest up from the long cross-country flight and see a bit of the town made famous by fraudulent land deals, cocaine trafficking, and Cuban cuisine. Braden and I quickly recognized additional advantages to both layovers: birding.

The evening of June 20, Amy, Tessa, Braden, and I flew to Portland. Amy's dad, Walter, picked us up at the airport, and the next morning, Walter and Carol's brother, Johnny, drove us to the Audubon sanctuary along Balch Creek on the west side of town. I had no idea what we might find, but on this day we outscored the Portland Trailblazers, racking up Western Tanagers, Brown Creepers, Song Sparrows, Black-throated Gray Warbler, Black-headed Grosbeak, Chestnut-backed Chickadees, Red-breasted Sapsucker, Spotted Towhee, and a Lifer for me, Wilson's Warbler. Braden had seen all but one of these (the Red-breasted Sapsucker) on his earlier trip to Washington with Amy, but the morning added five new species to my Big Year total, and all of us had a blast.

In comparison, Miami two days later proved to be the birding equivalent of the Bay of Pigs disaster. After a long day of flying, Braden and I eagerly arose the next morning and headed out in the minivan I'd rented for the occasion. A. D. Barnes Park had topped lists on several Miami birding websites, and we decided to head there first. When we arrived, we were dismayed to discover a lack of birds of any kind. Instead we entered a kind of Mirkwood Forest. Giant orb-weaving spiders hung between the trees, and hungry stray cats, like orcs, lurked behind every bush and building. I couldn't prove it, but I suspected that the feral felines had much to do with the avian Armageddon that had blighted the park.

"What should we do now?" I asked Braden.

As it had during our Big Weekend, a military intensity took hold in us. Hot and sweaty in South Florida's tropical climate, we needed help. Since returning from Texas, Braden had been texting Ted Wolff (of Red-cockaded Woodpeckers fame) every time we had enjoyed a great day birding.

Braden said, "I'll bet Ted has been to Miami. Maybe I should text him."

"Do it, Sergeant," I commanded.

Braden fired off a desperate plea for air support, and within moments Ted responded with coordinates for Brewer Park. We plugged it into Google Maps, and off we went. There we found a few good birds, including Yellow-crowned Night-Herons and Northern Cardinals. We also found more bird-eating invasive species— especially numerous large iguanas—prowling the park.

And that's pretty much how our morning went. We managed to find a Hill Myna nest in one park and glimpsed a pair of parrots disappearing over the horizon, but for us Miami remained depressingly devoid of birds. Taking pity on us, Ted texted, "Do you have Purple Swamphen and Egyptian Goose? Both are ABA countable. Swamphen in retention ponds at Dadeland Mall, west of Miami. Egyptian Goose at Metro Life Church at Dadeland."

By this time, the temperature and humidity were enough to steam a plantain, and Braden's blue eyes had lapsed into a thousand-yard stare. "Well, Sergeant," I said. "Should we at least go try to find the Egyptian Geese? There could be a promotion in it for you."

"Sure," he said, showing clear signs of birder battle fatigue.

We set off depleted of both energy and optimism, but exactly where Ted had told us, we found the geese—a flock of handsome critters who, like countless previous waves of immigrants, had carved out a comfortable existence in South Florida. As we headed back to the hotel, however, we crossed off Miami as a future birding destination while consoling ourselves with memories of great birding in Oregon.

Two mornings later we landed on the tiny island of Baltra.

JUNE BIRD LIST

Sneed's List (15)	Braden's List (13)
Calliope Hummingbird	Evening Grosbeak
Williamson's Sapsucker	Nashville Warbler
Hammond's Flycatcher	Calliope Hummingbird
Cassin's Vireo	Williamson's Sapsucker
Orange-crowned Warbler	Hammond's Flycatcher
American Three-toed Woodpecker	Cassin's Vireo
Evening Grosbeak	Orange-crowned Warbler
Red-breasted Sapsucker	American Three-toed Woodpecker
Chestnut-backed Chickadee	Pacific Wren
Bushtit	Red-breasted Sapsucker
Pacific Wren	Egyptian Goose
Wilson's Warbler	Magnificent Frigatebird
Egyptian Goose	Common Hill Myna
Magnificent Frigatebird	
Common Hill Myna	

CHAPTER 23

birding across borders

A chunk of rock the size of an ostrich egg, Baltra is the site of one of two main Galápagos airports. Although the Galápagos Islands belong to Ecuador, landing there is in many ways like entering a separate, sovereign nation—one with extremely strict standards for what tourists can and cannot bring in. As with Hawaii, Tahiti, New Zealand, and countless other major island groups, invasive species have already made major impacts on the Galápagos, and, to their credit, Ecuadorian officials work hard to prevent further damage.

After spending more than an hour being interrogated by immigration officials and having our bags and packs inspected, we boarded buses for a short drive down to the docks, where we would catch inflatable Zodiacs out to our waiting vessel. Even as the bus trundled down the hill, we spotted our first interesting avifauna—frigatebirds hovering like pterodactyls over the harbor. As we stepped off the bus, dozens of smaller brown birds darted and swooped around us, many snatching up food from the harbor surface.

I turned to Braden and demanded, "What are those?"

"I'm not sure."

"They look like terns."

Braden quickly checked one of our guidebooks. "Brown Noddies," he confirmed. Then, not two beats later, he shouted, "Blue-footed Booby!"

I pivoted one direction, then the other. "What? Where? Are you kidding?"

"There!"

Braden pointed to a large bird with a white body and brown wings flying by.

"Wow!" I exclaimed, high-fiving Braden. "I never thought we'd see them so quickly!"

As soon as we climbed into our Zodiac, Braden and I added another Lifer to our lists—White-vented (or Elliott's) Storm Petrels, small seabirds that feed at the water's surface and that for the next week would turn out to be our most faithful avian companions.

For our cruise, Amy's parents had booked us on the National Geographic *Endeavour*, run by Lindblad Expeditions, and it was about the most pleasant vessel I'd ever been aboard. One of the largest ships cruising the Galápagos, the *Endeavour* held ninety-odd passengers and an almost equal number of crew. As the ship weighed anchor, Braden and I settled into Cabin 104, a narrow, comfortable berth with two twin beds. Amy and Tessa occupied Cabin 106 next door, while Carol and Walter took Cabin 108. After lunch and the ship's briefing, we all disembarked for our first Galápagos excursion, to Playa las Bachas on Isla Santa Cruz.

We rode to shore with Vanessa, one of half a dozen naturalists on the ship and a native of the Galápagos, and she led us on a beach walk that made me feel like I was starring in a PBS episode of *Nature*. Within a few steps we saw our first marine iguanas—the only lizards on earth that dive underwater to graze on marine algae. Scampering among them were Sally Lightfoot crabs whose red, orange, and blue exoskeletons were so vivid that I wondered what the *Endeavour*'s crew had slipped into my fruit drink. Blue-footed Boobies, frigatebirds, and noddies swirled offshore, but the day's major birding discovery took us totally by surprise.

Yellow Warblers!

Although the warblers were the same species we had back in Montana, we quickly determined that these were not the same birds. For one thing, the males sported handsome chocolate-colored skullcaps. Even more important, these warblers—like most other species in the Galápagos—proved delightfully tame. As any student in island biogeography can tell you, a recurring feature of island species is that many evolved in the absence of predators, a situation that has rendered them unafraid of almost everything.

The Yellow Warblers were a case in point. As we walked along the beach, they darted into exposed bushes alongside us and hopped in the sand right next to our feet. Others scoured the black lava rock in the intertidal zone, hunting for insects next to basking marine iguanas and the psychedelic Sally Lightfoot crabs.

It wasn't until the following day, however, that the true nature of Galápagos birdlife began to reveal itself.

The next morning, after breakfast, the Zodiacs shuttled us to North Seymour Island. There another skilled Ecuadorian naturalist, Walter—not to be confused with my father-in-law—led us on a spectacular walk through one of the Galápagos's most important nesting grounds. Within a few yards of our beach landing we almost tripped over Blue-footed Boobies nesting at our feet. Some pairs incubated only one or two eggs, but others had more, thanks to the recent departure of the El Niño weather phenomenon.

For those unfamiliar with it, El Niño occurs when east-to-west trade winds weaken or disappear across the equatorial Pacific. This shift in wind patterns allows warm surface waters, normally pushed toward Asia, to creep eastward toward the Americas. In different parts of the globe, El Niño unleashes different impacts ranging from unusually wet to unusually dry weather. In the Galápagos Islands, it replaces normally cool waters with a slug of warm water, triggering a cascade of mostly negative effects. The warmer waters kill off the leafy green algae that the marine iguanas need to survive, often leading to mass starvation. They also drive away the shoals of anchovies and sardines that boobies and other seabirds rely on. Fortunately when cooler waters return so do the fish, and most of the seabirds can resume or even increase their reproductive output.

"This year," Walter exulted, "we are seeing more Blue-footed Boobies laying *three* eggs than ever before."

He quickly taught us how to identify male versus female BFBs, as we began to call them.

"Look at the eyes," he explained. "The male boobies have small pupils, while the pupils of the females are much larger."

Joining the boobies, male Magnificent and Great Frigatebirds crowned dozens of low-lying bushes that covered the island. Almost all serious birders—and a great many non-birders—have seen nature documentaries about these amazing creatures. With deeply forked tails and wingspans exceeding seven feet, frigatebirds are impossible to mistake for any other tropical birds. What captures the most film footage are the astonishing red throat pouches males display during courtship—a ritual we got to observe up close.

Walter pointed out a half-dozen males perched just yards from where we stood. Each had assembled its own crude stick nest, hoping to attract a mate.

"Watch what happens when a female flies over," Walter told us.

On cue, a female slowly swept over the males and, as one, they raised their beaks skyward, inflated their throat pouches into garish red balloons—gular sacs—and began vibrating their wings in ardent supplication. It was their way of saying, "Choose me! I'm a sharp dresser and a good provider. Even better, I've already built you a house—and the mortgage is paid!" To make doubly sure their intentions could not be misunderstood, the male frigatebirds rattled their beaks against their gular sacs, and, by golly, it *worked*. We watched in astonishment as the female made her choice, landing next to one of the males only thirty feet from where we stood.

The boobies and frigatebirds were far from the island's only attractions. As we slowly made our way through the nesting bird colonies, we witnessed one of the world's most handsome gulls, the Swallow-tailed Gull, perched on nearby lava rocks. Several times we had to step around sea lions and five-foot-long land iguanas blocking our path. Following the trail inland through a ghostly forest of Palo Santo trees, we discovered a beautifully adorned Galápagos dove nesting in a cup formed by two prickly pear cactus pads. Like many doves its overall coloration left nothing to write home about, but the bird stood out by sporting vivid red feet and an iridescent blue ring around each eye. Since we were in South America, neither the dove nor any of the other Galápagos birds counted toward our Big Year lists, but Braden and I didn't care. We were just enchanted by the variety and distinctness of the birds we encountered.

Surrounded by delicate doves, garish boobies, and exuberant frigatebirds, we almost overlooked a number of small black or brown birds pecking at the ground and perched in trees. Back home we might have mistaken them for pesky starlings or House Finches. In many ways, however, these small, nondescript birds were the most important we would encounter.

CHAPTER 24

the bird feeders of evolution

Entire books have been written about the role of the Galápagos finches in helping Darwin tease out the basics of natural selection and evolution. I'm not going to write another one now. For the increasing number of Americans who have not heard the story, here are the main talking points:

- Naturalist Charles Darwin visits the Galápagos aboard the *Beagle* in 1835.

- Darwin finds a lot of finches with various beak shapes and sizes and different behaviors. He kills a bunch and takes them home to England.

- Back home, one of his colleagues informs him that many of the finches are actually different species.

- Darwin starts to think, "Hmm. Maybe these finches all came from a common ancestor. Maybe environmental conditions favor some features—such as beak size or shape—over others, leading to greater reproductive success for individuals with those features. Maybe this leads to changes in species over time. Need a name for this process. 'Nature's weeding'? No. 'Better living through biology'? No. Ah, I've got it! I'll call it 'natural selection'!"

Darwin, of course, didn't just depend on the finches to make his monumental intellectual breakthrough. Galápagos mockingbirds kicked it off, and the giant tortoises contributed. The finches, though, get most of the credit, and I found myself paying more and more attention to these little brown birds as we moved from island to island. That's not to say that I worked hard to learn to distinguish the different species. Taxonomic differences between finches can thwart even the most accomplished experts, so I left the IDs up to Braden. Most of what we saw, however, fell into the categories of small, medium, or large ground or tree finches. And even though I couldn't usually tell which was which, it gave me small shivers to look at these birds and reflect on what a revolutionary impact they—with Darwin's help—have made on our understanding of how we and every other living thing on the planet got here.

The remainder of our Galápagos week offered one delight after another. Every day we hiked. We snorkeled. We sea-kayaked. At Puerto Ayora we visited the Charles Darwin Research Station and then an outlying farm to observe wild Galápagos tortoises migrating from the lowlands to higher elevations where there was more food during the dry season. One afternoon on the east coast of Isla Isabella we took a Zodiac ride along a rocky shore to see Galápagos Penguins emerging from their lairs to feed in the ocean. It was yet another bucket-list moment, as everyone in our family had always wanted to see penguins in the wild. None of us were prepared for just how well adapted these cute little animals were to their marine habitat. As we watched, one penguin dove into the water and zoomed away as if it were wearing a jetpack.

Braden and I looked at each other, jaws agape. "Wow!" Braden exclaimed. "Did you see how fast it was?"

"Incredible!" was all I could say.

On that same ride we watched a pair of Flightless Cormorants perform an elaborate aquatic courtship ritual—all as a second

A highlight of our Big Year was observing this neighborhood nest of Pileated Woodpeckers.

TOP LEFT Bruce and the goats catch up on some journaling against the backdrop of the Dragoon Mountains.

BOTTOM LEFT This spectacular Vermillion Flycatcher gave us an early indication of the birds we would experience at Half Moon Ranch.

TOP RIGHT As this Greater Roadrunner attests, the lots next to gas stations provided some of the best birding and biggest surprises of our Big Year travels.

BOTTOM RIGHT Setting out to explore a nearby draw in the Dragoons

TOP LEFT Bruce and Braden with the Chiricahua Mountains in the far distance

BOTTOM LEFT "Desert cardinals," Pyrrhuloxias, welcomed us our very first day of birding in Arizona.

TOP RIGHT Sunrise "burns down" Cochise Stronghold in the Dragoons.

BOTTOM RIGHT Braden takes the initiative to record our bird sightings at Jesse H. Jones Park & Nature Center near Houston.

TOP LEFT Braden with Ted Wolff at High Island

BOTTOM LEFT Avocets on the Bolivar Peninsula, the angry Gulf of Mexico a portent of calamity to come

TOP RIGHT A trio of White-faced Ibises

BOTTOM RIGHT A definite Bird of the Day, Scissor-tailed Flycatcher

Nesting birds, mainly egrets, Roseate Spoonbills, and Neotropic Cormorants, at the Rookery in High Island

LEFT The poster bird of the Galápagos, the Blue-footed Booby, entertained us throughout our weeklong excursion.

TOP RIGHT Amy (far right), Braden, and Tessa share a moment with the Patron Saint of Biologists, Charles Darwin.

BOTTOM RIGHT One of the finches that helped inspire Darwin's world-changing revelation

TOP LEFT A Magnificent Frigatebird solicits a companion.

BOTTOM LEFT A Galápagos Penguin prepares to do some fishing.

RIGHT Up-close and personal with Long-eared Owls courtesy of Denver Holt's Owl Research Institute team

TOP LEFT A Yellow-breasted Chat at Pirogue Island State Park near Miles City, Montana

BOTTOM LEFT Braden and Nick (left) with noted biologist Dick Hutto, shortly after Nick bagged his Lifer Black-backed Woodpecker

TOP RIGHT Searching for California Condors at Grimes Point Overlook on California's legendary Highway 1

BOTTOM RIGHT Our 2016 Bird of the Year, Northern Pygmy-Owl

Braden goes winter birding with our new bird dog, Lola.

hapless male looked on. Another moment out of a nature documentary, and we got to see it from only twenty feet away.

As too often happens, our adventure quickly drew to an end. A week after we flew to Baltra, we said goodbye to the wonderful crew of the *Endeavour* and boarded a flight from Isla San Cristobal to Guayaquil. Before returning home to Montana, though, Braden and I managed to squeeze in one more birding adventure.

Ideally I would have planned for us to spend at least an extra week in Ecuador to sample the mainland. Amy and I agreed, however, that her parents would need assistance getting back home—a prediction that turned out to be accurate, especially during our hellish transit of the Miami International Airport, the most dysfunctional airport I had experienced throughout my years of international travel.

Nonetheless, on our return from the Galápagos we would have a free afternoon in Guayaquil, and I asked Amy what we might do with it.

"I think my parents will be pretty tired after the cruise," Amy said. "Tessa and I will probably just hang out at the hotel pool with them."

"Okay," I said, already hatching an alternative.

With a bit of web searching, I located Carlos Vinueza, who runs a small company known as Tumbesian Birding. Via emails Carlos and I arranged to have a guide pick Braden and me up at our hotel upon our return to Guayaquil. Our objective: an afternoon of birding at nearby Cerro Blanco National Park.

Paul Abad was waiting for us when, laden with binoculars and cameras, Braden and I came down to the hotel lobby. Young, personable, and enthusiastic, Paul led us to his car and drove us north through Ecuador's largest city. I eagerly anticipated the excursion not only for the birding but for a chance to see a bit of mainland Ecuador outside of airports and hotels.

Guayaquil made a much more favorable impression than I'd expected. Years earlier I'd read a guidebook that, if I'm remembering correctly, described the city as a "coastal cesspool." Now, driving north with Paul, I had to disagree. Sure, the city consisted mostly of modern cement buildings and lacked visible pockets of charm, but for a major city in a developing nation it looked pleasant enough.

The traffic wasn't even as bad as Houston or Phoenix, although the concept of staying in a particular vehicle lane apparently hadn't reached this part of South America.

Paul drove us twenty minutes out of town and then pointed to a large forest-covered hill. "That's Cerro Blanco," he said.

A guard opened a chain-link fence to let us in, and Paul relayed our intentions in Spanish. The guard nodded agreeably, and we drove several hundred yards down a rough road before pulling over to park.

I had visited tropical forests in Asia, Australia, and Costa Rica, but I'd never seen one like this. The canopy reached perhaps thirty to fifty feet, with occasional emergent trees rising to seventy or eighty feet, and the forest exuded a scruffy appearance, with lots of dead leaves and bare branches. My first thought was that the area had been logged, but Paul corrected me.

"This is a dry tropical forest," he said. "That's why a lot of the trees are bare this time of year. It's much greener during the rainy season."

Paul went on to explain that the park had been created to protect one of South America's most critically endangered species, the Green Macaw.

Braden and I looked at each other. "Do we have a chance of seeing one today?" Braden asked.

"Probably not," Paul admitted. "There are only about six nesting pairs left, and they live high in the park. Last year I camped up there and got to see one, but they don't often come down this low."

Never mind. Almost anything we saw would likely be a new species—if not a totally new family. We followed Paul down a trail and right away were rewarded with a clear if brief view of a beautiful large brown bird with a long tail.

"Squirrel Cuckoo!" Paul shouted enthusiastically. "That's a really good bird. You don't see them every day in here."

Braden and I grinned at each other, and we continued to hike.

Unfortunately, after our prized cuckoo, the birding took a nosedive. Paul led us off onto a series of trails that cut through thick forest, and, though we heard a lot of birds, seeing them proved difficult. Overcast conditions exacerbated the problem. We'd hear something call above us and look up to see only a tiny, backlit silhouette flitting among heavy foliage. We did manage to pick up dark views of Amazilia Hummingbirds and Blue Gray Tanagers. Paul identified other species by their calls, but clear looks eluded us.

After an hour of trekking, both Braden and I were starting to feel frustration—along with dehydration. We quickly drained the one water bottle I'd brought with us, but it wasn't nearly enough, and I started to feel the heat and humidity in my legs as I forced myself up a creek drainage.

My frustration peaked when Paul and Braden spotted a pair of birds down the slope in thick brush off the trail.

"Gray-and-gold Warblers!" Paul exclaimed. "Do you see them?"

Braden got a great look at one, but I saw only flashes of movement before the shapes darted into the understory.

"No," I said, trying to control my impatience.

"They're moving down the streambed," Paul said, hurrying down the trail. I followed, vainly trying to glimpse the birds, but kept missing them.

Braden did his best to encourage me. "Do you see them now, Daddy?" he asked.

I sighed. "No."

"Here, use my binoculars."

Recently we'd discovered just how much better Braden's optics were than mine, and I gratefully swapped with him. The warblers continued to do their best to avoid me. Finally, after a ten-minute chase, they must have figured that I'd suffered enough and paused on an exposed rock across the creek.

"Wow," I said, bringing the pair into focus. "They're stunning!"

It was especially gratifying to see a warbler species different from any that we could find in our usual stomping grounds. Like most American birders, I tended to think of warblers only in terms of the ones that live or breed in the United States, but this gray-and-gold pair reminded me that at home I see only a slice of what's going on in the world and that there's a lot more to discover.

Despite our sighting of the warblers, Paul could probably tell that Braden and I had been less than wowed by the park. It wasn't Paul's fault. The sky was lousy, and we were hitting the forest at a tough time of day. I could tell that Paul was hoping for more, as were we.

"Let's go down along the road," he suggested. "It's more open there, and it will take us to an overlook where we might see parrots."

"Sounds good," I told him, trying to bolster my enthusiasm.

We made our way back down the creek drainage until we reached a wide dirt road. I have to admit that, as much as I love forests, tropical forests can make me feel claustrophobic with their dense canopy and intense humidity. Out on the road I breathed easier, and almost immediately our luck began to improve.

We saw two more Blue Gray Tanagers, then a pair of flycatchers with brilliant yellow breasts, perched on an open branch.

"Are those Kiskadees?" I asked, remembering similar birds from Costa Rica.

Paul focused his binoculars. "Boat-billed Flycatchers, I think. Yes, definitely."

Other birds also began to emerge: Fasciated and Superciliated Wrens, Tropical Kingbird, Ecuadorian Thrush, and a fleeting glimpse of what Paul said was an Ecuadorian Piculet.

Speaking of piculets, as we'd set off from the hotel Paul had asked what birds we'd most like to see. Braden had answered "parrots," while I had replied "woodpeckers." If I'd gotten a good look at the piculet, I could have checked that off my list since piculets are in the woodpecker family of birds. As it was, I began to realize that my odds of a solid woodpecker sighting were growing longer with the growing evening gloom.

Then suddenly Braden cried, "Woodpecker!"

My adrenaline pumped.

"Yes! Good eye!" Paul confirmed, hurrying forward with me on his heels. As we got closer, I stopped to raise my camera.

"What kind is it?" I eagerly asked.

"Black-cheeked," Paul said.

And right then the setting sun dipped below the cloud layer, focusing a thick beam of golden light on the bird and the tree it clung to. I fired off at least thirty frames as the woodpecker cooperated with its best Calvin Klein pose.

I turned to Braden and grinned.

Hardly a minute passed before Paul called, "Look! There's another woodpecker!"

We easily picked up the second species—a bird unlike any we'd ever seen.

"Oh," Paul exclaimed, delighted. "It's a Scarlet-backed."

"Do you see it, Daddy?" Braden asked. After my frustration with the warblers, my son had taken it upon himself to make sure that I didn't miss anything, and I inwardly smiled at this parent-child role reversal—something that seemed to be happening more and more as our Big Year progressed.

"Yeah!" I replied.

While the Black-cheeked presented a similar black-and-white appearance to a Hairy or Downy, the Scarlet-backed sported a bold, solid-red back and wings. It left no doubt that Braden and I weren't in Kansas anymore—or Montana, Arizona, or Texas. I tried to get a good photo of the bird, but it apparently didn't feel as cooperative as the Black-cheeked, which continued to peck happily away at a hole on its own tree trunk. Still, all three of us were elated by this unexpected woodpecker exhibition, and for me it justified the entire excursion.

In the tropics, however, sunrises and sunsets don't mess around. One moment you have plenty of light, and the next moment you're stumbling around like a drunk in a cave. We all decided we'd better use our dwindling daylight to scamper up to the overlook Paul had recommended. While Paul and Braden bounded ahead of me, I forced myself to keep moving up the slope. By this point I harbored little doubt that dehydration was catching up with me, but I pushed forward, calculating that I'd be able to gut it out before the onset of serious consequences.

Finally reaching the overlook, we spotted a flock of parrots in the midst of their nightly migration from the distant mangroves up into the forest hills, but the birds flew too far away for us to ID them. We did see some other great birds—White-tailed Jays and a Bananaquit—and on the way back to the car heard the call of a Forest Falcon—but just like that, the curtain of darkness crashed down on us and our outing.

To celebrate our afternoon of birding, I asked Paul if we could take him to dinner at one of his favorite local places, and he drove us to a perfect little restaurant in a modern mini-mall. We sat down to huge platters of tasty chicken, beef, rice, and beans, and I spent the next hour interrogating him about all things Ecuadorian. Though the birding hadn't been what I expected, Braden and I were content. We knew one thing for sure: our afternoon adventure beat sitting around the hotel pool.

ECUADOR AND GALÁPAGOS BIRD LISTS

Sneed's List	Braden's List
GALÁPAGOS (37)	**GALÁPAGOS (38)**
Elliot's Storm-Petrel	Elliot's Storm-Petrel
Blue-footed Booby	Blue-footed Booby
Brown Pelican	Brown Pelican
Brown Noddy	Brown Noddy
Galápagos Dove	Galápagos Dove
Great Blue Heron	Great Blue Heron
Ruddy Turnstone	Ruddy Turnstone
Lava Gull	Lava Gull
Galápagos Mockingbird	Galápagos Mockingbird
Yellow Warbler	Yellow Warbler
Small Ground-Finch	Small Ground-Finch
Medium Ground-Finch	Medium Ground-Finch
Galápagos Shearwater	Galápagos Shearwater
Magnificent Frigatebird	Magnificent Frigatebird
Great Frigatebird	Great Frigatebird
Semipalmated Plover	Semipalmated Plover
Swallow-tailed Gull	Swallow-tailed Gull
Small Tree-Finch	Small Tree-Finch
Nazca Booby	Nazca Booby
Galápagos Hawk	Galápagos Hawk
Flightless Cormorant	Flightless Cormorant
Striated Heron	Striated Heron
American Oystercatcher	American Oystercatcher
Whimbrel	Whimbrel
Galápagos Martin	Galápagos Martin
Yellow-crowned Night-Heron	Yellow-crowned Night-Heron
Wandering Tattler	Wandering Tattler
Galápagos Penguin	Galápagos Penguin
Galápagos Flycatcher	Galápagos Flycatcher
Large Tree-Finch	Large Tree-Finch
Large Ground-Finch	Large Ground-Finch
Common Cactus-Finch	Common Cactus-Finch
White-cheeked Pintail	White-cheeked Pintail
Common Gallinule	Common Gallinule
Smooth-billed Ani	Smooth-billed Ani
Wedge-rumped Storm-Petrel	Wedge-rumped Storm-Petrel
Red-footed Booby	Red-billed Tropicbird
	Red-footed Booby

GUAYAQUIL, ECUADOR (29)	GUAYAQUIL, ECUADOR (29)
Black Vulture	Black Vulture
Turkey Vulture	Turkey Vulture
Crane Hawk	Crane Hawk
Ecuadorian Ground-Dove	Ecuadorian Ground-Dove
White-tipped Dove	White-tipped Dove
Squirrel Cuckoo	Squirrel Cuckoo
Amazilia Hummingbird	Amazilia Hummingbird
Black-cheeked Woodpecker	Black-cheeked Woodpecker
Scarlet-backed Woodpecker	Scarlet-backed Woodpecker
Red-lored Parrot	Red-lored Parrot
Pacific Parrotlet	Pacific Parrotlet
Streak-headed Woodcreeper	Streak-headed Woodcreeper
Southern Beardless-Tyrannulet	Southern Beardless-Tyrannulet
Boat-billed Flycatcher	Boat-billed Flycatcher
Baird's Flycatcher	Baird's Flycatcher
Tropical Kingbird	Tropical Kingbird
Rufous-browed Peppershrike	Rufous-browed Peppershrike
White-tailed Jay	White-tailed Jay
Fasciated Wren	Fasciated Wren
Superciliated Wren	Superciliated Wren
Tropical Gnatcatcher	Tropical Gnatcatcher
Ecuadorian Thrush	Ecuadorian Thrush
Tropical Parula	Tropical Parula
Gray-and-gold Warbler	Gray-and-gold Warbler
Blue-gray Tanager	Blue-gray Tanager
Blue-black Grassquit	Blue-black Grassquit
Bananaquit	Bananaquit
Streaked Saltator	Streaked Saltator
Scrub Blackbird	Scrub Blackbird

CHAPTER 25

bucking for birds

Returning home left us seriously discombobulated. International travel always does that to some extent, but usually it is caused by jet lag and the vast cultural differences between a foreign destination and one's native land. This time my sense of dislocation had more to do with the intensity of our travel experience and the short time we'd been gone than with culture shock. I suspect the same was true for Amy, Braden, and Tessa. On the trip we had all become so immersed in exploring nature that it was jarring to have it end so abruptly.

During our first couple of days home, whenever I glanced into Braden's room I saw him poring through Galápagos brochures and our South American bird guides. A couple of mornings after we returned, Tessa came downstairs and said, "I woke up wondering where we would take the Zodiacs today. Then I remembered that we weren't on the ship anymore."

Amy and I laughed, but I knew how she felt. As we resumed our routines, Braden, Tessa, Amy, and I frequently asked each other, "Were we really just watching Blue-footed Boobies a week ago? Do you know that at almost exactly this time last Thursday we were snorkeling with sea turtles?"

We all relished such memories, but I couldn't afford to dwell on them for long. On July 10, just four days after returning from our trip, I had to pick up a rental car and hit the interstate for a different kind of adventure—to teach a weeklong writing camp to high school students in Miles City, Montana.

I greeted the prospect with some trepidation. Though I'd spoken to thousands—make that hundreds of thousands—of students during my career, I'd never before committed to teaching one group of kids for an entire week. Before the Galápagos trip I had worked furiously to prepare enough exercises and lectures to keep these unknown students of mine occupied, but I worried: *What if they really don't care about learning to write? What if I don't have anything to teach them? What if they stage a coup and decide to hang me from the nearest Dairy Queen sign?* They were teenagers, after all.

Despite these concerns, I made up my mind to at least enjoy the five-hundred-mile drive east across the state. I bought a deliciously violent, politically incorrect Wilbur Smith novel on CD, and, even better, I packed my binoculars and camera so that I could search for birds along the way.

I started my journey at dawn and at eight pulled over at my favorite truck stop outside of Butte to hit the restroom and pick up breakfast. One hundred fifty miles later I spotted my first Big Year bird of the trip—a trio of White Pelicans on the Yellowstone River near Big Timber.

By one o'clock my body screamed for a break, and I decided to stretch my legs at a place I'd visited once before, Pompey's Pillar National Monument. Located half an hour east of Billings, the park preserved the only deliberately placed evidence of Lewis and Clark's entire expedition. Here, on a large sandstone outcrop overlooking the Yellowstone River, Clark had paused at least long enough to carve his signature. Why here and nowhere else on the trip? No one will ever know. Maybe the full impact of what he and his crew had accomplished had started to sink in. Perhaps as the end of the journey approached he began looking inward, sensing his own mortality. Maybe he finished reading all his books and needed something to do. Whatever the reason, I decided this would be an ideal time to carve my own signature into the rock next to his.

Not really.

In fact I didn't even walk up to look at Clark's famous scrawl. Instead I set out to see what birds might be hanging around the park. As soon as I climbed out of my car, I spotted several robins, two American Goldfinches, a trio of Cedar Waxwings, and a blue flash I later identified as a Lazuli Bunting. Hoping to beat an ominous storm cloud sweeping in from the west, I slung my camera around my neck, locked the car, and rushed to see what else I might find in a thick stand of cottonwoods along the river.

I especially hoped to see a Red-headed Woodpecker. They almost never reach western Montana, but out here, in the south-central part of the state, they at least make an occasional appearance, and as soon as I began walking I heard drumming in the surrounding trees. I excitedly began turning in all directions, looking for the source but couldn't pinpoint it.

Probably a Downy, I convinced myself.

Continuing along the trail, I saw House Wrens and Yellow Warblers and heard tweets and chirps I couldn't identify. A couple of miles away, lightning split the sky, and I began hearing raindrops hit the green canopy of foliage above me, but I hurried on, reaching the river and then curving back toward the west end of Pompey's Pillar itself.

Suddenly I stopped.

In a nearby cottonwood tree, a yellow and black bird busily investigated a branch fifteen feet above the ground.

Townsend's Warbler? I thought excitedly, not realizing that both the location and habitat were way off. I continued to watch the bird flit from one branch to another and managed to get a couple of ID photos before it disappeared for good. Then I continued walking.

Hundreds of swallows flew above and around Pompey's Pillar, and I saw at least one White-throated Swift. Peering into the sagebrush south of the pillar I also saw Vesper Sparrows and what I'm pretty sure was a Say's Phoebe. That mysterious yellow and black bird, though, gnawed at me.

What was it? I kept wondering.

Back at the car I dug out my Kaufman's guide and began flipping through the pages. I stopped on page 320.

"No way!" I shouted aloud. "Yellow-breasted Chat!"

I know. I know. To many of you birders, especially from the South or Midwest, chats are probably as common as houseflies, but this was a Lifer for me, and I got so excited that I called Braden to tell him about it.

"You saw one?" he asked in a sad voice.

"Yeah!" I told him. "But I didn't call to get you down. I just wanted to share it with you."

"I know. But I'll probably never get to see one," he lamented.

"Of course you will," I tried to console him.

I understood his disappointment. At the same time, I'd been hoping that by age thirteen he'd begin developing the ability to set his own wants aside and just be glad for my discovery. *Then again,* I told myself, *I doubt I would have been mature enough to do that at his age. Still, it's a parent's job to lead him in the right direction.*

"They're all over," I continued, trying to be encouraging. "I'll bet you even see one this year."

"But how?"

"I don't know," I said, "but be happy for me, okay?"

His voice cheered up. "Okay. Good job. Call me if you see anything else."

"You got it."

Two hours later I rolled into Miles City.

Though home to fewer than nine thousand souls, Miles City is considered Montana's major eastern outpost. For those living outside of the state, the town's chief claim to fame is that it featured in the popular novel and television miniseries, *Lonesome Dove*, serving as the ultimate destination for the two main characters, Woodrow F. Call and Augustus "Gus" McCrae, and their herd of Texas cattle. For Montanans, Miles City holds another, albeit less literary, claim: the annual Miles City Bucking Horse Sale.

Begun in 1951 as a way for local ranchers to auction off their excess stock to rodeo producers, the sale had by the 1960s turned into a regional affair known for its rodeo events and for wild, drunken celebrations that attracted thousands of cowboys, college students, and anyone else who wanted to party. Though the festivities have calmed somewhat since then, I became so intrigued by the sales history that in 2010 I wrote a book about the event. In the strange, often unpredictable ways of the world, it was that book that led to my invitation to teach the writing camp now.

I had arranged to bunk with a wonderful family I'd become friends with over the years, the Freeses. Shelley Freese was a terrific artist and writer and often helped me out by delivering copies of my *World Famous Miles City Bucking Horse Sale* book to local stores. Her husband, Bart, had gained as much fame for his dashing pirate's mustache as he had for serving as the dynamic principal of Miles City's Sacred Heart School. Rounding out the family were the couple's smart, funny teenage girls, Cecelia and Lila.

Because I arrived in town earlier than expected, I decided not to intrude upon the Freeses right away. Instead I bought myself a mocha (yes, they can be had in Miles City) and made my way to the southwest side of town and Spotted Eagle Recreation Area, which eBird listed as a hotspot for Red-headed Woodpeckers. I spent more than an hour walking the trails of the park, scouring cottonwood groves and fields, and strolling along the shore of Spotted Eagle Lake. I didn't see a single woodpecker but did notch ten other species, including at least half a dozen Yellow Warblers and a big surprise skulking along the edge of some cattails—a Brown Thrasher. Braden and I had seen this chestnut-colored, long-billed bird in Sabine Woods in Texas, but I hadn't realized they summered in Montana. To make certain I wasn't imagining things, I consulted the range map in Kaufman's guide and, sure enough, confirmed that I was in thrasher territory. None of the afternoon's finds contributed to my Big Year list, but I didn't mind. I was just having fun looking for birds.

The following days passed quickly. My writing camp group of eight girls and one boy demonstrated genuine interest in improving their craft, and only once or twice did I experience any fear they might string me up or burn me at the stake. Even better, prior to teaching each day I rose to the blasts of the 6:00 a.m. coal train rumbling through town, grabbed a pastry at Main Street Grind, and headed out to bird.

My first morning in Miles City I returned to Spotted Eagle and again saw a nice assortment of birds, though not a single woodpecker. The morning after that, my exhausting schedule caught up with me and I slept in, but the day after that I discovered a real gem, Pirogue Island State Park.

Located on the north shore of the Yellowstone River, Pirogue had been set aside as a Lewis and Clark historical area, but to me its real value lay in its wildlife habitat. The first morning I set out for the park, Google Maps misrouted me and landed me half an hour from my goal. As a result, I spent only forty-five minutes birding the park. The next day, I returned to Pirogue with plenty of time to spare.

The park offered a mix of sagebrush, grasslands, and cottonwood forest and hosted a wide variety of bird species, from pewees, House Wrens, and chickadees to Western and Eastern Kingbirds, Bald Eagles, and Killdeer. My main quarry continued to be Red-headed Woodpeckers, and—I didn't find them. I did see a pair of Downies and at least half a dozen flickers, including my first Yellow-shafted variety. Walking along the river I also paused to listen to a very strange, almost cooing, call that I'd never heard before. After quietly waiting for ten minutes, I finally saw that it was coming from my new friend Yellow-breasted Chat! Unlike its brethren at Pompey's Pillar, this one posed in full sunlight while I fired off half a dozen clear, crisp photographs.

The real value of my week of birding was not checking off new birds. It was that out there on my own I became more familiar with common species. The birds' calls still befuddled me. Part of this was my crummy hearing, but I was also realizing that I just didn't retain birdcalls in my brain. Nonetheless, I gained great confidence in picking out wrens, kingbirds, and other common Montana birds by sight. As much as I loved birding with Braden, I recognized that at least some of the time, I learned more by struggling over IDs on my own.

After a farewell to the Freeses and my students, I raced back across the state, though I did squeeze in a stop at Madison Buffalo Jump State Park, where I had a surprise, close-up encounter with a group of Rock Wrens. I arrived back home with only three new Big Year birds—American White Pelican, Yellow-breasted Chat, and Common Nighthawk, which I'd spotted one evening while strolling through Miles City's Riverside Park. I brought home something even more important, however: a bundle of birding knowledge that promised to serve me well during the remainder of our Big Year.

CHAPTER 26

dog days

Alas, the rest of July proved pathetic for Braden's and my Big Year lists. Braden picked up Common Nighthawk, a species I'd seen in Miles City, but that was it. Schmatta. Nada. Niente. Part of the issue, as usual, was that my writing schedule left little time for birding. A bigger problem was that the birds had gotten tougher to find. Most species had stopped nesting, and their babies had fledged. As a result they grew a lot quieter and moved away from nests and territories where we could easily locate them. According to Dick Hutto, a lot of birds moved up in elevation or to riparian areas this time of year, where food was more plentiful. Others, such as hummingbirds, had already begun migrating south.

On July 30, we sent Braden on the first of two weeklong Boy Scout camps, this one to Camp Parsons on the Olympic Peninsula in Washington.

"I'm guessing you'll pick up at least ten new species out there," I predicted.

"Really? You think so?" His voice betrayed skepticism.

"Maybe," I hedged. "You'll be right on Puget Sound. You might get a ton of shorebirds. Maybe even some Pigeon Guillemots. You could also pick up forest species."

Part of me wished I could go with him. As at the airport in Houston, dropping him off to catch his ride to Washington left a lump in my stomach. Amy and I had sent him to other camps and on trips by himself, but this time felt different.

Since we'd started our Big Year, Braden had grown as tall as me, and he moved through life with more independence. I attributed some of that to normal physical, intellectual, and emotional development, but I also gave credit to the Boy Scouts of America. It wasn't a flawless organization, but it offered boys the chance to grow in ways that few other groups did. It taught them invaluable practical skills, but it went far beyond that. Being in a troop and communicating with each other and with adults, scouts learned how to cooperate and become part of something bigger than themselves. Braden was no exception.

I recognized, though, that birding had also had a huge positive impact on my son. His expanding birding skills and knowledge gave him more confidence as a young man. At the beginning of our Big Year, we'd had more of a typical parent-child relationship, with me doing all the planning and telling him what to do. Now, as I'd witnessed on our birding trip with Paul Abad in Ecuador, Braden was much more of an equal partner. He led the way with bird identifications, and he pitched in with the nuts and bolts of planning, traveling, and more.

It all pointed to one, irrefutable conclusion: my son was growing up. And as much as I had enjoyed his early childhood years, I took huge satisfaction in our current relationship too. Watching him leave for Washington, I couldn't help lamenting that in five fast-paced years Braden would be gone. Many other parents had assured me, "Take our word for it, by the time he's eighteen you'll be ready to have him go," but I didn't believe it. I couldn't think of anything sadder than living without my children under our roof. And the worst part? There was absolutely nothing I could do about it.

Not surprisingly, Braden had a blast at Camp Parsons.

"Daddy," he told me when he returned. "I think that was my favorite thing I've done in Boy Scouts."

"Really? How come?" I asked.

"Well, they let us choose what we wanted to do," he said, "and the counselors came up with all kinds of activities to make it fun."

As we drove back to our house, he recounted humorous stories involving new scouts that he'd met and adventures he'd had taking sailing lessons and going on a treasure hunt with his tentmates.

"I'm thinking I might like to be a camp counselor there next year," he told me.

"Huh," I said, pleased by his enthusiasm.

The only downside to Camp Parsons was that my birding predictions had careened wildly off the mark. During his week in Washington, Braden picked up only two Big Year birds: Western Gull and Pigeon Guillemot. A couple of weeks after he returned, we again sent him off with his scout troop—this time for a week of camping and service work in Glacier National Park. All indications were that he'd spend most of the week painting benches, pulling weeds, or doing trail maintenance, but the troop hit the volunteer jackpot. Instead of inhaling lead-tainted paint dust and digging splinters out of their flesh, the boys were assigned the task of recording plants and animals around the park. As a result, they got to hike every day—and on some of Glacier's most spectacular trails.

One day they traveled to the Many Glacier Valley on the park's east side. Our family had a special connection to this stunning area. It's where I had spent a summer cooking at the Swiftcurrent Motor Inn after my second year of college and is where I proposed to Amy.

For Braden, the magic continued. Right near the little bridge that crossed over to the Many Glacier Hotel, he spotted a bird we had both longed to see since we had started birding: Harlequin Duck. One of America's most stunningly beautiful birds, Harlequins display graphic black, chestnut, gray, and white markings that would look more at home in the Metropolitan Museum of Art than out in the wilderness. Harlequins also happen to be ducks of special concern. Found only in high-quality, roaring streams and rivers, they quickly disappear from any area that has suffered logging or other serious disturbance. Glacier, in fact, is one of the few places in the Lower 48 where Harlequins breed, and it was a major score for Braden to see and identify one. It was the only new bird he picked up during the week, but was worth ten other Big Year birds put together.

While Braden soaked up a glorious week in Glacier, Amy and I agreed that Tessa could use her own outdoor adventure. Though Tessa had recently joined the Girl Scouts, she and other Girl Scouts got severely short-changed on camping experiences. Because of our Galápagos trip, Amy couldn't take any more time off work, so I decided to take Tessa for a weeklong daddy-daughter trip to one of my all-time favorite places: Banff. Birding wasn't the purpose of the trip, but as we threaded our way up through Eureka and across the Canadian border, I couldn't help thinking I might see something new.

My hopes were soon confirmed. That first afternoon, arriving at the Radium Springs Campground, I saw a pair of ground birds crossing the road in front of us.

"Look! Ptarmigans!" I shouted to Tessa.

"Daddy, we are not here to look at birds."

"I know. I know. But aren't they cool?"

Later, while riding our bikes around the campground, we almost rode over another one of the chicken-like creatures.

Well, at least I added one new bird to my Big Year list, I thought.

A few days later, when Tessa and I hiked up Johnston Canyon near Banff, I thought I might get a shot at Black Swifts, a fairly uncommon species known for nesting behind waterfalls. Tessa and I observed enormous flocks of Japanese and Chinese tourists but not a single swift or any other new birds for the entire trip. To make matters worse, my one new bird—White-tailed Ptarmigan—later flapped into the Not Bloody Likely category.

A week after returning from our trip, I showed Braden and Nick Ramsey the one horrible photo of the bird I'd taken with my phone.

"Hmm, Daddy," Braden informed me. "That doesn't look much like a ptarmigan."

"Could have been a Ruffed Grouse," Nick said.

"Or Dusky Grouse," Braden added.

Argh!

The bottom line: while August had provided us all with loads of fun and adventure, it seized the trophy for Year's Worst Birding Month, with Braden racking up a single species, and me a big fat zilch. It left Braden's and my Big Year counts on life support with 270 and 267 species respectively—far from our new "Super Target" of 350 and even well short of our previous target of 300.

As September arrived and leaves began to turn, Braden and I both came to a sober realization: to turn in any kind of serious Big Year numbers, we would have to take desperate measures. Fortunately we had already begun planning for such a predicament.

JULY BIRD LIST

Sneed's List (3)	Braden's List (1)
American White Pelican	Common Nighthawk
Yellow-breasted Chat	
Common Nighthawk	

AUGUST BIRD LIST

Sneed's List (0)	Braden's List (1)
Big Squat Zilch Bird	Harlequin Duck

CHAPTER 27

california

Even before August had been squashed flatter than a road-killed robin, Braden and I knew that we had our birding backs against the wall. If we wanted to be able to show our faces in the birder community during the coming year, we would have to dig deep. There was only one place we could do that without taking out a second mortgage on the house.

California.

The Golden State not only offered plenty of endemic birds that we couldn't find anywhere else, it was *on the ocean*. That meant we had the possibility of dozens—perhaps scores—of coastal and pelagic species.

In the weeks before school started, Braden and I began mapping out a California itinerary.

"How long can we stay?" Braden asked me.

"Now that you'll be in eighth grade, it's going to be tougher to pull you out of school," I told him. "You'll have more homework, and the schools start to whine about unexplained absences. Also, your legions of girlfriends will raise hell that you're gone."

He punched me in the shoulder. "Ha-ha."

"That said," I continued, "if we leave on Wednesday night, September 21, and come back the following Monday, that should give us four and a half days of solid birding, and, since there's no school on Monday, you'll only miss two days of classes. How's that sound?"

"Good," he said, looking over my shoulder as I marked it down on my calendar.

That still left the big question of where to go, but as we debated possible birding options, one location emerged as a clear winner: Monterey Bay.

If you've seen the movie *The Big Year*, you will remember the character of Annie Auklet, the feisty boat captain who led pelagic birding tours out of Washington State and nurtured a major grudge against the character played by Owen Wilson. Annie, brilliantly played by Angelica Houston in the film, was modeled after Debi Shearwater, who leads similar tours not from Washington but from Monterey Bay.

"Our top priority has got to be one of Shearwater's pelagic trips," I told Braden.

"Agreed."

"I'm also thinking we should try to see California Condors."

Braden's voice filled with awe. "You think we can?"

"Maybe. They've been reintroduced to Pinnacles National Park, and that's only about an hour from San Jose, where we'll be flying in."

The possibility thrilled me as much as it did Braden. In the 1960s and '70s, I'd spent most of my childhood living just over the mountains from the world's last living California Condors, but, despite more than a dozen backpacking trips into Condor country, I never glimpsed so much as a single tail feather. By the time I turned twenty-seven—and the condor population had plunged to the exact same number—I figured I'd forever missed my chance at watching these magnificent, doomed birds.

Then, in 1987, in a heavily criticized, desperate move, the US Fish and Wildlife Service spearheaded the capture of the last of the wild condors and began overseeing an intensive captive-breeding program. Against mighty odds the program succeeded—to the point that wildlife workers had been able to release condors in Pinnacles, Utah, Arizona, and Baja California. By 2016 the total condor population had swelled to 446 birds, capping one of the world's truly great conservation stories. The idea that I might get to see one in the wild—and with Braden by my side—well, it seemed as miraculous as the Boston Red Sox coming back from three games to none to defeat the Yankees in the 2004 American League Championship Series.

As we continued planning, I emailed an old friend of mine, Andrea Weiss, who lived near Monterey and had become a birder herself in recent years. I told her our plans and proposed we get together.

"Oh," Andy emailed back. "Are you coming out for the Monterey Bay Birding Festival?"

Birding festival? Huh?

I quickly looked it up, and Andy was right. The weekend of our California trip corresponded exactly with the birding festival. Braden and I excitedly pored over the many field trips that the festival offered and picked an all-day trip called California Specialties.

As we counted down the days, our Big Year's last big adventure was starting to seem like destiny.

On the afternoon of September 21, Braden and I caught our flight to San Jose via Salt Lake City. We flipped through my Kaufman guide on our way down and discussed which birds we most hoped to see—and which did and didn't seem likely. For me, Nuttall's Woodpecker topped my most-wanted land birds list. It was a woodpecker I'd never seen and one that could be found mainly in California.

"I want to get Black Phoebes," Braden said.

"I think we'll get those for sure. I remember that they are really common."

"I know, but we missed them in Arizona."

"What else do you want to see?"

"Well, everything," he told me. "The only two that I think we might *not* get are Wrentits and White-tailed Kites. Wrentits stay hidden a lot, and I don't know how common White-tailed Kites are."

"Did White-tailed Kites used to be called Black-shouldered Kites?"

"Yeah."

"I used to see those all the time in the Central Valley, flapping over fields."

"Do you think we'll get them?"

"Geez, I don't know."

After picking up our rental car, we reached our hotel in Morgan Hill just before midnight. Our intent for the following day—the last official day of summer—had been to get up early and take a shot at condors in Pinnacles National Park. Upon further deliberation, we realized that we had a good chance of picking them up at Big Sur too—and, if we did that, we could work in a visit to the Monterey Bay Aquarium. Added to this argument was the fact that my son had caught his first back-to-school cold, complete with sore throat and sniffles. Instead of speeding off to see condors, we slept in and then leisurely made our way down to one of my all-time favorite places.

It had been twenty years since I'd visited the Monterey Bay Aquarium, but it never had lost its spot at the top of my Best Aquariums list. Entering the complex I realized that it had become even more spectacular than I remembered. Braden and I walked past immense tanks full of living kelp, sea otters, and giant tuna and were equally captivated by the smaller displays of jellies, cephalopods, and coral reef fishes.

Though other aquariums boasted bigger tanks and larger animals, they often failed in their education departments. I recalled how disappointed I'd been by Atlanta's Georgia Aquarium, which offered whale sharks and beluga whales as if they were amusement rides instead of educational opportunities. I'd visited the place twice and watched as thousands of kids rushed through like the Gulf Stream. Were they excited? Sure. Did they learn anything? Hard to tell.

Monterey offered a much different experience. Walking through the exhibits not only wowed visitors, it gave them a greater understanding of the ocean and how its marine life all fit together. The fact that you could step out onto the balcony and observe wild sea otters floating in *real* kelp beds lifted Monterey above all contenders.

Braden and I spent a blissful four hours soaking up everything the aquarium had to offer, then dashed off to check into the Monterey Hampton Inn, where, in the parking lot, we spotted our first new bird of the trip—one that had eluded us in Arizona and sat atop Braden's most-wanted list: Black Phoebe. With that auspicious beginning, we headed out for our first real California birding, in the company of Andrea Weiss.

I'd first met Andy in 1987 while attending the *Highlights for Children* weeklong workshop at Chautauqua, New York. Andy had been an assistant editor for the magazine, and we'd immediately hit it off.

I recognized her as smart, funny, and insightful. Even after she left *Highlights* we ran into each other at conferences. She had visited me once in Santa Barbara, and I had returned the visit when she worked as an editor for *American Girl* in Madison, Wisconsin.

It had been more than five years since I'd seen Andy, however, and during that time, she had undergone a remarkable professional transformation, from editor to naturalist and recreational director at the elite Carmel Valley Ranch near Monterey.

She met me with a hug at the clubhouse, and I introduced her to Braden. "Welcome to California," she told us. "Why don't you two hang out here while I change into some hiking clothes?"

No problem there. As soon as Andy disappeared, raucous Acorn Woodpeckers and California Scrub-Jays called and swooped over our heads, sending Braden into a photographic frenzy.

When Andy reemerged, she led us out for a glorious two-hour walk through chaparral and oak woodlands.

"This is my kind of country," I exulted, inhaling the aroma of sage and dried oak leaves.

We walked downslope through grapevines full of sparrows and juncos, then headed uphill toward a trail that led to a mountain high above the ranch. As Braden walked ahead to bird, Andy and I caught up on each other's lives. I learned how she'd finally parted ways with educational publishing, how she'd begun volunteering as a naturalist at a nearby park, and how that had led to her current position with the Carmel Valley Ranch. I gave her details about the kids and Amy and my last few years as a writer. I also filled her in on Braden's and my Big Year exploits.

As we talked, we frequently stopped to watch birds in the undergrowth or oak branches above us, and Braden's and my Big Year tallies grew. Around the horse stables, we spotted plenty of juncos, flickers, Savannah Sparrows, and a new Lifer for Braden, California Towhee. As we climbed higher up the mountain, we surprised a group of California Quail. Braden's cold rendered him less than 100 percent, but he still birded enthusiastically, and on our descent made a terrific discovery.

As Andy led us toward a meditation platform used by the ranch's upscale guests, we spotted a bird in the brush.

"What is that?" I asked. "Wren?"

"I think it's a Song Sparrow," said Andy.

Braden interjected. "I think it's a Wrentit."

"I don't think so," said Andy. "I've been here four years and have never seen a Wrentit. I hear them, but they never come out of the bushes."

Just then a small gray-brown bird with a bluish face ventured out onto a branch. I took a good photo of it with my zoom lens, and Braden and Andy crowded around to look at my LCD screen.

"It *is* a Wrentit!" Braden exclaimed.

"Wow!" said Andy. "That's amazing! It came out just for you."

Braden grinned like he'd just eaten a bowl of Goldfish crackers. One unlikely bird down. One to go.

CHAPTER 28

pitching and tossing

"Black-crowned Night-Heron!" Braden shouted.

It was 6:15 a.m., and we had just climbed out of our rental car in the parking lot of Monterey's Fisherman's Wharf.

"Where?" I asked, doing my birder bobblehead impersonation.

Braden pointed up into a tree, and I finally saw one of the birds that had eluded us all year.

"Good eye," said a man standing nearby.

He and a friend wore binoculars around their necks, so I hazarded a guess. "You here for the pelagic birding trip?"

"Yep," the man said and pointed toward the pier. "Right that way."

"Thanks," I said. As Braden and I began walking, I took in the wharf and the bay beyond it. "Buddy, can you believe we're here?"

"I know," Braden said. "And we already got one of our nemesis birds."

"How'd you know it was a Black-crowned?"

"Yellow-crowned don't live on the West Coast."

Well, duh. Guess it pays to study the range maps, huh?

Walking out to the pier, we passed a line of tacky tourist seafood and trinket shops, all still closed at this early hour. The smell of dried fish guts, the fresh breeze, and the Western Gulls wheeling overhead all lightened my step. A good thing too, since thanks to some partying neighbors I'd only logged six hours of sleep the night before.

We soon found our destination: Her Majesty's Ship *Check Mate*. Okay, just kidding about the HMS designation. I actually was surprised how small the boat was and wondered if it could accommodate the two dozen or so intense avian enthusiasts swarming the adjacent dock. None of them seemed concerned, however, as they stood talking in small groups, eager to board the boat so they could add hard-to-see pelagic bird species to their year and Life lists.

One reason for their zeal may have been that over the summer, while Braden and I were pursuing our own modest Big Year goals, things had gotten downright insane nationally. By July 18, two birders had obliterated Neil Hayward's ABA Big Year record of 749, with a flock of other hardcore birders in hot pursuit. As the new record kept bounding, past 755 and then 760 species, no one knew where it would top out. To make sure they didn't wind up with the short end of the tail feather, the country's elite birders had launched into a jet-setting frenzy in attempts to claim the all-time Big Year record. For all Braden and I knew, some of those birders might even be joining us on the cruise.

"Where are you from?" I asked a stout man about my age.

"Des Moines, Iowa."

"We're from Montana," I said. "Have you been out with Debi before?"

He nodded. "This is my sixth time in the last eight days."

I stared at him blankly. "*Really?* Are you looking for something special?"

"Hawaiian Petrel."

"Oh. Have you seen one?"

"No. They're rare out here, but they do show up occasionally."

Before I could fully process the man's dedication—make that, obsession—a no-nonsense blonde woman cleared her throat.

"Hello, everyone! I'm Debi Shearwater. Welcome to our cruise."

As Braden and I rocked from one foot to the other, full of anticipation, Debi proceeded to give us a list of instructions for the day, including stern warnings about open-toed shoes, all forms of tobacco, and seasickness.

"Do *not* throw up over the bow!" she told us. "Go to the back of the boat so that your breakfast doesn't end up all over everyone else's fleece jackets!"

After these admonitions, Debi used a clipboard to check us in one by one as we climbed aboard.

When the *Check Mate* left the launch, my new friend from Iowa advised, "You want to be on the port side as we leave."

I assumed his advice had something to do with where people chose to regurgitate their breakfasts, but I discovered that the port side offered both a stunning panorama of Monterey in the rosy morning light and great views of birds crowded in among the sea lions on the harbor's rock jetty.

"Most of those are Brandt's Cormorants," Debi announced over the boat's PA system. "You'll also see Brown Pelicans, plenty of Western Gulls and—oh, looks like we have a Surfbird, right under the number 11!"

Surfbird? I'd never heard of one, but I located the big white 11 painted on the jetty and, sure enough, glassed a nondescript gray bird I could have mistaken for a gull.

"Do you know about Surfbirds?" I asked Braden.

"They put them in with turnstones," he told me.

Of course they do.

Just then Debi announced, "Oh, and it looks like our resident Peregrine Falcon is up on the radio tower."

In one synchronized move, the twenty of us trained our binoculars on the massive red-and-white steel tower rising over the peninsula. About a quarter of the way from the top, I spotted a dark form surveying its domain.

I nudged Braden. "Peregrine Falcon. Didn't think we'd get that today."

"We don't have a very good look at it," he objected.

"Well, if she says it's a Peregrine, it's probably a Peregrine, don't you think?"

"Well, yeah," he grudgingly admitted.

That encounter set the tone for much of the rest of the day. As we turned away from shore and headed out into the open ocean, we passed a number of birds such as Common Murres and Black-vented

Shearwaters that we got good close looks at. Many of the other birds flew or floated hundreds of yards from the boat—or raced by so quickly that we couldn't possibly get them in focus before they vanished over the horizon. When Debi or one of her naturalists called out "Tufted Puffin" or "Pomarine Jaeger," we often just had to believe them.

It didn't take long for that dilemma to emerge in conversations I had with other birders. One problem, apparently, was that bird numbers were down this year. Evidently less food (read: anchovies and sardines) filled the bay, so naturally fewer birds hung out there.

Massive declines in seabird populations were also a concern. In 2015 a major scientific study reported that seabird abundance had dropped by almost 70 percent in the preceding sixty years. Both the causes and species affected are widespread, but two major culprits are birds mistaking plastic for food and getting caught in fishing gear. Invasive species, flooding of nest sites due to global warming, and reductions in prey also are having major impacts.

One final gripe among the birders on board was new, stricter enforcement of anti-chumming regulations. In *The Big Year* the boat crew ladled a vile stew of raw fish guts and oil into the water as an attractant. That brought swarms of birds right into the boat, where birders could study, photograph, and identify them up close, but those days were gone. Apparently the powers that be had doubled-down on this activity saying that it harmed birds and marine life. It was a testy topic and still evolving (Debi was in the process of obtaining a chumming research permit as I wrote this story), but one anti-chumming argument I fully agreed with was that absent the smell of fish guts, people were less likely to get seasick.

As we ventured farther from shore, the ocean swell grew larger and larger until it reached a good four or five feet—enough to make any landlubber queasy even without the perfume of fish guts wafting over the boat. Once again I thought of *The Big Year*, especially the scene in which Owen Wilson psyches out Steve Martin by warning him of seasickness—"Pitching and tossing. Pitching and tossing"—until Martin loses his breakfast over the side.

As a veteran of several research cruises, I took precautions against such a performance by staying next to the boat rail and keeping my eyes to the horizon. Others were not so fortunate—including my son. I had warned Braden to keep his eyes fixed to the farthest points possible, but after an hour or two he succumbed to the rolling waves and, with an admirable lack of fanfare, redeposited his morning bagel into the sea.

I glanced around to see if the chumming police might show up and arrest him for so blatantly trying to attract seabirds, but they apparently missed this gross violation of environmental ethics.

Alas, Braden ended up spending the next couple of hours curled up with his eyes closed inside the cabin. I sat with him for much of that time, rubbing his back, assuring him that this happened to everyone. When Debi or one of her naturalists called out a new bird, I'd rush out to try to see it, but Braden wisely took a break from the action and fell asleep. When he awoke an hour or so later, he felt much better and even nibbled some lunch.

Despite his seasickness and a low number of birds, Braden and I managed to rack up nineteen and twenty-one Big Year species respectively, most of them Lifers. They included Ashy Storm-petrel, Rhinoceros Auklet, Buller's Shearwater, and Pink-footed Shearwater. The day's highlight: a group of eleven Black-footed Albatrosses following a research boat from the Monterey Bay Aquarium and undoubtedly hoping for some chum from the scientists.

I put my arm around Braden's shoulders. "Albatrosses! We saw some!"

Neither of us had seen a wild albatross before, and we never dreamed we'd see so many together—or so close. Our boat drifted to within a hundred yards of the birds, giving us extended looks at these handsome charcoal-colored ocean wanderers with their seven-foot wingspans. I even got some decent photos of one taking off from the water's surface right in front of us.

The rest of the day we cruised north, almost to Santa Cruz, before heading back down toward Monterey. We saw more birds and, in the distance, a few whales. Only a few miles from the harbor we encountered Risso's Dolphins diving for squid. When we climbed off the boat around 3:00 p.m., we thanked Debi and her crew for a memorable, productive day. Spent, but content, we beelined to a Panera in Seaside to eat a real meal, rest, and catch up on our journals before heading to stay with friends at our next destination, Santa Cruz.

peregrine shortcake

I had met Craig Himmelwright and Adrianne Waite in 1984, while working on a water quality study on the Pit River near Burney, California. While I rambled around in a beat-up, red Ford F-150 taking water samples and measuring temperatures, Craig had worked the raptor part of the study, an attempt to figure out how to optimize water flows to benefit both trophy rainbow trout and Bald Eagles. It was especially fitting that Braden and I were visiting him and Adrianne during our Big Year because Craig had been the first person ever to take me birding—and to introduce me to the particular joys of raptors. I clearly recalled going out with him and his team as they removed two juvenile Bald Eagles from their nest, tagged them, and then hauled the befuddled fledglings back up their tree. From that point on, I'd been hooked by raptors.

Craig greeted me with a crushing hug at the door and shook hands with Braden. Though it had been more than twenty years since I'd seen Craig, he hardly seemed to have changed. Six-three and equipped with a booming voice, he filled the room with a friendly, passionate enthusiasm, and we wasted no time catching up. Since I'd last seen him he'd gone to UC Davis to become a veterinarian but had since returned to his first love, field biology. In the past two decades he'd worked on everything from Golden Eagles to desert tortoises.

As he was telling me about his desert tortoise work, his wife, Adrianne, came home, setting off another round of greetings and storytelling. Adrianne worked at University of California, Santa Cruz, and had always been one of my favorite people, quieter than her husband but just as passionate about animals, education, women's rights, and other progressive issues. In the time since I'd seen them, they'd raised two sons, one of whom was off doing his own field research in Cameroon. While we three adults conversed, Braden slipped away to peruse Craig and Adrianne's extensive library and before long curled up on a couch with a couple of raptor reference guides. Craig and Adrianne could see that the Pacific Ocean had taken a toll on both of us, however, so after an hour or so of visiting we agreed to turn in early.

The next morning, well-rested after our first good sleep in days, Braden and I climbed into Craig and Adrianne's minivan, and we all headed north to a place I'd heard about for years but had never visited: Año Nuevo State Park.

Named for both a prominent coastal point of land and a small offshore island that was once a lighthouse station, Año Nuevo is most famous for the ten thousand or so elephant seals that gather there to mate and give birth to their young—and for the great white sharks that feast on this fat-filled smorgasbord of marine delicacies. As added bonuses, the preserve offers stunning coastal scenery and, you guessed it, birding opportunities.

That doesn't mean it was easy to see. When we arrived, we discovered that the regular, direct trails out to the point were mysteriously under repair, so we had to embark on a meandering, sandy hike of two miles through brush and open fields to get to where we were going. Along the way, we spotted more Wrentits, Black Phoebes, and scrub-jays. Suddenly Adrianne called "Incoming!"

We whipped around to see a Peregrine Falcon flying in low from the south. We all got our binoculars up in time to watch the bird pass less than fifty yards from us.

"Wow! That was a great look!" Braden said when the falcon had passed.

I nudged him with my elbow. "Does that make up for the tower Peregrine yesterday?"

"Yeah," he said with a smile.

It seemed like ancient history to someone as young as Braden, but in the post–World War II years, Peregrine Falcons (along with a host of other birds) had been decimated by the widespread use of DDT, which weakened the birds' egg shells, rendering them unable to reproduce. One of Craig's early biology jobs had been to help reintroduce Peregrines and other falcons throughout the West—a project that had succeeded wildly. "These days," Craig told us, not without some pride, "this whole area is lousy with Peregrines."

It was good news—and another example of the dramatic impact a few determined people can make to save a species.

For Braden an even greater reward came a couple of hundred yards later when we noticed two white birds perched in a tree a quarter mile away.

My son quickly raised his binoculars. "White-tailed Kites!" he shouted.

"That they are," Craig confirmed, also gazing through his binoculars.

The kites sat as if they'd been waiting for us.

"Not bad, huh?" I said to Braden.

He turned to Craig and Adrianne. "I told my dad that the two birds we might not see on this trip were Wrentits and White-tailed Kites. Now we've got both of them."

Craig laughed. "Glad we could get them for you."

It was one of those rare days along the coast with full sun and not a cloud or even a cool breeze. By the time we reached North Beach, where a couple of dozen elephant seals lounged in the sun, all four of us were sweating profusely, but for some reason we had decided not to carry water with us. I know—you'd have thought I'd smarten up after getting dehydrated in Ecuador. Nonetheless, before slogging back to the minivan, we paused for twenty minutes to enjoy the "shark bait" and watch Black Oystercatchers and Black Turnstones work the tide pools below us.

Leaving Año Nuevo, we desperately needed water and a caloric pick-me-up. In the spirit of the abundant Peregrines trolling the area, we decided to stoop on the Swanton Berry Farm to pick off some especially satisfying prey—the best strawberry shortcake ever.

"Oh, man, that is *good*," I said, cramming a sinful gob of shortcake, strawberries, and whipped cream into my mouth. I glanced at Braden for his reaction, but my son was too busy inhaling his own portion to comment.

"We've stopped by many a time after a long day of hiking or birding around here," Craig informed us, and I had to use every ounce of willpower to keep from buying and scarfing down a second helping.

Refreshed, we proceeded to our next stop: a nearby beach to try to find Snowy Plovers. The birds didn't cooperate.

"I'm wondering if they're farther south, tucked into a more protected beach along Monterey Bay," Craig mused, scanning the empty beach.

"Where are we going next?" Braden pressed.

"How about we stop by campus to see if we can find that hummingbird?" Adrianne suggested.

Only a few days before, Adrianne had observed a rare leucistic form of Anna's Hummingbird at the Santa Cruz Arboretum. The bird had been hanging out there for several weeks and had caused a stir in the local press. Leucism is caused by the lack of melanin pigment in an animal, and it renders an individual lighter than its conspecifics. Unlike albinos, leucistic animals still retain their dark eyes and other darker body parts. They just look lighter and brighter than they should.

After driving to UC Santa Cruz, Adrianne led us into the arboretum. "The bird hangs out in the Australian section," she explained, and as we approached, we thought we spotted it zoom past us. We couldn't be sure, though, so we plopped down on a shady bench and spent the next half hour enjoying the spot and waiting for the bird to return. The leucistic never did reappear, but many other hummingbirds did, giving us plenty of entertainment as they took advantage of the profusion of red brushy flowers nearby.

Since we were there, I asked Adrianne and Craig to give us a quick tour of the campus, since UCSC was a school I thought might interest Braden as a potential college candidate. Adrianne drove us around the spectacular, heavily forested grounds, pointing out the various residential colleges and academic buildings and talking about some of the interesting foreign exchange programs and research opportunities the school offered. I kept glancing at Braden throughout, but his face failed to betray any particular interest or lack of interest in UCSC except as potential bird habitat.

Leaving the university, we headed home for showers and then enjoyed an early dinner at the hopping El Palomar restaurant. It had been thirty years since I'd visited downtown Santa Cruz, and it seemed much nicer than I remembered. The buildings looked spruced up, and plenty of people gave the place a lively, happening vibe. At the local, independent Bookshop Santa Cruz, I picked up *Salt*, by Mark Kurlansky, and a book Craig recommended, *Four Fish*, by Paul Greenberg. I also took a deep breath and introduced myself to one of the store's managers.

One of my least favorite parts of being an author is selling myself, and over the years I'd acquired a bit of a bad attitude about it. Children's science books, after all, almost never ended up on bookstore shelves, and, when they did, they gathered more dust than an Oklahoma cattle ranch.

Still, *Fire Birds* had been attracting a fair bit of attention from adult audiences and, with a vigorous wildfire raging around Big Sur, I thought it might be worth a word to the store buyer. To my surprise, he seemed interested and took careful notes about where to order it.

With that, we all headed back to Craig and Adrianne's house. Braden and I had picked up only one Big Year bird for the day—White-tailed Kite—but it had been a fun, interesting time in the company of good friends and fantastic scenery. Nevertheless, we were eager to call it an early night because the next day would be the make-or-break day for our trip—and quite possibly for our entire Big Year.

CHAPTER 30

golden state dash

The orange rind of a new day had barely backlit the Santa Cruz Mountains when we parked on the top level of the Watsonville Civic Plaza parking lot the next morning. It was only 6:20 a.m., but already this unlikely staging area for the Monterey Bay Birding Festival swarmed with binocular-wielding zealots committed to kicking birder butt and taking names. Braden and I picked up our registration packets and joined a man holding a yellow sign that read "California Specialties." His name was Kumaran Arul, and he would be our intrepid leader for the day.

One of the most pleasant people I'd ever met, Kumaran greeted us all warmly and then reviewed his list of fanatics—er, registrants— for the trip. Among the twenty-odd birders standing around him, I noticed several from our pelagic trip two days earlier—including at least one who, like Braden, had deposited her breakfast into the rough seas. Also joining us was Kumaran's nine-year-old son, Julian. Braden and I introduced ourselves to Julian, and I asked him, "Are you a birder like your dad?"

"I like birds, but my sister's the real birder in the family," the boy confided to us. "She's sixteen but couldn't come today."

In an earlier email, Kumaran had informed everyone that we would be starting our day inland and work our way back out to the coast. After finishing his birder count, he said, "Because of the tides today, I think we're going to change our plans a bit. We'll first start down at Elkhorn Slough and then work our way inland."

"Do you think we'll get condors?" someone asked.

"No, probably not," Kumaran said. "Every once in a while you can see one where we're going, but not often. We will be trying for about one hundred bird species, though."

Braden and I looked at each other.

"One hundred!" I mouthed to him.

If we came even close to that, it would shatter our one-day record of seventy-eight that we'd tallied in and around High Island, Texas, in April.

"Are there any species people especially want to see?" Kumaran asked.

One woman said, "Yellow-billed Magpies."

"We've got a good chance at those," Kumaran replied.

I said, "Nuttall's Woodpecker."

Braden added, "Snowy Plover."

Kumaran nodded, processing the information. Then he directed everyone who was driving to line up across the street. Ten minutes later we were following his minivan out to Highway 1, heading south.

On our way to Santa Cruz two days before, Braden and I had passed the giant twin smokestacks that mark the hamlet of Moss Landing and the tidal wetlands known as Elkhorn Slough. In fact, it had set off a major row between us as I tried to locate a nearby place to bird. Unfamiliar with the area, I'd made several fruitless turns without finding anywhere to stop and, faced with heavy rush-hour traffic on Highway 1, had grumped, "Forget it. Let's keep going."

"What? Why?" Braden had demanded.

"Well, look at the traffic!" I'd snapped, angry that he didn't recognize the driving difficulties confronting me. "It's not always just about the birds."

"But we might not get to bird here again," he'd huffed.

I hadn't replied, but after sulking our way up the highway, I apologized for losing my temper and he graciously did likewise. Still, it was a relief to both of us that we were returning to Elkhorn with Kumaran, who knew what he was doing.

When we turned right, west, off Highway 1 that morning, the first things to catch our attention weren't birds but flotillas of sea otters hanging out in the protected lagoons between the highway and the beach.

"Look at 'em all!" I told Braden, firing off a burst of photos. "There must be twenty or twenty-five."

"More," Braden corrected me.

As always, the marine mammals totally disarmed everyone with their charm and almost pathological cuteness. But only for a moment.

Almost immediately the oohs and ahs over otters were replaced by bird names flying through the air: Great Egret, Black-necked Stilt, Long-billed Curlew. After moving a couple of hundred yards down the road we picked up Bewick's Wren and White-crowned Sparrows before following a sandy trail across the dunes to the beach.

Kumaran raised his binoculars. "If you look carefully about midway between here and the water," he told us, "you'll see a number of Snowy Plovers. They like to sit in little depressions in the sand."

Someone said, "I see them. They're beautiful!"

Understatement. Glassing the beach with my binoculars, I counted at least a couple dozen of the adorable white-and-gray birds, sitting low, trying not to draw attention to themselves.

"Looks like Craig was right," I told Braden. "They've moved to the more sheltered beaches farther into the bay."

While the other birders turned their attentions to Sanderlings, Heermann's Gulls, and Elegant Terns, I crept down to try to get good pictures of the plovers. They let me approach only to within fifty feet before they started twitching nervously, but that was close enough for my 100–400 mm lens to do its job.

From Moss Landing, the Kumaran caravan headed a couple of miles inland to a spot well known to local birders—the Moonglow Dairy. Here Kumaran had promised us Tricolored Blackbirds, and, sure enough, we found the small, understated critters in abundance, foraging among the dairy cow stock pens. The Tricoloreds proved to be only a dung-scented appetizer, however. In the waters next to the stockyards, we spotted American White Pelicans, Northern Shovelers, and Long-billed Dowitchers, and Braden impressed everyone by identifying a Green-winged Teal. I tried to top that by pointing out a Peregrine Falcon sitting in a distant eucalyptus tree, but the other birders responded with a collective yawn.

Speaking of eucalyptus, after scanning the waters Kumaran led us on a walk through the exotic forest that had sprouted up on the dairy's property. Before describing that, I must pause for a little rant.

Eucalyptus trees played a prominent role in my childhood in Southern California. The trees grew everywhere in and around Goleta and Isla Vista where I lived, and my friends and I spent many a happy hour exploring the dark, cavernous woods, inhaling the menthol aroma from their leaves and peeling six-foot-long strips of bark from the trees' hard, bone-like trunks.

One thing I noticed, even as a child, is that very little lived among the eucalyptus. I never questioned why, but years later, when I was in college, my friend Scott Callow provided a shocking explanation: Eucalyptus trees aren't native to California. They are from Australia!

It turns out that these pleasant-looking trees had been planted the world over because they grew easily and people thought they would provide great timber. And while it's true that the trees became widely used for pulp and building material in many countries, only later, after eucalyptus had swallowed up tens of millions of acres, did their many drawbacks also emerge. These range from the trees' inferior timber and firewood properties to their toxic leaves and the extreme fire hazard they present. Perhaps the worst feature of eucalyptus trees is that they suck water tables dry, destroying streams and lakes and rendering life more difficult for millions of people living nearby.

My own beef with the trees is that they are basically biological deserts. Sure, eucalypt groves provide winter roosting sites for monarch butterflies, and a few animals have adapted to them, but all you have to do is walk through a large, mature stand to see that very few critters forage or make their homes there. Since educating myself about invasive species, I had made it a point of denigrating eucalyptus to anyone who would listen. I felt a bit annoyed, therefore, when Kumaran decided to walk us through the eucalyptus at the Moonglow Dairy.

We're not going to find anything in here but crows and rats, I thought. I was in for a surprise.

Even before entering the eucalyptus, our fellow birders began calling out Yellow Warblers around the grove's perimeter. Neither Braden nor I saw those, but inside the shady glade we observed Chestnut-backed Chickadees, Dark-eyed Juncos (Oregon variety), Brown Creepers, and—this just blew me away—Townsend's Warblers. Not just one either. We spotted at least four or five of the birds as we walked through the woods.

"What are these birds doing here?" I demanded. "There's no food in here, is there?"

"Well," Kumaran said. "Some insects do come in here, but mostly I think the birds are here because of the structure of the trees."

"You mean they are finding shelter here?"

"Yes," he said.

"Huh."

As we also picked up Downy Woodpeckers and Hermit Thrushes, though, I wondered if the birds really did well in this habitat, or if they were here mainly because of the shortage of native trees in the immediate area. I guessed the latter, but seeing the birds here at all proved one of the giant surprises of the day and reinforced the basic fact that I don't understand half as much as I would like.

One undeniable feature of the eucalyptus grove is that, while we were sheltered in its embrace, it kept us nice and cool. As we left the refuge of the trees, the sun slammed into us like a mallet.

"I know it's hot," Kumaran told us, "but before we go, let's head out onto the dikes to see if we can pick up some other birds."

Despite temperatures that already cracked ninety degrees, it was a good call. Closer to the main slough we spotted a dozen more species, including Clark's, Western, and Eared Grebes, Lesser Goldfinches, and my personal favorite of the bunch, Braden's and my first-ever Golden-crowned Sparrow. The sparrow's plumage stuck to the brown-and-gray template of most other sparrows, with one very notable exception: a spectacular helmet of black and yellow. As we were leaving the dikes a male landed on a fence post not twenty feet away and looked directly at us, brilliantly showing off its golden forehead.

"That thing is spectacular!" I said to Braden.

I raised my camera to take a picture, but the bird immediately sparrowed out of range.

Braden and I had already recorded sixty species by the time we turned away from the coast and headed inland—way inland. The landscape changed dramatically from misty, conifer-covered head-lands to drought-parched beige hills embroidered with patchy oak woodlands. As the landscape grew drier and more agricultural, we kept expecting to see one of the day's main targets, Yellow-billed Magpies, but the birds had other ideas. After a refreshment stop at a roadside mini-mart, we pulled into San Benito County Historical Park shortly after eleven o'clock.

Driving in, Braden regarded the dry, dusty park and its few oak trees with disdain. "This doesn't look like a great birding spot. I won-der why we're here."

"I don't know," I said. "But you never can tell. This might be our best shot at Nuttall's Woodpeckers."

We all climbed out of our cars, and Kumaran told us, "You can eat lunch here, but if you want to do a bit of birding first, you're welcome to do that too."

Braden and I felt more than ready to inhale our peanut butter and honey sandwiches, but when we spied two other birders staring up into a nearby oak tree, we grabbed our optics and hurried over to them.

"What do you see?" I asked a couple I recognized from the pelagic trip.

The man replied, "White-breasted Nuthatch and Nuttall's Wood-pecker, but I don't see it now."

Then I detected movement in an adjacent oak. "There's some-thing," I said, raising my camera. "Braden, it's a Nuttall's!"

Two of them, actually. For woodpeckers, the Nuttall's were drab—bird "farm folk" who saw no good reason to get all fancied up when there was work to be done. They looked almost identical to the Ladder-backed Woodpeckers we'd seen in Arizona, but to me they were fabulous. That was primarily because they ranged only through coastal California and into northern Baja and were impossible to see anywhere else.

San Benito held other treasures as well. After we watched the Nut-tall's for a few minutes, Kumaran pointed out Oak Titmice and Lark

Sparrows—both Lifers for Braden and me. Next we strolled the edge of the park, hoping for a California Thrasher. Kumaran got a glimpse of one, but most of us saw only quivering branches. We did pick up another Wrentit, Western Bluebirds, and Say's Phoebe—further improving Braden's initially dour opinion of the park and its habitat.

Daylight was a-wasting, and we still lacked one of our major objectives: Yellow-billed Magpie. After San Benito, three drivers peeled off for home, but Kumaran directed the rest of us to stop at the turnoff to La Gloria Road, twenty minutes up the highway.

Temperatures simmered in the mid-nineties, and I asked Braden, "Do you think we should call it a day too?"

Braden still had a cold, and I didn't want to push him too hard, but he responded, "I think we should keep going."

That was my feeling too, and I was proud of him for pushing himself even when he felt less than optimal.

At the entrance to La Gloria Road, Kumaran pulled over and parked, and the rest of us followed suit. We didn't know why until he pointed to a farmhouse right across the highway. There, finally, we got a look at Yellow-billed Magpies. Not a *great* look, mind you. Several of the magpies were hanging out in the deep shade of a carport while others preferred the yard in back, which was partially obscured by trees and hedges. But at least we could add the bird to our lists.

Bigger rewards lay up La Gloria Road itself. At two cattle watering holes, we encountered a virtual bird safari of Fox Sparrows, Northern Flickers, California Towhees, Bell's Sparrows, Lesser Goldfinches, and one of the stars of the day, Lawrence's Goldfinches. Kaufman describes these rare yellow-gray-and-black songbirds with the phrase, "Uncommon, elusive, unpredictable," but at the second watering hole they gathered in abundance, flying back and forth from a nearby oak into the reeds poking out of the pond.

Our band of birders spent a good half hour enjoying the Lawrence's and other birds frequenting the watering hole while keeping an eye on thirty California Quail milling around the far side of the pond. The quail performed a hilarious slapstick routine à la Buster Keaton or the Marx Brothers, darting from one bush to another and every once in a while approaching the pond only to reel away again for some incomprehensible reason.

Suddenly, as they neared the pond for the tenth time, a scrub-jay flew by, startling the quail and sending them scurrying back, but in the next instant, an even larger bird swooped in like it meant business.

"Accipiter!" I shouted without even thinking about it.

It could have been almost anything from a Peregrine to a Red-tailed, but for once I was right.

"Cooper's Hawk!" Kumaran confirmed.

As we watched, the bird scattered the quail. It made a try at one, but the quail zigged or zagged and easily avoided the predator's grasp. Just like that, the hawk lost its advantage and flew up to sulk on a nearby oak branch.

"Wow! Did you see that?" I asked Braden. "Cooper's Hawk!"

"Nice ID," he told me, holding up his hand for a high five.

It was yet another bird that had eluded us all year, and to get it in this fashion felt like we'd just seen a lion attack a zebra at a South African watering hole. It seemed to place an exclamation mark on the entire day.

After the Cooper's Hawk, you could have put a fork in us. Baked and buttered, Braden and I thanked Kumaran for an awesome day and wearily climbed into our rental car for the long drive back to Santa Cruz. At the last moment, we took along two women from Watsonville who had carpooled with someone else earlier but, like us, had exhausted their birding stamina. As the four of us bumped back along La Gloria Road, Braden quickly added up our species for the day.

"Eighty-seven," he told me.

"Eighty-seven? That blows away our previous one-day record, doesn't it?"

"Daddy, it doesn't just blow it away. It dismembers it and scatters its bones everywhere—and you can quote me on that if you ever write about it."

I laughed.

"Too bad we couldn't make it to ninety," Braden mused. "Do you think we could see three more species on the way back?"

One of our passengers asked, "Did you see a Red-shouldered Hawk today?"

"No, we didn't," said Braden.

"Well, we might see one of those."

I was skeptical. From my experience with them in Southern California, I considered Red-shouldereds to be hard-to-see canyon birds rather than anything that might be flying out in the open. Right before we reached the highway, we did finally get a good look at a Yellow-billed Magpie, sitting on a fencepost. I pulled up slowly and the bird continued to strike a pose while Braden got great photos through the car window.

"Well, that was nice of him," I said, but the generosity of the birds had not yet spent itself.

Driving back toward Highway 101, we picked up Mourning Dove for species number eighty-eight of the day. Then, a few miles later, I spotted a dark shape on the ground next to the road. At first I thought it was a rock, but I called it out anyway, and as we zipped by we got an incredible view of it.

"Red-shouldered Hawk!" Braden rejoiced.

The women in back confirmed it, and I shook my head. "That's amazing. I've never seen one just sitting by the road like that."

"Do you think we'll get one more species?" Braden asked.

Again I doubted it. It was late in the day. We were driving fast. *The birds have probably all headed home for dinner with their families,* I thought.

Then, just as we approached Highway 101, Braden noticed a white shape flying slowly above us.

He leaned forward to get a better look through the front windshield. "What is that?"

The rest of us craned our heads and at first couldn't figure it out. Then one of the women in back said, "It's a White-tailed Kite, isn't it?"

"Yeah!" we exclaimed.

The kite brought our day's count to ninety species, demolishing our single-day record. Thanks to Kumaran's careful planning, we'd also racked up twenty-two Big Year birds for the day.

Braden and I couldn't have felt more pleased.

But one task remained.

CHAPTER 31

din tai dilemma

As tired as we were, Braden and I had one more important decision to make before going to bed that night. Although the trip had been spectacular so far, we still stared at a glaring hole in our birding list: California Condors. Our flight didn't leave San Jose until 4:45 p.m. the following day, so we had plenty of time to try for condors the next morning, but we faced a complicating factor.

Din Tai Fung.

One of the highlights of our family trip to Taiwan two years earlier had been getting to eat at what is probably Taiwan's most famous restaurant, Din Tai Fung. A Michelin star restaurant, Din Tai Fung dished up a wide assortment of mouth-watering delicacies, but one soared above all others: Xiao Long Bao.

Pork soup dumplings.

Just the thought of these delicious, soupy, porky morsels sent the kids and me into paroxysms of yearning and salivation. Conveniently, even as we had ordered basket after basket of dumplings in Taipei, Din Tai Fung had been expanding its culinary empire across

Asia and, even better, to America's West Coast. In the past couple of years we'd managed to eat at Din Tai Fung locations in L.A. and Seattle. By exquisite timing, the latest restaurant had opened up in the Westfield Valley Fair mall in Santa Clara—a dumpling's throw from the San Jose airport.

Two weeks earlier—not knowing we'd still need condors—I had made early lunch reservations for 11:15 a.m. Tragically, that did not leave adequate time both to search for condors and quench our desire for Xiao Long Bao.

"So," I asked Braden on this final night of our trip. "Condors or Din Tai Fung?"

"Well, we *have* to try for condors," he said, his tone leaving no room for debate.

"You're right," I acknowledged, "but then I'll have to cancel our lunch reservations."

His face fell. "Don't you think that if we go early, we can still do both?"

"If we look for condors first, there's no way we'll make it to Din Tai Fung by eleven fifteen. Remember, the birds don't take flight until it warms up a bit."

"Can't you change the reservation until later?"

"I tried," I told him. "They don't have anything until two—too late to still make our flight."

Braden considered this for a moment, then nodded. "Okay. I guess you'd better cancel."

We both sighed.

The sacrifices we birders make.

As always on these birding trips, Braden and I awoke to our last day filled with a mixture of excitement and sadness. While we packed the car, Adrianne was getting ready to go to work and Craig was sipping his first of twenty or thirty morning coffees in preparation for his own busy day, so we had only a few minutes to chat. Once our bags were loaded, Craig walked us out to the street.

"Come visit us in Montana," I told him.

"Yeah, Ade and I definitely need to get up there soon," he said. Then, turning to Braden, he stuck out his hand. "It was great to meet you, Braden. Keep up the great birding, okay?"

Braden shook Craig's hand. "I will."

As we pulled away from the curb, Braden said, "It's always the people I end up missing the most."

I passed my hand through his thick brown hair. "You make good friendships even in a short time. That's one of many special things about you."

"Do you think we'll get to see Craig and Adrianne again?"

"I'm sure of it," I told him.

"I hope so."

With that, we turned south, toward Monterey.

Especially since we'd gone inland the day before, Braden and I had decided to try for condors around Big Sur instead of the hotter, drier Pinnacles National Park. It had become part of our Big Year routine to patronize at least one Denny's restaurant on every trip, and we fulfilled that obligation with a Grand Slam breakfast in Monterey. As we resumed our journey south through Carmel's heavy traffic, I pointed out the window.

"That's Monastery Beach," I told Braden, "where I learned to scuba dive. I got seasick there more than once."

Braden grunted, and I wondered whether my reminiscences meant anything to him.

Probably not, I guessed, but I felt parentally bound to offer these nostalgic morsels just in case he might value them later.

We kept driving, past Mal Paso and on toward Big Sur. Eventually traffic thinned, and we entered the spectacular stretches of coastline that make Highway 1 one of the most famous roads in the world. Glancing to my right, I was pleased to see hundreds of acres of kelp forests floating in dark blue ocean waters, and rocky cliffs and outcrops that made me want to stop and stare at every turn.

Craig had given us detailed directions to our destination, a roadside pullout at a place called Grimes Point. Several birders from our field trip the day before had said they'd had luck with condors there, so we kept our fingers crossed as we approached. Where the road began a deep indent toward the mountains, I spotted the distinctive A-frame house Craig had said to watch out for.

"It's right up here," I told Braden. "Keep your eyes peeled."

After a final sharp bend in the road, we braked into a dusty pullout no more than fifty feet long and perched at least five hundred feet above the Pacific Ocean. Braden and I piled out and did a quick survey of the skies above and cliffs below. Two Peregrines flapped and darted around us—the fourth day in a row we'd seen these magnificent hunters—but not a single condor graced the skies.

Just a few yards from us, a road crew with a heavy rig prepared for a day's work, and I decided to walk over to them. "Good morning. You haven't seen any condors around have you?"

The workers took a genuine interest in my question.

"No, not today," one of them said.

It was nine thirty and unusually warm, and I began to suspect that the birds had gotten an early start—not good news.

"There's a visitor's center down at Pfeiffer State Park," one man suggested. "You might go check in with them."

Another said, "There's a tree down there where one's been perching a lot."

"Thank you," I said. "I appreciate it."

Braden and I climbed back into the car and continued our way south. We stopped at several more pullouts to scope the skies but saw only a couple of Turkey Vultures.

Braden sighed heavily. "I guess we're not going to see them today."

"Hey," I said, irritated by his attitude. "We didn't come down here to give up so easily. Keep looking."

At the entrance to Julia Pfeiffer Burns State Park, I spied a man bent over a spotting scope, and we pulled in behind him.

"See anything?" I asked the man.

He grunted, obviously less than pleased to have company. "There are a couple of condors up above that ridge."

We strained our eyes and could barely make out two black dots several miles away, but when I looked through my binoculars, I was 99 percent sure I saw the flash of white beneath the wings as one of the birds pivoted on a thermal.

"Braden, it's them!" I said, excitedly.

My son wasn't convinced. "Are you sure?" he said, also staring through his binoculars. "I can't see them well enough."

"I saw the flash of white under their wings."

"But they could be Red-taileds or Turkey Vultures," Braden insisted.

"They're not Turkey Vultures," the other man said, with a hint of superiority. "Only condors are that big."

Braden still wasn't buying it. Instead of being happy, he looked as miserable as I'd seen him on the entire trip—make that the entire year. As the condors drifted even farther away, we got back into our car and headed north. Tears pooled in Braden's eyes.

"Braden," I asked, "why are you so upset? We saw *condors!*"

"Maybe *you* did," he said, "but now I don't know whether to put them down or not. It's even worse this way than not seeing them at all."

I tried to convince him and give him a little kick to improve his attitude. "Well, *I* saw condors. I'm sure of that. It wasn't a great look, but that guy was right. Those birds couldn't have been anything else. Anyway, keep looking. Maybe we'll see more."

Braden gathered himself and kept staring out the windows. As we drove around a bend, suddenly I saw a large bird and skidded into the dirt. We pointed our binoculars.

"Turkey Vulture," Braden said.

A few minutes later, the same thing happened again, this time with a Red-tailed Hawk.

As we once again approached Grimes Point, I knew that our chances for condors were soaring away fast. Finally I saw the Grimes Point pullout ahead. Unfortunately, it was on the opposite side of the road, and to stop I would have to cross a lane of traffic—right in front of a blind, dangerous curve.

Is it worth the risk? I asked myself.

At the last possible moment, I jerked the wheel left just as another car whipped around the corner heading straight toward us. My heart hammered, but we slid into home plate throwing up a cloud of dust.

Safe.

Despite my heroic driving, I harbored almost no hope of seeing condors here.

It's just too late, I thought. *The birds are riding thermals far inland, looking for dead cows and deer—or maybe other birders who perished trying to find condors!*

When my pulse had slowed, however, I glanced through the windshield up at a nearby ridge.

"Braden!" I shouted. "Get out!"

Cameras in hand, we scrambled out of the car to see two enormous birds circling a hilltop of parched brown grass less than a mile away. The birds quickly disappeared from view, and my heart sank. Moments later, though, came one of the most dramatic sights

I have ever witnessed. As we watched, six California Condors soared back over the ridge like a squadron of B-52s. This time, there was no question about the IDs. Not only did the distinct white streaks of their wings clearly show, they flew solid and stable—like nothing else in the sky.

Braden and I fired off more than a dozen pictures each. When we were finished, I looked over at him. "Are you convinced now?"

Braden grinned sheepishly. "I didn't think we were going to see them."

"But we did," I said, resisting the urge to lecture him about not giving up. Instead, I said, "Condors, man! Can you believe it?"

"Yeah!"

We continued to watch these stunning birds circle, their dramatic black-and-white bodies stark against the blue sky. It was a miracle, really, that we could be watching them after they'd come so close to extinction.

"They are just so cool," Braden said, his voice filled with wonder.

"They are," I said, squeezing his shoulder. I breathed in deep lungfuls of the fresh sea air and tried to be present in a moment that I felt sure would never come again.

Another car pulled up—the man with the spotting scope from down the road.

"Do you see anything?" he asked.

I pointed. "Right up there."

"Oh! These are much closer than the ones I was looking at."

The man's tone had miraculously become friendlier than before. "I was driving by," he told us, "and I saw you here, so decided I'd better take a look. I pulled a quick U-turn. I'm glad I did."

I'll bet, I thought.

"That makes nine I've seen today," he boasted.

Neither Braden nor I responded. For us, one would have been enough. It was a bonus that this most exalted of birds left Braden and me tied at 322 species for our Big Year count.

As we headed back north, Braden texted Ted Wolff. "Guess what was the last bird of our California trip?"

"California Condor?" Ted texted back.

"Yeah!" Braden wrote.

"Really?" Ted texted. "Along the cliffs? You're a lucky guy!"

Braden and I agreed.

Which left only one question: was there any possible way we could still make it to Din Tai Fung?

It was noon by the time we got back to Monterey. I had Braden run a quick Google Maps calculation and our best ETA for Din Tai Fung looked to be an hour and forty-five minutes—and only in the highly unlikely event we didn't hit traffic.

"Even if they can get us in quickly," I told Braden, "that's going to be cutting it close for eating, turning in our rental car, and getting back to the airport."

"Should we still try for it?"

"I don't know," I said. "Let's see how the drive goes."

Miraculously, as the mileage signs for San Jose ticked down from 80 to 40 to 10, the traffic gods kept smiling down on us. As we approached our decision point, I glanced at Braden. "What do you think? Go for it or not?"

"I think we should go for it," he said.

"Okay. Hang on," I shouted, swerving toward the I-880 turnoff.

As if to confirm our commitment, my phone buzzed with a text from Delta Airlines notifying us that our flight would be delayed an hour. "We'll have plenty of time, now," I rejoiced. "If Din Tai Fung can seat us, that is."

Google Maps guided us to the Valley Fair parking lot, and, feeling triumphant, we hurried into the mall as condor-conquering heroes. Braden checked a directory and said, "It should be right around this corner."

We spotted the restaurant with only a small group of people waiting in line, and our hopes soared. I rushed up to the hostess. "We don't have much time," I said. "Is there any way you can give us a table? There's only two of us."

She studied her schedule—and delivered the devastating news: "We don't have anything until two thirty."

"Oh." My swagger wilted like a dandelion in the desert, and I meekly pleaded, "We have to catch a plane. Can we at least sit at the bar?"

She sadly shook her head. "No, I'm sorry. Even those seats are reserved."

I sighed and forced a smile. "Thank you."

I began to turn away when the hostess said, "You *could* order take out."

I whiplashed back toward her. "*Really?* How long would that take?"

"Only about twenty minutes."

Braden and I looked at each other but didn't need to confer. "Let's do that," I told the hostess, and quickly placed an order of Xiao Long Bao, veggie fried rice, and sesame buns.

While we waited for the text message that our order was ready, Braden and I perused two stores that could only be found outside of Montana—a Lego store and a shop that sold make-up and bling from Japan. When my phone finally vibrated, we collected our meal and took it upstairs to the food court.

The food didn't taste as fresh and hot as if we'd been served in the restaurant, but Braden and I agreed it was pretty darned good. Even better, it was the perfect way to cap an almost perfect trip—and what would likely be our final major Big Year adventure.

SEPTEMBER BIRD LIST

Sneed's List (54)	Braden's List (52)
Heermann's Gull	Heermann's Gull
Western Gull	Western Gull
Glaucous-winged Gull	Caspian Tern
Caspian Tern	Band-tailed Pigeon
Band-tailed Pigeon	Black Phoebe
Black Phoebe	California Scrub-Jay
California Scrub-Jay	Wrentit
Wrentit	Savannah Sparrow
Savannah Sparrow	California Towhee
California Towhee	Pink-footed Shearwater
Pink-footed Shearwater	Sooty Shearwater
Sooty Shearwater	Black-vented Shearwater
Black-vented Shearwater	Brandt's Cormorant
Brandt's Cormorant	Pelagic Cormorant
Pelagic Cormorant	Black-crowned Night-Heron
Black-crowned Night-Heron	Black Oystercatcher
Black Oystercatcher	Black Turnstone
Black Turnstone	Surfbird
Surfbird	Common Murre
Common Murre	Pigeon Guillemot
Pigeon Guillemot	Rhinoceros Auklet

Rhinoceros Auklet	California Gull
California Gull	Elegant Tern
Elegant Tern	Peregrine Falcon
Peregrine Falcon	Black-footed Albatross
Black-footed Albatross	Pomarine Jaeger
Pomarine Jaeger	Red-necked Phalarope
Buller's Shearwater	Tufted Puffin
Red-necked Phalarope	White-tailed Kite
Tufted Puffin	Surf Scoter
Ashy Storm-Petrel	Eared Grebe
White-tailed Kite	American White Pelican
Surf Scoter	Snowy Plover
Eared Grebe	Long-billed Curlew
Snowy Plover	Ruddy Duck
Long-billed Curlew	Western Grebe
Ruddy Duck	Clark's Grebe
Western Grebe	Least Sandpiper
Clark's Grebe	Long-billed Dowitcher
Least Sandpiper	Greater Yellowlegs
Long-billed Dowitcher	Pacific-slope Flycatcher
Greater Yellowlegs	Golden-crowned Sparrow
Pacific-slope Flycatcher	Tricolored Blackbird
Golden-crowned Sparrow	Nuttall's Woodpecker
Tricolored Blackbird	Oak Titmouse
Nuttall's Woodpecker	Lark Sparrow
Oak Titmouse	Cooper's Hawk
Lark Sparrow	Red-shouldered Hawk
Cooper's Hawk	Yellow-billed Magpie
Red-shouldered Hawk	Bell's Sparrow
Yellow-billed Magpie	Lawrence's Goldfinch
Bell's Sparrow	California Condor
Lawrence's Goldfinch	
California Condor	

CHAPTER 32

trumpeter tragedy

After returning from California, I had only a week to prepare for the first of five school visits and conferences ahead of me. The first journey, a road trip to Billings, offered a nice warm-up to the speaking season, with a light schedule that allowed plenty of afternoon birding time. Although I missed having Braden along, I continued to sharpen my own ID skills by exploring three different natural areas and got a chance to observe unusual late migrants such as Orange-crowned and Yellow-rumped Warblers.

With a bigger trip looming, I probably shouldn't have devoted any more days to birding around Missoula, but I couldn't help myself. Braden and I had signed up for the email-based Montana's Online Birders Group—also known as MOB—and by mid-October, MOBsters began reporting an assortment of rarities moving through Montana, from Surf Scoters to Palm Warblers to Gyrfalcons. Besides, Braden and I had promised to help a couple of newer scouts plunge into the Bird Study merit badge. More birding? What choice did I have?

On Saturday, October 14, we once again headed toward Lee Metcalf, this time with two scouts in tow, Wyatt and Will. As we drove south, Braden predicted we'd pick up two or three Big Year birds. I felt less optimistic but didn't really mind. Though overcast, it was another mild fall day, and I felt good about trying to get more young people involved in birding.

As usual, Lee Metcalf did not disappoint. At the ponds, we located Northern Shovelers, Green-winged Teal, Buffleheads, Pied-billed Grebes, Northern Pintails, American Wigeons, Gadwalls, and Mallards amid swarms of coots. On the forest trails, we saw our best-ever "mixed flock" of gleaners and forest birds with six Black-capped Chickadees, two White-breasted Nuthatches, two Ruby-crowned Kinglets, one Downy Woodpecker, and (we think) two Pacific Wrens. As we were driving back toward the exit, however, we looked out toward the main pond and even from a mile away, saw a large white spot gracing the water.

"Look out there!" Braden shouted.

"Could it be a swan?" I asked.

Wyatt, the more vocal of our two new birders, looked through my binoculars. "I think it is a swan."

"What kind? Trumpeter?" I asked.

"Probably," said Wyatt, who had evidently seen swans before.

We cautiously pulled up to within a hundred yards of the large white apparition and eased out of the car. Our proximity left no doubt we were looking at a swan, but what kind?

"It can only be a Trumpeter or a Tundra," Braden said, consulting the range maps in *Sibley*.

"I think it's a Trumpeter," Wyatt said. "Tundras have yellow below their eyes. They're also smaller."

"I don't see any yellow," Braden said.

"Neither do I," I said, "but *Sibley* shows that the Tundras don't always have yellow, either."

We agreed it was most likely a Trumpeter, but just to make sure, decided to drive over to the visitor's center.

For all the times Braden and I had visited Lee Metcalf, we'd never actually entered the visitor's center, but it grabbed our attention with a nice little shop and informative displays of stuffed wildlife. A friendly volunteer greeted us, and I wasted no time asking if that was indeed a Trumpeter Swan out there.

"Sure is," the man told us. "A hunter killed its mate this morning. He mistook it for a goose."

"What?" we all cried.

"Yep. That same swan had been coming to the refuge for about ten years, ever since I started working here."

I felt a lump in my stomach. I mean, we hear about such little tragedies all the time, but to see the other swan out there without its mate brought the challenges of conservation home on a personal level.

"Do you think it will find another mate?" I asked.

"Oh, sure. We had about fourteen other Trumpeters in last week."

That news didn't make me feel any better, but I decided not to make too big a deal about it in front of the boys. The world was full of enough bad news to make even the most stalwart young person sink into despair, and this was a day to nourish optimism, not extinguish it.

We thanked the man and decided to follow a trail near the visitor's center, where we saw a Bald Eagle and a group of Green-winged Teal. Then we headed back north.

We stopped in Lolo, where none of us had any trouble polishing off full meals of burgers and fries, and as we piled back into the minivan I asked, "So, how's everyone doing? Do you want to try Fort Missoula for Surf Scoters or are you too tired?"

Tired? Adolescents? Dumb question. We headed to Fort Missoula.

None of us had ever been to the gravel ponds behind the fort, but loons and Surf Scoters had shown up there in recent days, and I'd asked another member of MOB for directions. We parked at the military museum and walked downstream along the Bitterroot River for half a mile before coming to two expansive, water-filled pits. From the surrounding fence, all we could make out were Canada Geese and a lone Great Blue Heron, but we soon discovered a huge gap at the corner of the property.

"I don't see any No Trespassing signs, do you?" I asked the boys.

"Nope!" Will said.

I smiled. Though a bit quieter than Wyatt, and perhaps not as knowledgeable about wildlife, Will had stayed enthusiastic the entire day, and I appreciated his willingness to go for it.

We scrambled down a short embankment and then trudged across the muddy landscape to the ponds, keeping our eyes out for loons and scoters. I saw a couple of white shapes on the pond, but they turned out to be some kind of plastic floats or buoys.

Looking through my camera, I said, "Well guys, it looks like the loons and scoters have vamoosed."

"Yeah," Braden agreed.

As we kept walking around the shoreline of the pit, though, a new section of pond came into view, and I excitedly peered through my camera lens.

"Look," I shouted. "Western Grebe!"

There out in the middle of the water floated the beautiful black-and-white form of one of my favorite birds.

"Cool," Wyatt said. "Have you ever seen one before?"

I shook my head. "Not in Montana."

Like most grebes, this one held its head up high and moved through the water with grace, staying alert to everything around it—including us.

Moving on to the next pond, we saw more geese and three Ring-billed Ducks. Walking back across the muddy flats toward the trail, Braden suddenly froze like a pointer who's located a deer. Instead of raising his front paw, he raised his binoculars.

"There's some sparrows up there," he whispered to the rest of us. "I have a feeling this is a new Lifer for me."

We all spread out and crept forward, looking for movement in the weeds. I saw plant stems twitch and brown shapes dash back and forth, but couldn't get a clear look.

"They might be Vesper Sparrows," Braden said. "I saw some white on the tail, but they don't really look like Vespers."

Finally, after five minutes I got a fix on one of the birds. I lightly tapped a button on my camera to focus the lens and then fired off several quick shots. Braden hurried over.

"Let me see," he demanded.

I showed him a photo.

"Is it a Lincoln's?" I asked. As usual, we'd left the guidebooks back in the car.

"No, it's not a Lincoln's," he said, almost reflexively shrugging off my wild speculation.

"It could be—I'm thinking American Pipit."

"Really?" I asked.

"I think so."

Back at the car, *Sibley* and *Kaufman* left no doubt that Braden had once again guessed correctly. This time, he'd also correctly predicted our rate of success for the day. American Pipits and the Trumpeter Swan gave us two new birds, bringing our Big Year totals to 324.

Over the next couple of days, the death of the Trumpeter Swan continued to stab at my heart. I saw nothing about it in the news so decided to alert our local paper, the *Missoulian*. To my surprise, they jumped on it, publishing a preliminary story and then a follow-up with more details, under the headline "Swan Shot Was Popular" (October 18, 2016). Despite the awkward title, it was a good piece, detailing the successful efforts of the Confederate Salish and Kootenai tribes to reintroduce Trumpeters into the Flathead Valley over the preceding decade, and how the one that had been shot had dispersed from those efforts. People at Lee Metcalf had been hoping the swan—dubbed 5T1—would link up with a mate and breed, and, just before its violent death, it had started spending time with the swan we'd observed.

"People here knew that swan by heart," the article quoted Lee Metcalf manager Tom Reed saying. "It was a permanent fixture at the refuge. I just don't get how you mistake a swan for anything that's legal to hunt. It looks nothing like a snow goose. I was sick when I heard the news."

Exactly. In fact, while talking it over with several friends, most of whom were hunters, all of them expressed sorrow over the loss. The hunter in question at least had had the decency to turn himself in, but his (choose one) ignorance, stupidity, or lack of proper training would do nothing to bring back 5T1.

I decided to do a little research myself and was surprised to discover that Trumpeters are legal to hunt in parts of north-central Montana. Many are also accidently killed by hunters mistaking them for the much smaller Tundra Swan. Neither of these facts excused the killing of 5T1, since hunting for both species was clearly prohibited anywhere in western Montana where we lived.

The whole episode made me question the taking of many wild waterfowl species. I am not opposed to hunting. In fact, I'm a firm believer that we have to cull deer and other ungulate populations— and I wish to god hunters would acquire more enthusiasm for Canada Geese. I also see hunting as a great way for people to put healthy meat on the table. But what is the point of shooting a swan or a Sandhill Crane? A Hooded Merganser, Canvasback, or Wood Duck? Sure, hunters often eat them, but aren't there enough Mallards, Ring-necked

Pheasants, Canada Geese, and other common game birds around? My guess is that the main point to killing these other species is to hang them on the wall and brag about bagging this or that.

Just as we wisely outlawed the shooting of songbirds more than a century ago, it seems time to consider doing the same for more waterfowl species. And, yes, I can already hear the arguments that Ducks Unlimited has worked tirelessly to improve waterfowl habitat and that sort of thing. Well, great! I wholeheartedly applaud them. But has that been just so hunters can go out and shoot anything that flies in front of them? Haven't we moved beyond such purely self-interested motivation? I looked up North American duck populations and many seem to lurch dramatically up and down. According to the US Fish and Wildlife Service 2016 Waterfowl Survey (as reported by Ducks Unlimited), for instance, between 2015 and 2016, Blue-winged Teal populations dived 22 percent—in one year. It doesn't seem like it would take much to push many species over the edge, especially considering the increasing perils of climate change.

Was it possible to have a reasonable conversation about this? With the power of today's gun lobby, I doubted it.

A few days later I left on my second fall speaking trip, a furious four-day race through DC, Maryland, and Pennsylvania. At the Keystone State Reading Association annual conference in Seven Springs, Pennsylvania, I squeezed in an hour of birding through deciduous woods and managed to see juncos, Red-bellied and Downy Woodpeckers, and a Ruby-crowned Kinglet, which I was proud to identify all on my own. Behind a promising rest stop along the interstate, I watched Blue Jays, more juncos, another Red-bellied, Turkey Vultures, and some kind of hawk hunting through the trees. I failed to find any new Big Year birds, though, so my count idled at 324.

Back on the home front, Braden and I weren't giving up. A number of Montana birds stood out on our Winter Hopeful List including:

- Snowy Owl
- Great Gray Owl
- Okay, *any* owl
- American Tree Sparrow
- Snow Bunting

- Red and White-winged Crossbills
- Gyrfalcon
- Prairie Falcon
- Tundra Swan

Even if we got all of these before the end of the year—a highly unlikely scenario—it still wouldn't push our total to our new magic number, 350, but it would make us feel better about ourselves.

I also had one more ace up my sleeve.

snipe hunting

As the presidential election accelerated into an unprecedented frenzy of accusations, lies, threats, and intrigue, my own pace of life and birding acquired an unanticipated intensity. With only a week between the East Coast trip and my next one, I buckled down to some serious writing but somehow couldn't keep myself from birding. Our new dog, Lola, helped out.

A stray, Lola had been found nursing eight puppies up near Polson, about an hour north of Missoula. Since the death of our last dog, Mattie, three years before, Tessa had been clamoring for another dog and finally in the past few months Amy and I had agreed that we all were ready. Tessa and I began scouring the Humane Society website and in mid-September spotted an adorable black Lab mix. A week later Lola joined our family.

Loving, smart, and enthusiastic, Lola didn't come without baggage. She was suspicious of anyone dressed in a uniform and growled at men, bicyclists, little dogs, joggers, and anything else that didn't fit her narrow definition of safe. Once, when I took out a broom to sweep the floor, she cowered and slunk to another room. We could only assume that someone had mistreated her in the year or two before we adopted her, but we all dedicated ourselves to helping her overcome her less-than-ideal puppyhood and let her inner good dog emerge. We smothered her with affection, took her for long walks, and controlled our temper when she devoured three loaves of bread and several six-packs of Costco chocolate muffins—apparently with no ill effects.

As part of her socialization process, I took Lola erranding wherever I went, and it didn't take her long to figure out that these trips usually led to bonus walks.

One day, on a whim, Lola and I decided to visit McCormick Park, down by the Clark Fork River. The park had a small fishing pond, and I wondered if anything fun might be dabbling around there. Even as I pulled up, I spotted a ducky bird with a white head and thought, *Cool! Bufflehead!*

Well, not quite. It was a Hooded Merganser—actually, several of them. A couple of days later, I returned with Braden and our cameras. The mergansers still paddled the pond, along with a lonely looking Pied-billed Grebe. Even better, in the Clark Fork a couple hundred yards away, we got great photos of a resplendent, sun-drenched male Wood Duck taking a final swim before heading south for the winter.

Lola seemed to enjoy this new activity called birding, and I debated whether to sign her up for eBird so that she could begin her own Life list. For dogs, that refers to how many ABA birds they can *eat* in a single year.

Lola opted out of eBird, but the next day I took Braden and his friend Eli up to Blue Mountain to search for Red Crossbills, birds that had dodged us all year. Eli had a sharp eye for wildlife, which wasn't at all surprising. His father, Rich, was a professional biologist, and several years after Braden and Eli became friends, Eli's mom, Susan, casually let slip that her own mother, Phoebe Snetsinger, had been one of the top birders of all time. I had just recently started reading Phoebe's autobiography, *Birding on Borrowed Time*, in which she recounted her adventures finding and identifying more than eight thousand bird species during her life—a life tragically cut short by an automobile accident during a birding expedition to Madagascar.

Eli hadn't acquired his grandmother's passion for birds, but he was always good company and, like Tessa, indulged Braden's and my enthusiasm for birding. On Blue Mountain the three of us discovered crossbills in abundance. After craning our necks high into the trees for half an hour, Braden said, "Hey, one landed over there." Lucky for us, the previous day's rain had left a ground-level watering hole for the birds, providing rare close-up views and yet another fantastic photo op.

Notably, it raised each of our Big Year counts to a cool 325. The problem is that when we reached 325 it made our goal of 350 all the more irresistible. Much like the Trump and Clinton teams, who were furiously poring over possible Electoral College numbers, Braden and I redoubled our discussions about possible routes to 350. Again we concluded that it would be tough—*very* tough. The last of the migrants were fleeing the state, and it didn't seem possible that twenty-six new winter birds would replace them. The number 335 seemed reachable with a little effort, but 350? Not without more travel.

But that's exactly what I was about to do—and back to a place that could bring me within striking distance of 350.

California.

After not being invited to speak in the Golden State for several years, I'd been surprised the previous spring to receive an invitation to visit six elementary schools in Merced, the heart of the Central Valley.

As the trip grew near, I began thinking, *Hmm, migrating waterfowl.*

Google Maps confirmed that not one, but two national wildlife refuges lay less than forty-five minutes from Merced, and it was an opportunity too good to pass up.

"I wish you could come with me," I told Braden before the trip.

"Me too," he lamented.

Unfortunately, our son had already missed a lot of school in the last twelve months, and our family budget could do without the stress of an added airline ticket and expenses. Nonetheless, in the days leading up to the trip, Braden helped me identify which species to look for. We already had most of the birds on our Big Year lists but not all.

"Look for Greater White-fronted Geese," he told me. "They should be there for sure. Also Lincoln's Sparrows."

I groaned. "Like I'll be able to identify *those*."

"You will," he assured me. "They're like immature White-crowneds, except that they've got a more yellowish breast."

If you say so. With their extremely similar, drab markings, I found sparrows to be some of the toughest birds to identify.

Still, I was looking forward to the trip and holding out hopes that a big basket of Big Year birds—birds that I could identify—would somehow make an appearance.

"If you can't identify something," Braden said the night before I left, "call me and I'll help you figure out what you're looking at."

The next morning—Tuesday, November 1—I caught the early flight out of Missoula. By ten fifteen I'd picked up my rental car in San Jose. By noon I'd eaten Xiao Long Bao at Din Tai Fung, and by two I was pulling into the San Luis National Wildlife Refuge parking lot.

Only one other car sat in the lot, and, by the enthusiasm with which Madeline, the naturalist, greeted me, I got the feeling that visitors here were rare. The birds, though, were waiting, and after enlisting Madeline to help me plot a course, I set out on two large driving loops. Although the refuge had been set up to protect the rare Tule elk population, I didn't spot a single elk—probably because I wasn't looking for one. Mammals? Who needs 'em! I was here for the birds, and they were everywhere. The numbers of raptors knocked me out. Rarely had I seen so many buteos concentrated into such a small area, and the harriers? Forget about it! Over the next three hours I would lose count of how many I saw, often observing two or three of the owl-like, low-flying hunters at a time.

Braden ought to be seeing this, I thought with more than a little guilt.

Largely because of my son, I especially worked to add sparrows to my Big Year list. This proved frustrating because for sparrow IDs I needed decent photos, and the sparrows refused to cooperate. While pursuing putative sparrows, however, I discovered a flock of Yellow-rumped Warblers and a Loggerhead Shrike along one tiny watercourse. I also saw what I felt sure must be a Prairie Falcon—only to later learn that it had almost certainly been a kestrel, the first of seven or eight I would see that day.

Soon after beginning my second driving loop, I notched my first definite Big Year bird of the trip when, just as Braden had predicted, I came upon a flock of Greater White-fronted Geese on one of the main ponds. On a nearby pond I found something even more delightful, a scattered group of about fifty Northern Shovelers. These ducks are known for their bills that splay wide like vacuum cleaner attachments. Braden and I had seen one or two earlier in the year, but only from a distance, and I spent a good ten minutes enjoying them—especially the males with their handsome chestnut-and-white flanks and shimmering green heads.

I had intended to spend only an hour or two at the refuge, but before I knew it the sun had sunk low in the west, and I stood watching hundreds of Sandhill Cranes stream into the refuge from the south. They put on an amazing show, one wave after another, honking and bickering like in-laws as they headed to their bedding grounds for the night. I watched them for several minutes and even called Amy and the kids to let them listen to the birds over the phone. Then, reluctantly, I headed to my own refuge for the night, the Merced Hampton Inn.

My schedule for the next ten days included three consecutive days of school visits, a three-day weekend in the Bay Area with friends and family, and three final days of school visits.

It was a schedule that should have allowed for plenty of birding, and I especially had one pie-in-the-sky bird chase in mind—running up to Yosemite to try to score and photograph a White-headed Woodpecker. Ever since Dick Hutto had told me about this bird, I had dreamed of seeing one, and this would be my first and only chance for the year. White-headed Woodpeckers live mainly at high altitudes in far western ranges and are almost never reported in Montana. Getting to Yosemite, though, was going to be tough. My only two windows of opportunity were on the two days when my school presentations ended early in the afternoon. Even then I faced a daunting two-hour drive each way, with only a couple of hours to bird.

My first short day, a Thursday, I felt too wiped to attempt it. Instead I opted for birding the nearby Merced National Wildlife Refuge, which proved enjoyable but didn't net any new Big Year birds.

After finishing my school visit the following day, Friday, I headed to El Cerrito to stay with my friends Roger and Claudia. Though not avid birders, they liked birds and had dabbled in birding. More important, they were contemplating retiring in the next few years and needed new hobbies to keep their bodies and brains from turning to compost. The night I arrived, I coaxed Roger into signing up for an eBird account, and over the weekend I dragged him and Claudia to several local birding hotspots. At the Richmond Marina, we scored more than a dozen species, including an unexpected Horned Grebe for my Big Year list. By the end of the weekend, we had pushed Roger's new eBird Life list to twenty-eight species.

Heading back to Merced on my fifty-seventh birthday, I resumed thinking about White-headed Woodpeckers. I was scheduled for a long school day the next day—Tuesday, Election Day. Wednesday, though, I would finish my school visit by one o'clock. *Maybe, just maybe, I can bolt up to Yosemite then.*

Two events put the kibosh on my plan—Daylight Savings Time and Donald Trump.

Like most Americans, I felt stunned watching the election results roll red Tuesday night. Though I had told Amy that I felt Trump was a possibility, I really never thought that so many voters would put their knee-jerk angst ahead of their common sense. I particularly never believed so many would vote for a man who clearly didn't care about anyone but himself. For the environment, Trump promised to be a disaster, as the new president-elect had pledged to dive back into fossil fuels, dismantle the EPA, and nominate Supreme Court justices sure to side with corporate interests over the planet's well-being—all promises, we now know, he pursued with blind abandon.

None of this directly affected my search for the White-headed Woodpecker—except for the fact that I woke up at three the next morning asking myself, *Is the world as we know it about to disintegrate?*

By the time I finished my school visit the next day, almost nothing sounded less appealing than four hours of breakneck driving in search of a bird that very likely wouldn't show up.

Besides, I reasoned, *this is a bird I really want to see with Braden one day.*

Instead of a frantic drive into the mountains, I devised a sensible alternative: I took a nap.

When I woke, however, I still had a few daylight hours left, so I headed back to the Merced National Wildlife Refuge with a new target in mind: Wilson's Snipe.

I had never ever seen a Wilson's Snipe, but a recent eBird post had reported more than forty of them at the refuge. *Even a nincompoop like me should be able to find one,* I thought as I followed straight rural roads south and west past farms and pastures.

At the observation platform near the refuge's main entrance, I paused to try to photograph some of those cursed sparrows that continued to thwart my identification attempts. I wasn't having much luck when another car pulled up and a woman slightly older than me walked up the ramp wearing binoculars. She waited patiently as I photographed a White-crowned Sparrow, and then we began to chat.

Her name was Bonnie Bedford-White, and she was stopping by the refuge on her way home from a dentist appointment in San Jose.

"Are you a birder?" I asked.

"I try," she said.

I suspected she might be sandbagging and said, "I'm looking for Wilson's Snipes and Lincoln's Sparrows, but I haven't seen either one."

"The sparrows are hard," she commiserated as we glassed a bunch of the little brown birds flitting in and out of some nearby bushes. She proclaimed them to be White-crowned and Song Sparrows, but not two minutes later she exclaimed, "Oh, there's a Wilson's Snipe!"

"Where?" I whispered excitedly.

She pointed to thick grass along the edge of the pond in front of us. "It's poking its head up and down. That's kind of what they do."

Suddenly I saw it. It looked just like its picture in the book—a handsome sandpiper-sized bird with bold white stripes on its brown head and back.

Then Bonnie said, "Oh, and I think that's a Lincoln's Sparrow!"

I quickly swung my binoculars to the bush she was pointing at, but the sparrow dived out of sight before I could focus.

Lousy, no-good, seed-eating sparrows.

Still, I was happy. Snipe on the list, I thanked Bonnie, got into my car, and cruised around the rest of the refuge. Shovelers, White Pelicans, and dowitchers were out in force, and I even spotted another snipe. The birds and the beautiful setting didn't make up for Trump, but they were a great way to wrap up a long, demanding trip—and put some salve on an uncertain future.

OCTOBER BIRD LIST

Sneed's List (3)	Braden's List (3)
Trumpeter Swan	Trumpeter Swan
American Pipit	American Pipit
Red Crossbill	Red Crossbill

CHAPTER 34

shots in the dark

The rest of November did little to fatten our Big Year lists. I blamed our incoming president. *The birds have probably heard about Trump's plans to gut environmental protections and build a wall along the Mexican border,* I reasoned. *They must have wisely decided to avoid the United States of Right-Wing Fanatics and migrate through friendlier territories.*

As tempting as it was to really embrace this explanation, I had to admit that our stagnating lists had more to do with my impending textbook deadline and the upcoming holiday season than with the not-so-democratically-elected Trumpster. I thought I might have a shot at some new birds during a four-day school visit trip to Wyoming, but when I landed in Gillette, I was greeted by weather so frigid that I barely ventured outside, let alone birded. In fact, Braden and I didn't manage to go birding again until the day after Thanksgiving, and it wasn't until a couple of days after that that we were able to gear up for another serious birding assault.

Our initial plan was to try for Jewel Basin, a high basin in the Swan Mountain Range northeast of Flathead Lake. The most recent eBird post from there had listed several coveted species including Gray-headed Rosy Finches, Bohemian Waxwings, and White-winged Crossbills. After consulting with two MOB members, however, we determined that road conditions would be particularly hazardous, so we shifted attention to another location: Ninepipe National Wildlife Refuge. Less than an hour from our house, the refuge offered a series of ponds and marshes sure to be irresistible to all manner of birds. What's more, Braden and I had never birded the area. Alas, I checked the refuge's website for directions and information—only to discover that it was closed until March.

"Look," I told my disappointed son, "This is a weird time of year, and I think our timing is off. Let's spend the day seeing what we can find around town. We can hit the quarry where we saw the pipits, and then bird Maclay Flat. Who knows? Maybe we'll finally see a Northern Pygmy-Owl."

The plan didn't make either one of us pirouette with joy, but Braden agreed that it probably was our best option given the circumstances. To spice up the possibilities, we decided to kick it off with a real long shot. A few days earlier, an eBird poster had reported hearing—possibly seeing—a Saw-whet Owl just up the street from our house. Braden and I pulled out of our driveway half an hour before dawn and drove to the location in a dark, quiet neighborhood. After an unbelievably warm fall, temperatures had finally plunged and as we got out of the car, we both wondered if we'd lost our minds—especially since we heard no signs of the owl.

"Play its call," Braden said, stomping his feet to stay warm.

I dug out my iPhone and played the Saw-whet's mesmerizing, repeating high note.

Nothing.

"C'mon," I said, "let's walk a bit to see if we can find it." We hurried through a half-mile loop of a nearby forest trail, and every hundred yards or so stopped to play the Saw-whet's call. No Saw-whet responded, but we did hear multiple Great-horned Owls—three at a time from one spot.

"That's cool," I said.

"Yeah," said Braden. "Should we go?"

I hated to give up so quickly, but the arctic temperatures were flash-freezing my extremities. "Yeah," I said. "Let's head out."

We double-timed back to my 4Runner, and I started it up. Before leaving the neighborhood, we stopped at one more spot close to Rattlesnake Creek. Shivering next to the car, we continued to hear the Great-horned Owls and spied a raccoon slinking along a nearby fence. Suddenly a single flute-like high note pierced the air.

"Did you hear that?" I hissed.

"Yeah," Braden said, concentrating on the dark forest in front of us.

The note didn't continually repeat itself as it did on the recordings we'd listened to, but the tone and duration were identical. A few moments later, we heard it again.

"That's got to be a Saw-whet, don't you think?" I asked.

"It sounded like it. Play the recording again."

I did as instructed, but we heard no more notes and witnessed no diminutive shapes flying through the dawn skies.

"Should we count it?" I asked as we climbed back into the car.

My son answered with an emphatic "No," but I was on the fence. It was true that we hadn't counted any other birds by ear this year, but this call was so distinct. What else could it be?

Twenty minutes later, over Egg McMuffins, I played other possible owl calls. To my dismay we discovered that our fleeting notes might have belonged to a Northern Pygmy-Owl. No matter. I was thrilled to have heard it—our first non-Great Horned Owl call ever—even if we couldn't tell exactly what it was or count it for our lists.

Excited by our owl encounter, and fortified with fat and protein, we headed for our next destination: the gravel quarry behind Fort Missoula. By the time we parked and climbed out of the car, temperatures had climbed into the mid-twenties, but we still walked briskly down the dirt road leading to the quarry ponds, all the while scanning for a Snow Bunting or two in the frosty fields on either side.

We didn't see buntings or much at the quarry ponds either. We had hoped for maybe a scoter or Red-throated Loon since they'd been reported there days earlier, but the cold weather had undoubtedly driven any birds with common sense south toward balmier resorts. As we approached a small thicket, Braden halted.

"Do you hear that?"

"No," I admitted.

"I hear chirps."

I cupped a hand behind my ear and twisted my head like a radar dish, futilely straining to pick up the signal. Then we saw movement.

"American Tree Sparrows!" Braden announced.

I fumbled for a good look through my binoculars. "How do you know?" I asked. "Do you see the two-colored bill?"

"No," he said. "But that's them for sure."

My son offered no better explanation, but I figured his ID was based on his hours of study and comparing these birds to the other sparrows that he'd seen. Just as he'd kept me honest with the Saw-whet, however, I wasn't going to confirm tree sparrows until I had seen the one definite distinguishing mark that I knew about—the bicolored bill. The sparrows didn't make it easy. I followed a little group of six for almost ten minutes before I got a clear look at one. Then, finally, I observed that the bird's bottom bill showed yellow while its upper bill was dark.

"Year bird!" I exulted.

"Can we go now?" Braden asked, shivering.

After our trip to the quarry, we agreed that we needed another shot of fat and sugar to combat the subfreezing temperatures, so in the spirit of our new president-elect we continued our patriotic support of corporate America by beelining to Starbucks for hot cocoa and chocolate-filled pastries. Then, well on my way to a diabetic coma, I steered us toward our third and final destination of the day: Maclay Flat.

This was our first visit to the Forest Service's Maclay Flat Nature Trail all year. Sitting on the south edge of town, the natural area borders the Bitterroot River and offers an intriguing mix of riparian and flatland habitats. One reason we'd probably ignored Maclay was that our last visit here had underwhelmed us. On the other hand, two years before this had also been where we'd seen our first and only Great Gray Owl. Just as enticing, friends had recently informed us that pygmy-owls often frequented the woods next to the parking lot. Braden and I didn't really think we'd see an owl of any kind, but as soon as we pulled in we optimistically scanned the parking area through the 4Runner's windshield. One of our best mixed-flocks of the year greeted us. It included chickadees, nuthatches, and a Brown Creeper—but, alas, no pygmy-owl.

"C'mon," I said, opening the car door, "Let's walk."

Armed with binoculars and cameras, we headed counterclockwise onto the two-mile loop trail. During the first three-quarters of the loop, we glimpsed only a few of the songbirds that we'd seen back in the parking lot and got a distant, frustrating look at some kind of falcon. As we passed a noisy throng of moms, dogs, and kids, however, the nearby trees suddenly erupted with tiny birds.

Without hesitating, Braden launched himself into the forest after the feathered flock.

"What are they?" I asked, stumbling to keep up.

"I can't tell," he called back.

I couldn't get a good look either. At least a dozen of the birds flitted between the branches above us, but they moved so quickly I couldn't focus my binoculars on them, and the gray skies backlighting them made the job even harder.

Then, Braden said, "Wait."

"What?" I said, looking over at him.

"Golden-crowned Kinglets!" he shouted. "Do you see them?"

"No. Wait. Are you sure?" I demanded, desperately trying to draw a bead on one of the fast-moving, elusive shapes.

"Absolutely! Do you see it?"

"No!"

I was becoming seriously pissed at these creatures, but then a bird in my binoculars looked straight down at me. Almost unbelievably, it showed a blazing yellow head stripe in full royal glory.

"Yes!" I shouted. Two Big Year birds was two more than I'd expected from our morning excursion, and heading back toward the parking area, both Braden and I felt deliciously satisfied. Since we were still at Maclay, I figured we might as well take one last look for pygmy-owls.

Entering the parking area, we cut down to the forest edge and walked slowly toward our car. The mixed flock was back, and we happily watched it scour the trees for food.

Suddenly I saw a kind of blobby brown shape dive to the ground after a junco. I couldn't identify the blob but felt sure it was something we hadn't seen before.

"Braden!" I hissed, hurrying forward.

"What is it? Where?"

I stopped and pointed to a fallen log behind some brush thirty feet away. Even through my binoculars, I couldn't tell what I was looking at. Then two enormous yellow eyes swiveled directly towards me.

"It's a pygmy-owl!" I whispered.

"Really?"

I helped Braden find the owl, and we followed it as it flitted from one tree to another. The songbirds began mobbing their mutual enemy, driving the predator farther and farther away, so we never got a great study of it. Still, it was a Lifer for both of us—and a long-awaited nemesis bird to boot.

NOVEMBER BIRD LIST

Sneed's List (6)	Braden's List (3)
Greater White-fronted Goose	American Tree Sparrow
Horned Grebe	Golden-crowned Kinglet
Wilson's Snipe	Northern Pygmy-Owl
American Tree Sparrow	
Golden-crowned Kinglet	
Northern Pygmy-Owl	

CHAPTER 35

a christmas basket of birds

Our latest trio of birds brought Braden's Big Year count to 328. Thanks to my time in California and earlier trips east, my own count stood at 331. Even my slightly higher total seemed hopelessly out of range of our Big Year target of 350.

Desperate times, though, called for desperate measures.

"You know," I told Braden one evening, "I am thinking we should pool our lists."

Braden looked at me, intrigued. "Why?"

"Well, we've worked as a team all year. Don't you think it makes more sense to combine our numbers? Besides, it might be our only way to reach 350."

"It still might not work," he said.

"I know, but don't you think it's worth a try?"

"Okay," he said. "I'll go along with that."

It was an outrageous move, likely to provoke cries of "Foul!" from around the globe. At the same time, I'm not sure why we didn't do it earlier. We'd birded together most of the year, and it represented our group effort better to view our year's endeavors as one instead of individually. The bad news? Pooling our lists added only two species to our collective count. Braden had picked up Harlequin Duck and Nashville Warbler without me, while I'd picked up Canyon Wren, Yellow-breasted Chat, White-fronted Goose, Wilson's Snipe, and Horned Grebe, bringing Team Collard's total to 333—still an intimidating seventeen species shy of our goal.

And with only one month to go.

On December 2 I departed for my last school visit of the year, to Maryland. Though I had only one school booked, just outside of Baltimore, I left three days early to spend time with my oldest friend, Eric Dawson, and his son, Geoffrey. Before leaving Missoula, I warned Eric that I wanted to go birding, and, using eBird, Braden and I picked out a likely place for me to go—a seaside hamlet called North Beach.

"I could get ten new species if everything goes right," I mused, flipping through *Sibley.*

"That would be tough," Braden responded, "but it's possible."

There was just one problem: North Beach proved a total bust. By the time Eric, Geoffrey, and I drove to the marsh "hot spot," a cold front had swept in and, with the help of a low tide, driven all but a handful of species out of the area. To help me avoid getting totally skunked, Eric took me around a pond in Upper Marlboro where he lived. In a nice tract of woods, we saw a number of songbirds including, finally, a new Big Year bird and Lifer—White-Throated Sparrow.

The next morning I decided to take eight-year-old Geoffrey on a walk around the golf course surrounding Eric's neighborhood. I had no expectations for anything new, but the course had been abandoned seven or eight years before, and on previous visits I'd discovered that it was "decaying" into an excellent wildlife habitat.

If nothing else, I thought to myself, *the Geoffster and I will get in a nice walk before settling down to a day of watching football and eating chocolate.*

At the end of Eric's street, Geoffrey and I discovered Blue Jays, more White-throated Sparrows, and a Red-bellied Woodpecker. Then I spotted a new-looking bird that sent my juices boiling.

With my binoculars, I followed the bird to an oak tree trunk. As it came into focus, the bird's posture and pecking behavior told me that I was looking at some kind of woodpecker, but an obnoxious branch—curse it—prevented me from getting a clear look.

Then the bird struck a beautiful, fully lit side view pose.

"That's it," I coaxed. "Just stay still." And that's when I realized that I wasn't looking at just any woodpecker. I was staring at a sapsucker.

The possibility of seeing a sapsucker hadn't even skimmed my radar, but my heart pounded, both because the bird I was watching belonged to my favorite group of birds—woodpeckers—and because sapsuckers were always so unexpected.

But what kind is it? I wondered.

I didn't know squat about sapsucker distribution, but the bird showed yellow all down its front. That ruled out Red-naped and Red-breasted, leaving only Williamson's and what I truly hoped for, Yellow-bellied.

As soon as we got back to Eric's house, I rushed to open my Kaufman's guide and realized that I could only have been looking at one species—a Yellow-bellied Sapsucker. It was one of the most spectacular birds I'd seen all year and a Lifer for Team Collard. It and the White-throated Sparrows raised Braden's and my Big Year count to 335.

Sadly, by the time I returned home near midnight on December 6, our Big Year was running out faster than the Obama presidency. One bright spot was that Braden and I had signed up for our local Audubon chapter's Christmas Bird Count, to be held on December 17. For those unfamiliar with this event, it is an effort by the nation's birders to count as many species as possible on a single day. The various counts are held on different days in different locales but all fall within a week or so of each other, and the results are pooled.

Squeezing in birding time during the ten days before the count, however, would be tough, if not impossible. Braden's middle school was still in full swing, and, more critically, my textbook deadline was thundering toward me like a runaway train. The usual Christmas craziness also had crept into our lives, with school performances, holiday get-togethers, gift-buying, and, to top it off, a doctor's office visit for Braden's ingrown toenail.

Still, when Braden's Boy Scout "tarp campout" got canceled the following weekend, it gave us an unexpected chance to bird on the morning of December 11. We again decided to stay around town and, on a fencepost near the gravel quarry, got a brief but wonderful look at a Sharp-shinned Hawk—but no Big Year birds.

A few days later I was sneaking in a late afternoon nap when Braden rushed home from school and burst into my room.

"Daddy!" he exclaimed. "On the way home from the bus stop, I saw a big flock of Bohemian Waxwings. Do you want to come see them?"

"Not really," I moaned, but of course changed my mind within seconds. Similar to Cedar Waxwings but with rusty markings on the head and under the tail, Bohemian Waxwings summer in Alaska and northern Canada, but winter farther south. Braden and I had been waiting for these handsome little birds to show up for days, and it would be foolish to look a gift bird in the face.

Deciding that my nap could wait, I threw on my clothes and we drove several blocks to the tree where Braden had seen them. The birds were still there! We crept out of the car and took a couple of dozen photos, and, even better, located a second group of waxwings three blocks away.

Ka-ching! Number 336!

As the days continued to tick by, Braden and I hoped that the upcoming Christmas Bird Count might pad our list even more, but the weather dashed that prospect. Checking the forecast, I saw that the day of the count promised a high temperature of 1 degree Fahrenheit. Recalling our first day of birding for the year, I knew that such frigid temperatures were unlikely to produce many birds, and it seemed foolhardy to spend the day outside shivering miserably. I emailed the local Christmas Bird Count director to ask if he might consider rescheduling to a more temperate day—only to receive a reply about how that would be impossible around the holidays.

I understood but politely informed him we would not be joining them this year and took my family to see the new Star Wars movie instead.

As a further setback, that night, Braden dug out his camera and began looking at the photos he'd taken of the Bohemian Waxwings. I sat next to my son on the couch, reading the final chapters of Phoebe Snetsinger's memoir, but I couldn't help notice him looking back and forth between his photos and *Sibley*.

"What are you doing?" I asked him.

"I think these are *Cedar* Waxwings," he solemnly informed me.

"What?" I said, putting down my book. "You're sure they're not Bohemians?"

"They don't show the red under their rumps."

"But we saw the white wing bars," I protested.

"Yeah, but look. Cedars show some white next to the wings too."

I compared Braden's photographs to Sibley's guide and, after a few moments, conceded that once again my son was right.

"Well, crap!" I said.

Braden moaned. "We're never going to get Bohemians. I'll bet we don't get anything new for the rest of the year."

"Oh, c'mon," I told him. "We probably will. Plus, isn't it neat we saw all those Cedars?"

"Yeah," he replied unconvincingly.

I knew how he felt and guessed that, like me, he was wondering if our Big Year had petered out for good.

The answer turned out to be no. Even though we had bailed on the Christmas Bird Count, a few days later a MOBster from Kalispell reported a different Christmas Bird Count from around Ninepipe— the closed National Wildlife Refuge about an hour north of us. His count had included seven or eight species Braden and I still needed, including fourteen—count 'em, *fourteen*—Short-eared Owls!

At first I was confused.

How did they rack up so many birds if the refuge is closed for the winter? Did they get special permission to enter?

I wrote to the member who posted the report, and he promptly replied, explaining that they'd spotted all of their birds on the roads *around* the refuge, not in the refuge itself.

That cinched it. On the evening of Wednesday, December 21, I asked Braden if he had anything important going on the next day—his last day of school before the Christmas break.

He eyed me suspiciously. "I don't think so. Why?"

I gave an exaggerated sigh. "Well, I was just thinking that the weather is looking pretty good. I'm sure you'd *rather* go to school, but—"

"But what?"

"Well, you could also play hooky so we could go birding at Ninepipe."

His eyes narrowed. "Are you serious?"

I shrugged noncommittally. "I mean I understand if you don't want to—"

"Shut up!" he said, punching me on the shoulder. "Maybe we can finally see a Short-eared Owl!"

The next morning, Braden ditched school and we headed north under cold, partly cloudy skies.

It was awesome.

The Short-eared Owls failed to show, but covering thirty miles on the icy roads surrounding the refuge we saw more than fifty Red-tailed Hawks and a dozen Rough-leggeds. Even better, we restored Bohemian Waxwings to our list—with confirmation photos this time—and picked up another Big Year bird, Prairie Falcon. Braden also filled in Wilson's Snipe for his own Big Year list—all against the backdrop of some of America's most spectacular mountains, the Missions, which lead north into Glacier National Park.

As we drove back to Missoula, Braden said, "I love days like this."

I couldn't have said it better myself. As a bonus, while walking Lola along Rattlesnake Creek that afternoon, I added yet another bird to our list—Gray Partridge—raising Team Collard's Big Year total to 338.

CHAPTER 36

frozen

Our last-minute December successes made us more determined than ever to keep birding through the last week of the year. The next morning I showed Braden where I'd seen the Gray Partridges, but we couldn't relocate them. Afterward we had some Christmas shopping to take care of, and then planned to head to Council Grove State Park, a place we'd so far failed to bird and one that might produce surprises.

By the time we survived Staples, Target, and Barnes and Noble, however, our birding ambitions had taken a nosedive. Shopping, together with the previous day at Ninepipe, had drained our reserves, and cold, gray weather further dampened our enthusiasm.

"Should we just head home?" I asked, looking up at the oppressive sky.

I expected Braden to object, but instead he looked relieved.

"Yeah," he said. "I'm tired."

"Me too," I told him. "I guess yesterday wiped us out."

As we negotiated the heavy holiday traffic back toward our house, though, my son turned reflective. "It's been an amazing year," he said. "Can you believe the places we've gotten to go?"

"You're talking about birding, right?" I joked.

"Yeah. We've hit three of the Big Five birding places: Arizona, Texas, and California. The only ones we've missed are Alaska and Florida."

"We *did* go to Florida," I reminded him.

"And learned where *not* to bird," he emphasized. "We needed to go a little north or a little south of Miami."

"Well," I asked, continuing his original train of thought, "what was your favorite place we went—besides the Galápagos, I mean?"

It was a question we had debated several times as the year had progressed, but at this point, near year's end, it carried more weight. "Hmm," he said, "I'm going to say Arizona. And not just because of the birds. Because of the habitat down there."

"Yeah, I think Arizona was my favorite too," I said. "Getting to stay at the ranch with Pat and Bruce was the perfect base camp. We definitely should try to rent that place ourselves."

"You mean when we do our *really* big year?" Braden asked.

I smiled. "Yeah."

During the closing months of our Big Year, Braden and I had talked more and more about doing a serious, hard-core Big Year, perhaps after he graduated from high school. I loved the idea but didn't know if it would ever happen. Time and money would pose major obstacles, and a stark reality—one that reading Phoebe Snetsinger's book reinforced—is that none of us really know how much time or opportunity we will have. Life and the world could be humming along swimmingly, only to have it all crash down in an instant. Sure, total disaster didn't usually strike, but I constantly reminded myself not to take anything for granted.

I think that even at age thirteen, Braden had developed an awareness of these and other facts of life. He'd had a terrific childhood so far, but even in Montana the tragedies and tides of the world affected him, just as they affected the rest of us. With Trump in the White House, things were likely to get worse before they got better. Perhaps it was that very precariousness of life that helped us both appreciate what an amazing thing we'd accomplished this past year.

And what was that, exactly?

Well, a respectable Big Year list, for one thing, though I'm not sure our final number—even if we managed to reach 350—meant as much to us as our other Big Year accomplishments. More important was how much our pursuit of birds had taught us about bird identification and behavior. Even with my brain that easily forgot details and my hearing that failed to detect a great many songbirds, I felt I was twice—maybe three or four times—the birder I'd been at the beginning of the year. Braden had elevated his expertise even more.

During our Big Year we'd also explored corners of the country that wouldn't have rated a second thought if it hadn't been for birding. Many of those places—even the suburbs of Houston—had turned out to be wonderful landscapes that would leave permanent imprints on both of us, even if we never managed to return.

Visiting those places had helped us forge new friendships and deepen old ones. In fact, as soon as we got home from our Christmas errands, I sent Ted—our Chicago birding buddy—photos of some of our best Big Year birds. Since we'd met him in Houston, Ted had had an amazing Big Year of his own. His trip to Texas had really fired him up, and with one week of 2016 remaining he'd amassed an ABA year list of 502 species. Even more impressive, he'd seen 313 species in Illinois, missing only Northern Saw-whet, Red Crossbill, Golden Eagle, and a handful of other species to slam the door on his state list for the year.

After I sent him our photos, Ted texted back some comments on each and offered perspective on the real value of Braden's and my Big Year. He wrote, "I love the photographs. The Wood Duck and Hooded Merganser are gorgeous, and the woodpeckers are good too, but nothing more so than the Pileated feeding its young, what a great action shot. And the best pic of all might be you and your sweet boy enjoying the pelagic trip together, that's a great father and son photograph."

With that last sentence, Ted nailed the most important payoff of our Big Year. It had offered Braden and me an unforgettable way to spend time together, learn together, and stay connected when Braden was crossing the threshold into manhood. Though Braden and I didn't speak of it in such specific—or sentimental—terms, I could tell from his earlier introspection that we both recognized it and cherished what a unique experience it had been.

And it wasn't quite over. One afternoon, on a tip from Nick's dad, Phillip, we swung by the University of Montana campus to find hundreds—make that thousands—of Bohemian and Cedar Waxwings filling the skies. Since they both were already on our Big Year list, we felt free to just stand and stare, mesmerized by the immense flocks swirling, roosting, and feeding around us. We breathed in the crisp, cold air, felt the winter sunlight on our backs, listened to the birds' frantic flight calls, and simply enjoyed the spectacle nature offered up to anyone willing to take the time to look.

Speaking of Nick, Braden and I agreed that we wanted to get Nick involved in at least one of our final 2016 birding excursions. Like Ted, Nick had been birding hard all year, and, while Braden and I hovered just out of the top one hundred on the Montana State eBird list, Nick had cracked the top twenty. As much as we wanted to pad our own list, we wanted to help Nick too, so on the Wednesday after Christmas, Braden and I collected him at his mother's house in Missoula for a return trip to Ninepipe. Although we'd just visited the refuge, there was a chance of picking up a rare Rusty Blackbird that Nick especially wanted to see, and I wanted another crack at those perfidious Short-eared Owls. I mean, on the Christmas Bird Count, other birders had seen *fourteen* Short-eared Owls, yet we had seen exactly zero.

"Those owls are really pissing me off," I told Braden and Nick.

The boys laughed but knew exactly how I felt.

Predictably, the Short-eared Owls again mocked us. We spent an enjoyable day birding around Ninepipe and then headed to the nearby National Bison Range, but despite our efforts none of us picked up a single new bird.

With only three days left in the year, Team Collard's Big Year list remained frozen at 338.

CHAPTER 37

the final countdown

This is the chapter where in many books the main characters' final, heroic efforts allow them to vanquish their foes, achieve their quest, and earn permanent glory.

You picked the wrong book for that.

Not that you won't find it in other Big Year books. As I mentioned earlier, a remarkable thing about 2016 is that while Braden and I steadily worked on our own modest Big Year, a phalanx of semiprofessional birders rabidly pursued an unprecedented list of Big Year achievements. By December, four birders had smashed Neil Hayward's 2013 record of 749, and—with less than a week to go—John Weigel achieved the almost incomprehensible feat of notching his 780th ABA species for the year. Each of the top four birders also sighted two or three "provisional" species that the ABA was considering adding to its official list. If all are included, that will raise Weigel's total to an even more astounding 783.

As impressed as Braden and I were by these achievements, neither of us thought it was something we would ever try to duplicate, let alone top. True, we had talked about doing a major Big Year at some point, but, beyond financial and time considerations, I didn't see the point of trying to set a new record. What we *did* think might be possible was to enjoy seeing 600 or so ABA birds in a year—or, perhaps during a lifetime, trying to see every species that nested in the United States and Canada. Both of those goals held more of a learning incentive than bragging rights.

Of course, even as you read this, the numbers keep changing. The ABA constantly adds and subtracts species to its official list as new migrants show up and scientists "lump" and "split" birds into new species and groups. While Braden and I were winding down our Big Year, the ABA handed down one of its all-time whoppers of a decision—to bring Hawaii into the fold. That edict, which wouldn't go into effect for a year or two, would add more than one hundred new species to the ABA list, including a large number of exotics that have become naturalized in the islands.

What did it all mean?

The answer: whatever you wanted it to. And that was as it should be. As other big-time Big Year birders had admitted, getting too hung up on statistics and competition robbed people of the real joys of finding, observing, and learning about some of Earth's most amazing creatures. It was a trap I was determined not to fall into, and I think Braden felt the same way.

December 31, 2016, dawned cold and beautiful over western Montana. Braden and I loaded the minivan and then drove over to pick up Nick at his mom's house for a final half day of looking for our favorite critters. The pressure was off. None of us had any expectations of adding to our lists. We just wanted to enjoy a final session of birding before 2016 closed out forever. We decided to begin by hitting a place only Nick had been to before: Slevin's Island out at Fort Missoula. One of the bird guys down at MPG Ranch had reported a Saw-whet Owl there, and we thought that would make a fun bird to seek out.

Temperatures hung around twenty degrees, but the sun shone brightly under blue skies as we clomped through a foot of snow blanketing the island. We didn't find the Saw-whet but ran across chickadees and Red-breasted Nuthatches and discovered a surprising group of American Goldfinches at the west end of the island.

"Where to next?" I asked the boys as we headed back to the minivan.

Neither of them offered a strong opinion, so I suggested, "How about we return to Maclay Flat? Maybe we'll see a Great Gray Owl or at least get a better look at a pygmy?"

"Sure," they replied.

After a quick stop at Starbucks, we proceeded with the plan. I had to admit to feeling a bit of melancholy pulling into the Maclay Flat parking lot. This would be our last birding adventure of a remarkable year—one that Braden and I would always remember. Even though I didn't expect to see anything in particular, I felt grateful for all we'd done and seen, and I was especially happy that Nick could close out the year with us too.

We stayed in the minivan for a few minutes, watching the patch of forest where we'd seen our first Northern Pygmy-Owl a couple of weeks earlier, but nary a bird foraged in front of us.

"Okay, guys," I said, thrusting open my door. "Let's see what's out there."

As before, we began walking the two-mile loop trail counterclockwise. We passed through a small patch of Ponderosa forest and approached an open, marshy area bordered by cottonwoods.

As we broke out into the sun, Nick suddenly called out. "Pygmy-owl!"

"What?" I demanded, not sure that I believed him.

In a second my eyes zeroed in on what he was looking at—a small, oblong lump perched high in the bare branches of an aspen or birch tree a hundred yards distant.

Throughout my birding career, I had become an expert at finding "owls" made of broken stumps or leaves or other items in trees, and I knew I wasn't alone in having that skill. Looking at Nick's owl, however, I immediately sensed that he might be on to something. I whipped my binoculars to my eyes, focused, and—

"Yes!" I said. "Amazing! Do you see him, Braden?"

"I see him!"

The owl sat perfectly exposed in full sunlight, seemingly without a care in the world, and the boys and I scrambled to get into better positions to photograph it. We scooted down into a frozen canal, crawled up the other side, and slogged through the foot-deep snow until the owl's perch rose only twenty or thirty yards from us. The pygmy didn't even yawn.

By this time we weren't the only ones watching this grand, diminutive raptor. Half a dozen chickadees had located it too and were swarming it, trying to drive it away. The chickadees weren't stupid. They maintained a good five-foot distance, but their efforts were in vain. The owl would glance at one of them now and then, as if to say, *Oh, give it up already. You and I both know who has the upper beak here.* Then it would resume scanning for potential prey in the meadow where Braden, Nick, and I were standing.

We watched and photographed the owl for a good ten minutes before slogging back across the canal to the main trail, but our encounter hadn't ended. Back on the trail we spotted a Brown Creeper and were watching it through binoculars when Braden called out, "Hey, the owl just flew down into the trees."

I spun around. "Where?"

Braden pointed to a group of pines only twenty yards away, and Nick and I went to investigate. I crept slowly past one tree and peered into the inner branches of a second. I didn't expect to see anything, but there it was—the Northern Pygmy-Owl, sitting on a branch only fifteen feet from where I stood! Nick saw it a split second later, and we both slowly sank into sitting positions and removed the lens caps from our cameras.

"Braden," I whispered as loudly as I dared. "Come over here."

"What is it?" he asked, trying to get a good photo of the Brown Creeper.

"The pygmy!" I hissed.

"Pygmy Nuthatch?"

"No. The owl!"

As Braden hurried to join us, the owl remained poised on its perch. The three of us fired off more than a hundred photos of the spectacular animal while it watched a Red-breasted Nuthatch trying to harass it from above. A woman passed us with a dog, and two cross-country skiers slipped and scrabbled by on the icy trail. The owl didn't move.

We photographed the raptor from almost every possible angle until finally it flew off. The boys and I just looked at each other.

"Can you believe that?" I asked them, awe filling my voice.

None of us could. Even for Nick it was one of the most remarkable bird encounters of his life.

As we tromped back to the car, Braden asked, "What do you think, Daddy? Definite Bird of the Year?"

I ticked through the other candidates we'd discussed in recent weeks: Painted Redstarts, Vermillion Flycatchers, Roseate Spoonbills, even California Condors. They—and many other birds—had been spectacular and unforgettable, and each of them deserved a top spot. Still, for sheer stunning and emotional impact, I could think of nothing that outdazzled this one pint-sized owl.

"Yeah," I told Braden with a smile. "I think you're right. Bird of the Year."

DECEMBER BIRD LIST

Sneed's List (5)	Braden's List (3)
White-throated Sparrow	Wilson's Snipe
Yellow-bellied Sapsucker	Prairie Falcon
Prairie Falcon	Bohemian Waxwing
Bohemian Waxwing	
Gray Partridge	

epilogue

January 1, 2017

Braden and I kicked off our 2017 birding much as we'd begun it in 2016—by getting the minivan stuck in the snow. This time, we weren't on Highway 12 looking for Black-backed Woodpeckers. We were down at the MPG Ranch, trying to remember how to reach the main house so we could pick up Nick. As soon as we drove through the ranch's security gate, we made not one but *two* wrong turns and soon found ourselves driving up an unplowed road heading into the wilderness. Fortunately I realized our mistake and began slowly reversing, my head out the window, looking behind me. As a famous author once wrote, however, "The road was narrow and the minivan was wide." In less than a minute, I'd wandered off the main track and jammed us into a drift of frozen white stuff.

During the last few months of 2016, Braden and I had discussed our birding strategy for 2017, and he understood that I had neither the time nor resources for another nationwide birding year. I was surprised to discover, though, that Braden didn't necessarily want to do another ABA Big Year—at least not right away.

"I'm thinking," he told me during one of our discussions, "that we should do a Montana Big Year next year."

"Hmm, that's not a bad idea," I said. "How come?"

"Well, we still haven't seen a lot of Montana birds, especially in the eastern part of the state. I also just want to get better at finding and identifying the birds around here. I know some of the birds by song, but I want to learn other calls too, especially warblers and other songbirds."

I nodded appreciatively. My son's comments not only made sense, they showed how much deeper his passion for birds had become during the past year. From mainly "collecting" birds like he had once collected Pokémon cards, he had progressed to wanting to understand birds better and improve his skills. As his dad, I couldn't have been more pleased by this evolution.

"But you know," I told Braden. "I won't have as much time this year as last year. I really have to work hard and make some money."

"I know," he said. "But don't you think we could take a few trips around the state?"

I laughed. In some ways, my son knew me better than I knew myself.

"Yeah," I admitted. "Probably."

To build momentum for our new plan, we had agreed to pick up Nick on New Year's Day and see what we could see. A couple of feet of snow had already fallen in the preceding couple of weeks, but the roads had been cleared and were in good driving shape. As we prepared to set out, the weather report promised conditions that were just as dismal as for our first day of birding in 2016: cold and, worse, with the likelihood of a new snowstorm sweeping down from the north.

Nevertheless, when I woke, the snow hadn't yet fallen and temperatures hovered around a balmy fourteen degrees. I walked Lola, then returned home to wake Braden.

Even with the cold weather and approaching snow, the birds seemed active as we drove through Missoula and south toward the Bitterroots. As in 2016, our first year bird was a Black-billed Magpie, and we spotted flickers, Collared Doves, and a surprise Belted Kingfisher before we left the city limits. By the time we reached MPG, our 2017 bird count stood at seven, and we were revved to collect Nick and blow out our list.

Until we got stuck in the snow.

The good news? This year I'd brought snow shovels. After five minutes of digging, Braden and I were able to free ourselves of the snow's tenacious grip. It's true that I got us stuck one more time before we made it to Nick's, but at least we *did* make it there, and, by the time we arrived, Nick's own 2017 count already stood at six. He took us around to their backyard feeders to collect Dark-eyed Juncos and House Sparrows, and then we headed off to see what we could find around the rest of the ranch.

As before, our main targets were Snow Buntings, along with rosy finches, Horned Larks, and maybe a Long-eared Owl.

We saw none of them.

We did trudge up a snow-filled draw to see Clark's Nutcrackers and checked out another feeder to pick up American Goldfinches and Townsend's Solitaire. A flock of American Tree Sparrows settled onto a slope above the road, and we kept whittling away at birds that, though they weren't Code 3s and 4s, provided welcome additions to our lists.

With the snow front closing in, we finally abandoned MPG to "go ducking" at Lee Metcalf ten miles to the south. Arriving at the refuge, we were dismayed to see the ponds almost totally frozen over. Parking near the one tiny patch of remaining open water, we flushed a Common Goldeneye and a few Mallards, but after watching them for a few minutes, I told the boys, "Well, it doesn't look like we're going to set any records here today. You up for a walk around the forest trail?"

"I am," said Nick.

"Good," I said.

Driving down to the trailhead, we saw a small flight of Tundra Swans and a few Ring-necked Pheasants but no turkeys as we'd seen the previous year. The forest trail didn't offer much either. We picked up only dippers along the Bitterroot River, a lone Hairy Woodpecker, and a few chickadees before thick curtains of snow finally began to fall.

So much snow came down so fast that as we left the refuge I worried about making it safely back to town. I called Nick's dad, Phillip, and asked if he could meet us at the MPG gate so that I wouldn't get stuck again before heading back to Missoula.

"I have to go into town, anyway," Phillip told me. "How about if we just meet at your house?"

Whew, I thought. *Maybe we'll make it back okay after all.*

Cars were crawling at thirty miles per hour on the Eastside Highway, and my anxiety grew. We followed one Jeep that kept swerving out into the middle of the road, evidently unaware that traffic was speeding toward him in the opposite direction.

"We may have to perform some emergency first-aid soon," I told the boys.

Braden and Nick took me seriously—and I realized that I was only partly joking.

"What would that involve?" Nick asked.

I paused to consider it. "Well, out here, mostly stopping any bleeding, keeping people still, and most important, calling 911 and directing traffic," I told them.

To our relief, the driver of the Jeep eventually figured out that he was on a major two-lane highway and started keeping to the right.

We made it to Missoula without incident, our bird count at twenty-seven—just two more than on New Year's Day in 2016. As we turned up the Rattlesnake Valley toward our house, I saw a raven sitting in a tree.

"Stop! Merlin!" Braden shouted.

"You're kidding!"

I slowly circled the block, and, sure enough, a Merlin sat in a fruit tree next to the main road. The same bird that had garnered Bird of the Day honors on our first day of 2016 had swooped in at the last minute to retain its crown for 2017. Nick, Braden, and I all high-fived each other. Then, for extra measure, we drove around the neighborhood until we picked up Cedar and Bohemian Waxwings, pushing our 2017 total to thirty-one species.

None of us had any idea what the rest of the year would bring. We didn't know what birds we'd find or even how many birding opportunities we might have. We didn't know what disasters the world's megalomaniacs might rain down on the planet. What we did know is that this day, along with our adventures of 2016, reinforced one loud, unmistakable message: keep birding.

SNEED'S BIG YEAR LIST (336)

Acorn Woodpecker: Madera Canyon, Arizona, March
American Avocet: Bolivar Peninsula, Texas, April
American Bittern: San Bernardino National Wildlife Refuge, Arizona, April
American Coot: Lee Metcalf National Wildlife Refuge, Montana, January
American Crow: Rattlesnake Canyon, Montana, January
American Dipper: Bass Creek Trail, Montana, May
American Goldfinch: Our backyard, Montana, April
American Kestrel: Saguaro National Park, Arizona, March
American Pipit: Fort Missoula gravel quarry, Montana, October
American Redstart: Sabine Woods, Texas, April
American Robin: Georgetown Bench Trail, Maryland, February
American Three-toed Woodpecker: Pattee Canyon, Montana, June
American Tree Sparrow: Fort Missoula gravel quarry, Montana, November
American White Pelican: Moss Landing Harbor, California, September
American Wigeon: Lee Metcalf National Wildlife Refuge, Montana, March
Anna's Hummingbird: Saguaro National Park, Arizona, March
Arizona Woodpecker: Madera Canyon, Arizona, March
Ashy Storm-Petrel: Shearwater Journeys, California, September
Bald Eagle: Lee Metcalf National Wildlife Refuge, Montana, January
Band-tailed Pigeon: Carmel Valley Ranch, California, September
Bank Swallow: Lee Metcalf National Wildlife Refuge, Montana, May
Barn Owl: Bolivar Peninsula, Texas, April
Barn Swallow: Interstate crossing, Texas, April
Barrow's Goldeneye: Lee Metcalf National Wildlife Refuge, Montana, March
Bay-breasted Warbler: Sabine Woods, Texas, April
Bell's Sparrow: La Gloria Road, California, September
Belted Kingfisher: Kim Williams Natural Area, Montana, February
Bewick's Wren: Madera Canyon, Arizona, March
Black Oystercatcher: Monterey Bay pelagic tour, California, September
Black Phoebe: Carmel Valley Ranch, California, September
Black Tern: Bolivar Peninsula, Texas, April
Black Turnstone: Monterey Bay pelagic tour, California, September
Black Vulture: Capital Crescent Trail, Bethesda, Maryland, February
Black-and-white Warbler: High Island, Texas, April
Black-backed Woodpecker: Lolo Burn, Montana, May
Black-bellied Plover: Bolivar Peninsula, Texas, April
Black-bellied Whistling-Duck: High Island, Texas, April
Black-billed Magpie: Rattlesnake Canyon, Montana, January
Blackburnian Warbler: Sabine Woods, Texas, April
Black-capped Chickadee: Our backyard, Montana, January
Black-chinned Hummingbird: Madera Canyon, Arizona, March
Black-crowned Night-Heron: Monterey Bay pelagic tour, California, September
Black-footed Albatross: Shearwater Journeys, California, September
Black-headed Grosbeak: Greenough Park, Montana, May
Black-necked Stilt: Anahuac National Wildlife Refuge, Texas, April
Black-tailed Gnatcatcher: Desert Botanical Garden, Arizona, April

Black-throated Gray Warbler: Chiricahua Mountains, Arizona, April
Black-throated Green Warbler: Sabine Woods, Texas, April
Black-throated Sparrow: San Bernardino National Wildlife Refuge, Arizona, April
Black-vented Shearwater: Monterey Bay pelagic tour, California, September
Blue Grosbeak: Jesse H. Jones County Park, Texas, April
Blue Jay: Georgetown Bench Trail, Maryland, February
Blue-gray Gnatcatcher: Half Moon Ranch, Arizona, April
Blue-winged Teal: San Bernardino National Wildlife Refuge, Arizona, April
Blue-winged Warbler: Sabine Woods, Texas, April
Boat-tailed Grackle: Anahuac National Wildlife Refuge, Texas, April
Bobolink: Bass Creek Trail, Montana, May
Bohemian Waxwing: Ninepipe National Wildlife Refuge, Montana, December
Brandt's Cormorant: Monterey Bay pelagic tour, California, September
Brewer's Blackbird: Clubhouse Floodplain, MPG Ranch, Montana, May
Brewer's Sparrow: Saguaro National Park, Arizona, March
Bridled Titmouse: Madera Canyon, Arizona, March
Broad-billed Hummingbird: Madera Canyon, Arizona, March
Broad-tailed Hummingbird: Ramsey Canyon Preserve, Arizona, April
Brown Creeper: Maclay Flat Recreation Area, Montana, January
Brown Pelican: Bolivar Peninsula, Texas, April
Brown Thrasher: Sabine Woods, Texas, April
Brown-headed Cowbird: Clubhouse Floodplain, MPG Ranch, Montana, May
Bufflehead: Lee Metcalf National Wildlife Refuge, Montana, March
Buller's Shearwater: Shearwater Journeys, California, September
Bullock's Oriole: Orchard House, MPG Ranch, Montana, May
Bushtit: Portland Audubon Bird Sanctuary, Oregon, June
Cactus Wren: Saguaro National Park, Arizona, March
California Condor: Grimes Point, Big Sur coast, California, September
California Gull: Monterey Bay pelagic tour, California, September
California Quail: Lee Metcalf National Wildlife Refuge, Montana, May
California Scrub-Jay: Carmel Valley Ranch, California, September
California Towhee: Carmel Valley Ranch, California, September
Calliope Hummingbird: Blue Mountain Nature Trail, Montana, June
Canada Goose: Lee Metcalf National Wildlife Refuge, Montana, January
Canyon Towhee: San Bernardino National Wildlife Refuge, Arizona, April
Canyon Wren: Pictograph Cave State Park, Montana, May
Carolina Chickadee: Jesse H. Jones County Park, Texas, April
Carolina Wren: Jesse H. Jones County Park, Texas, April
Caspian Tern: West Point, Discovery Park, Washington, September
Cassin's Vireo: Blue Mountain Nature Trail, Montana, June
Cattle Egret: High Island, Texas, April
Cedar Waxwing: Half Moon Ranch, Arizona, April
Chestnut-backed Chickadee: Portland Audubon Bird Sanctuary, Oregon, June
Chimney Swift: High Island, Texas, April
Chipping Sparrow: Madera Canyon, Arizona, March
Cinnamon Teal: San Bernardino National Wildlife Refuge, Arizona, April
Clark's Grebe: Moonglow Dairy, California, September
Clark's Nutcracker: Discovery Ski Area, Montana, February

Cliff Swallow: Pictograph Cave State Park, Montana, May
Common Gallinule: High Island, Texas, April
Common Goldeneye: Lee Metcalf National Wildlife Refuge, Montana, January
Common Grackle: Jesse H. Jones County Park, Texas, April
Common Hill Myna: Miami, Florida, June
Common Merganser: Kim Williams Natural Area, Montana, February
Common Murre: Monterey Bay pelagic tour, California, September
Common Nighthawk: Miles City Park, Montana, July
Common Raven: Lee Metcalf National Wildlife Refuge, Montana, January
Common Tern: Bolivar Peninsula, Texas, April
Common Yellowthroat: Anahuac National Wildlife Refuge, Texas, April
Cooper's Hawk: La Gloria Road, California, September
Crested Caracara: High Island, Texas, April
Curve-billed Thrasher: Saguaro National Park, Arizona, March
Dark-eyed Junco: Our backyard, Montana, January
Double-crested Cormorant: High Island, Texas, April
Downy Woodpecker: Lee Metcalf National Wildlife Refuge, Montana, January
Dunlin: Bolivar Peninsula, Texas, April
Dusky Flycatcher: Lolo Burn, Montana, May
Eared Grebe: Moss Landing Harbor, California, September
Eastern Bluebird: Cumberland County, Pennsylvania, February
Eastern Kingbird: Sabine Woods, Texas, April
Eastern Wood-Pewee: Sabine Woods, Texas, April
Egyptian Goose: Miami, Florida, June
Elegant Tern: Monterey Bay pelagic tour, California, September
Eurasian Collared-Dove: Saguaro National Park, Arizona, March
European Starling: Rattlesnake Canyon, Montana, January
Evening Grosbeak: Pattee Canyon, Montana, June
Ferruginous Hawk: Mullan Road, Missoula, Montana, January
Forster's Tern: Bolivar Peninsula, Texas, April
Fox Sparrow: Seeley Lake, Montana, May
Gadwall: Lee Metcalf National Wildlife Refuge, Montana, May
Gambel's Quail: Ramsey Canyon Preserve, Arizona, April
Gila Woodpecker: Saguaro National Park, Arizona, March
Glaucous-winged Gull: West Point, Discovery Park, Washington, September
Golden Eagle: Lee Metcalf National Wildlife Refuge, Montana, March
Golden-crowned Kinglet: Maclay Flat Recreation Area, Montana, November
Golden-crowned Sparrow: Moonglow Dairy, California, September
Gray Catbird: Sabine Woods, Texas, April
Gray Jay: Discovery Ski Area, Montana, February
Gray Partridge: Pea's Farm Trail, Montana, December
Gray-cheeked Thrush: High Island, Texas, April
Great Blue Heron: Lee Metcalf National Wildlife Refuge, Montana, January
Great Egret: Jesse H. Jones County Park, Texas, April
Great Horned Owl: San Bernardino National Wildlife Refuge, Arizona, April
Greater Pewee: Ramsey Canyon Preserve, Arizona, April
Greater Roadrunner: San Bernardino National Wildlife Refuge, Arizona, April
Greater White-fronted Goose: San Luis National Wildlife Refuge, California, November

Greater Yellowlegs: Moonglow Dairy, California, September
Great-tailed Grackle: Saguaro National Park, Arizona, March
Green Heron: High Island, Texas, April
Green-winged Teal: Lee Metcalf National Wildlife Refuge, Montana, January
Hairy Woodpecker: Lolo Burn area, Montana, January
Hammond's Flycatcher: Blue Mountain Nature Trail, Montana, June
Harris's Hawk: Saguaro National Park, Arizona, March
Heermann's Gull: West Point, Discovery Park, Washington, September
Hepatic Tanager: Ramsey Canyon, Arizona, April
Hermit Thrush: Lee Metcalf National Wildlife Refuge, Montana, May
Hooded Merganser: Lee Metcalf National Wildlife Refuge, Montana, March
Hooded Warbler: Sabine Woods, Texas, April
Horned Grebe: Richmond Marina, California, November
Horned Lark: Pictograph Cave State Park, Montana, March
House Finch: Mullan Road, Missoula, Montana, January
House Sparrow: Mullan Road, Missoula, Montana, January
House Wren: Ramsey Canyon Preserve, Arizona, April
Hutton's Vireo: Ramsey Canyon Preserve, Arizona, April
Inca Dove: High Island, Texas, April
Indigo Bunting: Jesse H. Jones County Park, Texas, April
Killdeer: Lee Metcalf National Wildlife Refuge, Montana, January
Ladder-backed Woodpecker: Half Moon Ranch, Arizona, April
Lark Sparrow: San Benito County Historical Park, California, September
Laughing Gull: Bolivar Peninsula, Texas, April
Lawrence's Goldfinch: La Gloria Road, California, September
Lazuli Bunting: Orchard House, MPG Ranch, Montana, May
Least Sandpiper: Moonglow Dairy, California, September
Least Tern: Bolivar Peninsula, Texas, April
Lesser Goldfinch: Madera Canyon, Arizona, March
Lesser Scaup: Lee Metcalf National Wildlife Refuge, Montana, January
Lewis's Woodpecker: Clubhouse Floodplain, MPG Ranch, Montana, May
Little Blue Heron: High Island, Texas, April
Loggerhead Shrike: Interstate 191, Arizona, April
Long-billed Curlew: Moss Landing Harbor, California, September
Long-billed Dowitcher: Moonglow Dairy, California, September
Long-eared Owl: Long-eared Owl banding area, Montana, January
Lucy's Warbler: San Bernardino National Wildlife Refuge, Arizona, April
MacGillivray's Warbler: Lolo Burn, Montana, May
Magnificent Frigatebird: Miami, Florida, June
Magnificent (Rivoli's) Hummingbird: Madera Canyon, Arizona, March
Mallard: Lee Metcalf National Wildlife Refuge, Montana, January
Marbled Godwit: Bolivar Peninsula, Texas, April
Marsh Wren: Lee Metcalf National Wildlife Refuge, Montana, May
Merlin: Lee Metcalf National Wildlife Refuge, Montana, January
Mexican Jay: Madera Canyon, Arizona, March
Mottled Duck: Anahuac National Wildlife Refuge, Texas, April
Mountain Bluebird: Pictograph Cave State Park, Montana, March
Mountain Chickadee: Our backyard, Montana, January

Mourning Dove: Lee Metcalf National Wildlife Refuge, Montana, January
Neotropic Cormorant: High Island, Texas, April
Northern Cardinal: Cumberland County, Pennsylvania, February
Northern Flicker: Lee Metcalf National Wildlife Refuge, Montana, January
Northern Harrier: Lee Metcalf National Wildlife Refuge, Montana, May
Northern Mockingbird: Capital Crescent Trail, Bethesda, Maryland, February
Northern Pintail: Lee Metcalf National Wildlife Refuge, Montana, January
Northern Pygmy-Owl: Maclay Flat Recreation Area, Montana, November
Northern Rough-winged Swallow: San Bernardino National Wildlife Refuge, Arizona, April
Northern Shoveler: Lee Metcalf National Wildlife Refuge, Montana, May
Northern Shrike: Kelly Island Trails, Montana, January
Northern Waterthrush: High Island, Texas, April
Nuttall's Woodpecker: San Benito County Historical Park, California, September
Oak Titmouse: San Benito County Historical Park, California, September
Orange-crowned Warbler: Blue Mountain Nature Trail, Montana, June
Orchard Oriole: High Island, Texas, April
Osprey: Seeley Lake, Montana, May
Ovenbird: Sabine Woods, Texas, April
Pacific Wren: Portland Audubon Bird Sanctuary, Oregon, June
Pacific-slope Flycatcher: Moonglow Dairy, California, September
Painted Redstart: Madera Canyon, Arizona, March
Pelagic Cormorant: Monterey Bay pelagic tour, California, September
Peregrine Falcon: Monterey Bay pelagic tour, California, September
Phainopepla: Half Moon Ranch, Arizona, April
Pied-billed Grebe: High Island, Texas, April
Pigeon Guillemot: Monterey Bay pelagic tour, California, September
Pileated Woodpecker: Rattlesnake Canyon, Montana, January
Pine Siskin: Discovery Ski Area, Montana, February
Pink-footed Shearwater: Monterey Bay pelagic tour, California, September
Piping Plover: Bolivar Peninsula, Texas, April
Pomarine Jaeger: Shearwater Journeys, California, September
Prairie Falcon: Ninepipe National Wildlife Refuge, Montana, December
Prothonotary Warbler: Jesse H. Jones County Park, Texas, April
Purple Gallinule: High Island, Texas, April
Pygmy Nuthatch: Our backyard, Montana, January
Pyrrhuloxia: Saguaro National Park, Arizona, March
Red Crossbill: Blue Mountain Nature Trail, Montana, October
Red-bellied Woodpecker: Jesse H. Jones County Park, Texas, April
Red-breasted Nuthatch: Maclay Flat Recreation Area, Montana, January
Red-breasted Sapsucker: Portland Audubon Bird Sanctuary, Oregon, June
Red-cockaded Woodpecker: W G Jones State Forest, Texas, April
Red-eyed Vireo: Sabine Woods, Texas, April
Redhead: Lee Metcalf National Wildlife Refuge, Montana, May
Red-headed Woodpecker: Jesse H. Jones County Park, Texas, April
Red-naped Sapsucker: Chiricahua Mountains, Arizona, April
Red-necked Grebe: Placid Lake, Montana, May
Red-necked Phalarope: Shearwater Journeys, California, September
Red-shouldered Hawk: La Gloria Road, California, September

Red-tailed Hawk: Lee Metcalf National Wildlife Refuge, Montana, January
Red-winged Blackbird: Lee Metcalf National Wildlife Refuge, Montana, March
Rhinoceros Auklet: Monterey Bay pelagic tour, California, September
Ring-billed Gull: Pier 4, Baltimore Inner Harbor, Maryland, February
Ring-necked Duck: Lee Metcalf National Wildlife Refuge, Montana, March
Ring-necked Pheasant: Lee Metcalf National Wildlife Refuge, Montana, January
Rock Pigeon: Rattlesnake Canyon, Montana, January
Rock Wren: Orchard House, MPG Ranch, Montana, May
Roseate Spoonbill: Interstate crossing, Texas, April
Rose-breasted Grosbeak: High Island, Texas, April
Rough-legged Hawk: Lee Metcalf National Wildlife Refuge, Montana, January
Royal Tern: Bolivar Peninsula, Texas, April
Ruby-crowned Kinglet: Half Moon Ranch, Arizona, April
Ruby-throated Hummingbird: High Island, Texas, April
Ruddy Duck: Moonglow Dairy, California, September
Ruddy Turnstone: Bolivar Peninsula, Texas, April
Ruffed Grouse: Placid Lake, Montana, May
Rufous Hummingbird: Seeley Lake, Montana, May
Sanderling: Bolivar Peninsula, Texas, April
Sandhill Crane: Lee Metcalf National Wildlife Refuge, Montana, May
Sandwich Tern: Bolivar Peninsula, Texas, April
Savannah Sparrow: Carmel Valley Ranch, California, September
Say's Phoebe: Half Moon Ranch, Arizona, April
Scaled Quail: Chiricahua Mountains, Arizona, April
Scarlet Tanager: High Island, Texas, April
Scissor-tailed Flycatcher: Anahuac National Wildlife Refuge, Texas, April
Semipalmated Plover: Bolivar Peninsula, Texas, April
Sharp-shinned Hawk: Seeley Lake, Montana, May
Short-billed Dowitcher: Bolivar Peninsula, Texas, April
Snow Goose: Interstate 90 near Warm Springs, Montana, March
Snowy Egret: High Island, Texas, April
Snowy Plover: Moss Landing Harbor, California, September
Solitary Sandpiper: Anahuac National Wildlife Refuge, Texas, April
Song Sparrow: Seeley Lake, Montana, May
Sooty Shearwater: Monterey Bay pelagic tour, California, September
Spotted Sandpiper: Clubhouse Floodplain, MPG Ranch, Montana, May
Spotted Towhee: Chiricahua Mountains, Arizona, April
Steller's Jay: Discovery Ski Area, Montana, February
Summer Tanager: High Island, Texas, April
Surf Scoter: Moss Landing Harbor, California, September
Surfbird: Monterey Bay pelagic tour, California, September
Swainson's Hawk: Chiricahua Mountains, Arizona, April
Swainson's Thrush: Sabine Woods, Texas, April
Tennessee Warbler: High Island, Texas, April
Townsend's Solitaire: Ramsey Canyon Preserve, Arizona, April
Townsend's Warbler: Madera Canyon, Arizona, March
Tree Swallow: San Bernardino National Wildlife Refuge, Arizona, April
Tricolored Blackbird: Moonglow Dairy, California, September
Tricolored Heron: High Island, Texas, April

Trumpeter Swan: Lee Metcalf National Wildlife Refuge, Montana, October
Tufted Flycatcher: Ramsey Canyon Preserve, Arizona, April
Tufted Puffin: Shearwater Journeys, California, September
Tufted Titmouse: Jesse H. Jones County Park, Texas, April
Tundra Swan: Interstate 90 near Warm Springs, Montana, March
Turkey Vulture: Saguaro National Park, Arizona, March
Vaux's Swift: Lee Metcalf National Wildlife Refuge, Montana, May
Verdin: Half Moon Ranch, Arizona, March
Vermilion Flycatcher: Half Moon Ranch, Arizona, March
Vesper Sparrow: Orchard House, MPG Ranch, Montana, May
Violet-green Swallow: Chiricahua Mountains, Arizona, April
Warbling Vireo: Seeley Lake, Montana, May
Western Bluebird: Lolo Burn, Montana, May
Western Grebe: Moonglow Dairy, California, September
Western Gull: West Point, Discovery Park, Washington, September
Western Kingbird: Orchard House, MPG Ranch, Montana, May
Western Meadowlark: Clubhouse Floodplain, MPG Ranch, Montana, May
Western Sandpiper: Bolivar Peninsula, Texas, April
Western Tanager: Bass Creek Trail, Montana, May
Western Wood-Pewee: Clubhouse Floodplain, MPG Ranch, Montana, May
Whimbrel: Anahuac National Wildlife Refuge, Texas, April
White Ibis: High Island, Texas, April
White-breasted Nuthatch: Maclay Flat Recreation Area, Montana, January
White-crowned Sparrow: ARCO gas station, Arizona, April
White-eyed Vireo: High Island, Texas, April
White-faced Ibis: Anahuac National Wildlife Refuge, Texas, April
White-tailed Kite: Año Nuevo State Park, California, September
White-throated Sparrow: Schoolhouse Pond, Maryland, December
White-throated Swift: Half Moon Ranch, Arizona, April
White-winged Dove: Saguaro National Park, Arizona, March
Wild Turkey: Lee Metcalf National Wildlife Refuge, Montana, January
Willet: Bolivar Peninsula, Texas, April
Williamson's Sapsucker: Blue Mountain Nature Trail, Montana, June
Willow Flycatcher: Seeley Lake, Montana, May
Wilson's Snipe: Merced National Wildlife Refuge, California, November
Wilson's Warbler: Portland Audubon Bird Sanctuary, Oregon, June
Wood Duck: Brown neighborhood, Montana, April
Wood Thrush: Sabine Woods, Texas, April
Worm-eating Warbler: Sabine Woods, Texas, April
Wrentit: Carmel Valley Ranch, California, September
Yellow Warbler: San Bernardino National Wildlife Refuge, Arizona, April
Yellow-bellied Sapsucker: Marlborough Estates Golf Course, Maryland, December
Yellow-billed Magpie: La Gloria Road, California, September
Yellow-breasted Chat: Pompeys Pillar National Monument, Montana, July
Yellow-crowned Night-Heron: Sabine Woods, Texas, April
Yellow-headed Blackbird: Lee Metcalf National Wildlife Refuge, Montana, May
Yellow-rumped Warbler: Saguaro National Park, Arizona, March
Yellow-throated Vireo: Sabine Woods, Texas, April
Zone-tailed Hawk: Chiricahua Mountains, Arizona, April

BRADEN'S BIG YEAR LIST (330)

Acorn Woodpecker: Madera Canyon, Arizona, March
American Avocet: Bolivar Peninsula, Texas, April
American Bittern: San Bernardino National Wildlife Refuge, Arizona, April
American Coot: Lee Metcalf National Wildlife Refuge, Montana, January
American Crow: Rattlesnake Canyon, Montana, January
American Dipper: Lolo Burn area, Montana, January
American Goldfinch: Jumbo Saddle via Tivoli Trail, Montana, May
American Kestrel: Rattlesnake Canyon, Montana, January
American Pipit: Fort Missoula gravel quarry, Montana, October
American Redstart: Sabine Woods, Texas, April
American Robin: Chiricahua Mountains, Arizona, April
American Three-toed Woodpecker: Pattee Canyon, Montana, June
American Tree Sparrow: Fort Missoula gravel quarry, Montana, November
American White Pelican: Moss Landing Harbor, California, September
American Wigeon: Lee Metcalf National Wildlife Refuge, Montana, March
Anna's Hummingbird: Saguaro National Park, Arizona, March
Arizona Woodpecker: Madera Canyon, Arizona, March
Bald Eagle: Lee Metcalf National Wildlife Refuge, Montana, January
Band-tailed Pigeon: Carmel Valley Ranch, California, September
Bank Swallow: Lee Metcalf National Wildlife Refuge, Montana, May
Barn Owl: Bolivar Peninsula, Texas, April
Barn Swallow: Interstate crossing, Texas, April
Barrow's Goldeneye: Lee Metcalf National Wildlife Refuge, Montana, March
Bay-breasted Warbler: Sabine Woods, Texas, April
Bell's Sparrow: La Gloria Road, California, September
Belted Kingfisher: Kim Williams Natural Area, Montana, February
Bewick's Wren: Madera Canyon, Arizona, March
Black Oystercatcher: Monterey Bay pelagic tour, California, September
Black Phoebe: Carmel Valley Ranch, California, September
Black Tern: Bolivar Peninsula, Texas, April
Black Turnstone: Monterey Bay pelagic tour, California, September
Black Vulture: W G Jones State Forest, Texas, April
Black-and-white Warbler: High Island, Texas, April
Black-backed Woodpecker: Lolo Burn area, Montana, May
Black-bellied Plover: Bolivar Peninsula, Texas, April
Black-bellied Whistling-Duck: High Island, Texas, April
Black-billed Magpie: Rattlesnake Canyon, Montana, January
Blackburnian Warbler: Sabine Woods, Texas, April
Black-capped Chickadee: Our backyard, Montana, January
Black-chinned Hummingbird: Madera Canyon, Arizona, March
Black-crowned Night-Heron: Monterey Bay pelagic tour, California, September
Black-footed Albatross: Shearwater Journeys, California, September
Black-headed Grosbeak: Greenough Park, Montana, May
Black-necked Stilt: Anahuac National Wildlife Refuge, Texas, April
Black-tailed Gnatcatcher: Desert Botanical Garden, Arizona, April
Black-throated Gray Warbler: Chiricahua Mountains, Arizona, April

Black-throated Green Warbler: Sabine Woods, Texas, April
Black-throated Sparrow: San Bernardino National Wildlife Refuge, Arizona, April
Black-vented Shearwater: Monterey Bay pelagic tour, California, September
Blue Grosbeak: Jesse H. Jones County Park, Texas, April
Blue Jay: Jesse H. Jones County Park, Texas, April
Blue-gray Gnatcatcher: Half Moon Ranch, Arizona, April
Blue-winged Teal: San Bernardino National Wildlife Refuge, Arizona, April
Blue-winged Warbler: Sabine Woods, Texas, April
Boat-tailed Grackle: Anahuac National Wildlife Refuge, Texas, April
Bobolink: Bass Creek Trail, Montana, May
Bohemian Waxwing: Ninepipe National Wildlife Refuge, Montana, December
Brandt's Cormorant: Monterey Bay pelagic tour, California, September
Brewer's Blackbird: Clubhouse Floodplain, MPG Ranch, Montana, May
Brewer's Sparrow: Saguaro National Park, Arizona, March
Bridled Titmouse: Madera Canyon, Arizona, March
Broad-billed Hummingbird: Madera Canyon, Arizona, March
Broad-tailed Hummingbird: Ramsey Canyon Preserve, Arizona, April
Brown Creeper: Maclay Flat Recreation Area, Montana, January
Brown Pelican: Bolivar Peninsula, Texas, April
Brown Thrasher: Sabine Woods, Texas, April
Brown-headed Cowbird: Clubhouse Floodplain, MPG Ranch, Montana, May
Bufflehead: Lee Metcalf National Wildlife Refuge, Montana, March
Bullock's Oriole: Orchard House, MPG Ranch, Montana, May
Bushtit: Discovery Park, Washington, May
Cactus Wren: Saguaro National Park, Arizona, March
California Condor: Grimes Point, Big Sur coast, California, September
California Gull: Monterey Bay pelagic tour, California, September
California Quail: Lee Metcalf National Wildlife Refuge, Montana, May
California Scrub-Jay: Carmel Valley Ranch, California, September
California Towhee: Carmel Valley Ranch, California, September
Calliope Hummingbird: Blue Mountain Nature Trail, Montana, June
Canada Goose: Lee Metcalf National Wildlife Refuge, Montana, January
Canvasback: Interstate 90 near Warm Springs, Montana, March
Canyon Towhee: San Bernardino National Wildlife Refuge, Arizona, April
Carolina Chickadee: Jesse H. Jones County Park, Texas, April
Carolina Wren: Jesse H. Jones County Park, Texas, April
Caspian Tern: West Point, Discovery Park, Washington, September
Cassin's Vireo: Blue Mountain Nature Trail, Montana, June
Cattle Egret: High Island, Texas, April
Cedar Waxwing: Half Moon Ranch, Arizona, April
Chestnut-backed Chickadee: Discovery Park, Washington, May
Chimney Swift: High Island, Texas, April
Chipping Sparrow: Madera Canyon, Arizona, March
Cinnamon Teal: San Bernardino National Wildlife Refuge, Arizona, April
Clark's Grebe: Moonglow Dairy, California, September
Clark's Nutcracker: Discovery Ski Area, Montana, February
Cliff Swallow: Lee Metcalf National Wildlife Refuge, Montana, May
Common Gallinule: High Island, Texas, April

Common Goldeneye: Lee Metcalf National Wildlife Refuge, Montana, January
Common Grackle: Jesse H. Jones County Park, Texas, April
Common Hill Myna: Miami, Florida, June
Common Merganser: Kim Williams Natural Area, Montana, February
Common Murre: Monterey Bay pelagic tour, California, September
Common Nighthawk: Our backyard, Montana, July
Common Raven: Lee Metcalf National Wildlife Refuge, Montana, January
Common Tern: Bolivar Peninsula, Texas, April
Common Yellowthroat: Anahuac National Wildlife Refuge, Texas, April
Cooper's Hawk: La Gloria Road, California, September
Crested Caracara: High Island, Texas, April
Curve-billed Thrasher: Saguaro National Park, Arizona, March
Dark-eyed Junco: Our backyard, Montana, January
Double-crested Cormorant: High Island, Texas, April
Downy Woodpecker: Lee Metcalf National Wildlife Refuge, Montana, January
Dunlin: Bolivar Peninsula, Texas, April
Dusky Flycatcher: Lolo Burn area, Montana, May
Eared Grebe: Moss Landing Harbor, California, September
Eastern Bluebird: W G Jones State Forest, Texas, April
Eastern Kingbird: Sabine Woods, Texas, April
Eastern Wood-Pewee: Sabine Woods, Texas, April
Egyptian Goose: Miami, Florida, June
Elegant Tern: Monterey Bay pelagic tour, California, September
Eurasian Collared-Dove: Rattlesnake Canyon, Montana, February
European Starling: Rattlesnake Canyon, Montana, January
Evening Grosbeak: Our backyard, Montana, June
Ferruginous Hawk: Mullan Road, Missoula, Montana, January
Forster's Tern: Bolivar Peninsula, Texas, April
Fox Sparrow: Seeley Lake, Montana, May
Gadwall: Lee Metcalf National Wildlife Refuge, Montana, May
Gambel's Quail: Ramsey Canyon Preserve, Arizona, April
Gila Woodpecker: Saguaro National Park, Arizona, March
Glaucous-winged Gull: Discovery Park, Washington, May
Golden Eagle: Lee Metcalf National Wildlife Refuge, Montana, March
Golden-crowned Kinglet: Maclay Flat Recreation Area, Montana, November
Golden-crowned Sparrow: Moonglow Dairy, California, September
Gray Catbird: Sabine Woods, Texas, April
Gray Jay: Discovery Ski Area, Montana, February
Gray-cheeked Thrush: High Island, Texas, April
Great Blue Heron: Lee Metcalf National Wildlife Refuge, Montana, January
Great Egret: Jesse H. Jones County Park, Texas, April
Great Horned Owl: San Bernardino National Wildlife Refuge, Arizona, April
Greater Pewee: Ramsey Canyon Preserve, Arizona, April
Greater Roadrunner: San Bernardino National Wildlife Refuge, Arizona, April
Greater Yellowlegs: Moonglow Dairy, California, September
Great-tailed Grackle: Saguaro National Park, Arizona, March
Green Heron: High Island, Texas, April
Green-winged Teal: Lee Metcalf National Wildlife Refuge, Montana, January

Hairy Woodpecker: Lolo Burn area, Montana, January
Hammond's Flycatcher: Blue Mountain Nature Trail, Montana, June
Harlequin Duck: Swiftcurrent Lake, Glacier National Park, Montana, August
Harris's Hawk: Saguaro National Park, Arizona, March
Heermann's Gull: West Point, Discovery Park, Washington, September
Hepatic Tanager: Madera Canyon, Arizona, March
Hermit Thrush: Lee Metcalf National Wildlife Refuge, Montana, May
Hooded Merganser: Lee Metcalf National Wildlife Refuge, Montana, March
Hooded Warbler: Sabine Woods, Texas, April
Horned Lark: Pictograph Cave State Park, Montana, March
House Finch: Mullan Road, Missoula, Montana, January
House Sparrow: Mullan Road, Missoula, Montana, January
House Wren: Ramsey Canyon Preserve, Arizona, April
Hutton's Vireo: Ramsey Canyon Preserve, Arizona, April
Inca Dove: High Island, Texas, April
Indigo Bunting: Jesse H. Jones County Park, Texas, April
Killdeer: Lee Metcalf National Wildlife Refuge, Montana, January
Ladder-backed Woodpecker: Half Moon Ranch, Arizona, April
Lark Sparrow: San Benito County Historical Park, California, September
Laughing Gull: Bolivar Peninsula, Texas, April
Lawrence's Goldfinch: La Gloria Road, California, September
Lazuli Bunting: Orchard House, MPG Ranch, Montana, May
Least Sandpiper: Moonglow Dairy, California, September
Least Tern: Bolivar Peninsula, Texas, April
Lesser Goldfinch: Madera Canyon, Arizona, March
Lesser Scaup: Lee Metcalf National Wildlife Refuge, Montana, January
Lewis's Woodpecker: Clubhouse Floodplain, MPG Ranch, Montana, May
Little Blue Heron: High Island, Texas, April
Loggerhead Shrike: Interstate 191, Arizona, April
Long-billed Curlew: Moss Landing Harbor, California, September
Long-billed Dowitcher: Moonglow Dairy, California, September
Long-eared Owl: Long-eared Owl banding area, Montana, January
Lucy's Warbler: San Bernardino National Wildlife Refuge, Arizona, April
MacGillivray's Warbler: Lolo Burn area, Montana, May
Magnificent Frigatebird: Miami, Florida, June
Magnificent (Rivoli's) Hummingbird: Madera Canyon, Arizona, March
Mallard: Lee Metcalf National Wildlife Refuge, Montana, January
Marbled Godwit: Bolivar Peninsula, Texas, April
Marsh Wren: Lee Metcalf National Wildlife Refuge, Montana, May
Merlin: Lee Metcalf National Wildlife Refuge, Montana, January
Mexican Jay: Madera Canyon, Arizona, March
Mottled Duck: Anahuac National Wildlife Refuge, Texas, April
Mountain Bluebird: Pictograph Cave State Park, Montana, March
Mountain Chickadee: Our backyard, Montana, January
Mourning Dove: Lee Metcalf National Wildlife Refuge, Montana, January
Nashville Warbler: Hiawatha Trail, Idaho, June
Neotropic Cormorant: High Island, Texas, April
Northern Cardinal: Saguaro National Park, Arizona, March

Northern Flicker: Lee Metcalf National Wildlife Refuge, Montana, January
Northern Harrier: Lolo Burn area, Montana, January
Northern Mockingbird: Saguaro National Park, Arizona, March
Northern Pintail: Lee Metcalf National Wildlife Refuge, Montana, January
Northern Pygmy-Owl: Maclay Flat Recreation Area, Montana, November
Northern Rough-winged Swallow: San Bernardino National Wildlife Refuge, Arizona, April
Northern Shoveler: Lee Metcalf National Wildlife Refuge, Montana, May
Northern Shrike: Kelly Island Trails, Montana, January
Northern Waterthrush: High Island, Texas, April
Nuttall's Woodpecker: San Benito County Historical Park, California, September
Oak Titmouse: San Benito County Historical Park, California, September
Orange-crowned Warbler: Blue Mountain Nature Trail, Montana, June
Orchard Oriole: High Island, Texas, April
Osprey: Greenough Park, Montana, April
Ovenbird: Sabine Woods, Texas, April
Pacific Wren: Rattlesnake National Recreation Area, Montana, June
Pacific-slope Flycatcher: Moonglow Dairy, California, September
Painted Redstart: Madera Canyon, Arizona, March
Pelagic Cormorant: Monterey Bay pelagic tour, California, September
Peregrine Falcon: Monterey Bay pelagic tour, California, September
Phainopepla: Half Moon Ranch, Arizona, April
Pied-billed Grebe: High Island, Texas, April
Pigeon Guillemot: Monterey Bay pelagic tour, California, September
Pileated Woodpecker: Greenough Park, Montana, February
Pine Siskin: Discovery Ski Area, Montana, February
Pink-footed Shearwater: Monterey Bay pelagic tour, California, September
Piping Plover: Bolivar Peninsula, Texas, April
Pomarine Jaeger: Shearwater Journeys, California, September
Prairie Falcon: Ninepipe National Wildlife Refuge, Montana, December
Prothonotary Warbler: Jesse H. Jones County Park, Texas, April
Purple Gallinule: High Island, Texas, April
Pygmy Nuthatch: Our backyard, Montana, January
Pyrrhuloxia: Saguaro National Park, Arizona, March
Red Crossbill: Blue Mountain Nature Trail, Montana, October
Red-bellied Woodpecker: Jesse H. Jones County Park, Texas, April
Red-breasted Nuthatch: Maclay Flat Recreation Area, Montana, January
Red-breasted Sapsucker: Portland Audubon Bird Sanctuary, Oregon, June
Red-cockaded Woodpecker: W G Jones State Forest, Texas, April
Red-eyed Vireo: Sabine Woods, Texas, April
Redhead: Lee Metcalf National Wildlife Refuge, Montana, May
Red-headed Woodpecker: Jesse H. Jones County Park, Texas, April
Red-naped Sapsucker: Chiricahua Mountains, Arizona, April
Red-necked Grebe: Placid Lake, Montana, May
Red-necked Phalarope: Shearwater Journeys, California, September
Red-shouldered Hawk: La Gloria Road, California, September
Red-tailed Hawk: Lee Metcalf National Wildlife Refuge, Montana, January
Red-winged Blackbird: Lee Metcalf National Wildlife Refuge, Montana, March
Rhinoceros Auklet: Monterey Bay pelagic tour, California, September

Ring-billed Gull: Washington Middle School, Montana, March
Ring-necked Duck: Lee Metcalf National Wildlife Refuge, Montana, March
Ring-necked Pheasant: Lee Metcalf National Wildlife Refuge, Montana, January
Rock Pigeon: Rattlesnake Canyon, Montana, January
Rock Wren: Orchard House, MPG Ranch, Montana, May
Roseate Spoonbill: Interstate crossing, Texas, April
Rose-breasted Grosbeak: High Island, Texas, April
Rough-legged Hawk: Lee Metcalf National Wildlife Refuge, Montana, January
Royal Tern: Bolivar Peninsula, Texas, April
Ruby-crowned Kinglet: Half Moon Ranch, Arizona, April
Ruby-throated Hummingbird: High Island, Texas, April
Ruddy Duck: Moonglow Dairy, California, September
Ruddy Turnstone: Bolivar Peninsula, Texas, April
Ruffed Grouse: Placid Lake, Montana, May
Rufous Hummingbird: Jumbo Saddle via Tivoli Trail, Montana, May
Sanderling: Bolivar Peninsula, Texas, April
Sandhill Crane: Lee Metcalf National Wildlife Refuge, Montana, May
Sandwich Tern: Bolivar Peninsula, Texas, April
Savannah Sparrow: Carmel Valley Ranch, California, September
Say's Phoebe: Half Moon Ranch, Arizona, April
Scaled Quail: Chiricahua Mountains, Arizona, April
Scarlet Tanager: High Island, Texas, April
Scissor-tailed Flycatcher: Anahuac National Wildlife Refuge, Texas, April
Semipalmated Plover: Bolivar Peninsula, Texas, April
Sharp-shinned Hawk: Seeley Lake, Montana, May
Short-billed Dowitcher: Bolivar Peninsula, Texas, April
Snow Goose: Interstate 90 near Warm Springs, Montana, March
Snowy Egret: High Island, Texas, April
Snowy Plover: Moss Landing Harbor, California, September
Solitary Sandpiper: Anahuac National Wildlife Refuge, Texas, April
Song Sparrow: Jumbo Saddle via Tivoli Trail, Montana, April
Sooty Shearwater: Monterey Bay pelagic tour, California, September
Spotted Sandpiper: Clubhouse Floodplain, MPG Ranch, Montana, May
Spotted Towhee: Chiricahua Mountains, Arizona, April
Steller's Jay: Discovery Ski Area, Montana, February
Summer Tanager: High Island, Texas, April
Surf Scoter: Moss Landing Harbor, California, September
Surfbird: Monterey Bay pelagic tour, California, September
Swainson's Hawk: Chiricahua Mountains, Arizona, April
Swainson's Thrush: Sabine Woods, Texas, April
Tennessee Warbler: High Island, Texas, April
Townsend's Solitaire: Fairmont Hot Springs, Montana, February
Townsend's Warbler: Madera Canyon, Arizona, March
Tree Swallow: San Bernardino National Wildlife Refuge, Arizona, April
Tricolored Blackbird: Moonglow Dairy, California, September
Tricolored Heron: High Island, Texas, April
Trumpeter Swan: Lee Metcalf National Wildlife Refuge, Montana, October
Tufted Flycatcher: Ramsey Canyon Preserve, Arizona, April

Tufted Puffin: Shearwater Journeys, California, September
Tufted Titmouse: Jesse H. Jones County Park, Texas, April
Tundra Swan: Interstate 90 near Warm Springs, Montana, March
Turkey Vulture: Saguaro National Park, Arizona, March
Vaux's Swift: Lee Metcalf National Wildlife Refuge, Montana, May
Verdin: Half Moon Ranch, Arizona, March
Vermilion Flycatcher: Half Moon Ranch, Arizona, March
Vesper Sparrow: Orchard House, MPG Ranch, Montana, May
Violet-green Swallow: Chiricahua Mountains, Arizona, April
Warbling Vireo: Seeley Lake, Montana, May
Western Bluebird: Jumbo Saddle via Tivoli Trail, Montana, May
Western Grebe: Moonglow Dairy, California, September
Western Gull: West Point, Discovery Park, Washington, September
Western Kingbird: Orchard House, MPG Ranch, Montana, May
Western Meadowlark: Clubhouse Floodplain, MPG Ranch, Montana, May
Western Sandpiper: Bolivar Peninsula, Texas, April
Western Tanager: Bass Creek Trail, Montana, May
Western Wood-Pewee: Clubhouse Floodplain, MPG Ranch, Montana, May
Whimbrel: Anahuac National Wildlife Refuge, Texas, April
White Ibis: High Island, Texas, April
White-breasted Nuthatch: Maclay Flat Recreation Area, Montana, January
White-crowned Sparrow: ARCO gas station, Arizona, April
White-eyed Vireo: High Island, Texas, April
White-faced Ibis: Anahuac National Wildlife Refuge, Texas, April
White-tailed Kite: Año Nuevo State Park, California, September
White-throated Swift: Half Moon Ranch, Arizona, April
White-winged Dove: Saguaro National Park, Arizona, March
Wild Turkey: Lee Metcalf National Wildlife Refuge, Montana, January
Willet: Bolivar Peninsula, Texas, April
Williamson's Sapsucker: Blue Mountain Nature Trail, Montana, June
Willow Flycatcher: Seeley Lake, Montana, May
Wilson's Snipe: Ninepipe National Wildlife Refuge, Montana, December
Wilson's Warbler: Discovery Park, Washington, May
Wood Duck: Brown neighborhood, Montana, April
Wood Thrush: Sabine Woods, Texas, April
Worm-eating Warbler: Sabine Woods, Texas, April
Wrentit: Carmel Valley Ranch, California, September
Yellow Warbler: San Bernardino National Wildlife Refuge, Arizona, April
Yellow-billed Magpie: La Gloria Road, California, September
Yellow-crowned Night-Heron: Sabine Woods, Texas, April
Yellow-headed Blackbird: Lee Metcalf National Wildlife Refuge, Montana, May
Yellow-rumped Warbler: Saguaro National Park, Arizona, March
Yellow-throated Vireo: Sabine Woods, Texas, April
Zone-tailed Hawk: Chiricahua Mountains, Arizona, April

chirps and tweets

When Braden and I began our Big Year, we had little idea how many wonderful people would befriend us and how many of them would make major contributions to our 2016 birding adventures. Perched at the top of the list, of course, are my wife, Amy, and daughter, Tessa, who remained enthusiastic and supportive of our peregrinations the entire year and good-naturedly helped us with Big Year opportunities. Nick and Phillip Ramsey also played prominent roles both in inspiring and abetting our Big Year plans and in educating us about Montana avifauna. A special shout-out to the members of the Montana's Online Birding (MOB) Group too, for their enthusiasm and generosity in posting bird sightings and, when asked, sharing information for how to locate and identify species.

With these keystones out of the way, I would like to offer additional heartfelt thanks to the following birding support crew, in approximately chronological order: Denver Holt (www.owlinstitute.org), for sharing with us his vast knowledge of owls and reviewing the chapter of this book in which he is featured; Bruce Weide and Pat Tucker for providing us with a once-in-a-lifetime opportunity to stay at Half Moon Ranch and explore one of the most spectacular corners of our country; Steve Kaye (www.stevekaye.com) for his enthusiasm, blogs, and help working through my camera issues; Paul Queneau, also for his camera help and wildlife insights; Ted Wolff for his friendship, birding expertise, and support throughout the year; Wes Homoya and the other guides at Tropical Birding (www.tropicalbirding.com), for helping us wade into shorebirds; Johnny Gibson, for a terrific day birding around the Audubon Society of Portland's Balch Creek sanctuary; Carol and Walter Ratzlaf for making our dream of a Galápagos visit come true; our amazing Galápagos guides: Emma Ridley, Vanessa Gallo, Socrates Tomala, Enrique Silva, Walter Perez, Jonathan Aguas, and Jason Hellmann; and finally, in Ecuador, Paul Abad (www.facebook.com/paul.abad.355) for his passion and excellence in showing us the birds of Guayaquil.

Back stateside, we owe gratitude and thanks to Steve Isaacson, Carol Milne, and their daughters, Mara and Jasmine, for never turning down a chance to take us birding; the family of Bart and Shelley Freese (www.dancingcowstudio.com) for once again providing me with a home away from home in eastern Montana; Dick Hutto, for inspiring a love of birding and for his go-to information on wood-peckers, warblers, and other families of birds; Andy Weiss for her friendship and introducing us to the wonders of Carmel Valley; Craig Himmelwright and Adrianne Waite for taking me birding for the very first time and helping make Braden's first birding journey to California memorable; Debi Shearwater (www.shearwaterjourneys.com) and her guides for answering questions and continuing to provide some of the best pelagic birding outings anywhere; NOAA contractor Sophie De Beukelaer for clarifying chumming policies inside Monterey Bay National Marine Sanctuary; Richard Gibbons of the Houston Audubon Society (www.houstonaudubon.org) for answering my questions about High Island; Kumaran Arul for leading us on our excellent, record-breaking transect of California; Bonnie Bedford-White for showing me my first Wilson's Snipe; Rhonda Sancibrian for inviting me to an unforgettable week in Merced; and Roger and Claudia Kohn, and Eric and Geoffrey Dawson, for indulging the strange new passions of their longtime friend.

I'd like to acknowledge the Montana Arts Council, which is funded by the State of Montana and the National Endowment for the Arts. Its support for writers and artists throughout the state helps make Montana a richer, more vibrant, and smarter place to live—and proves yet again that government can and should play a vital role in all our lives.

Finally, my warm thanks to the many editors and staff working for and at Mountaineers Books for believing in this book and devoting so much time and effort to making it sing.

about the author

Before beginning his writing career, Sneed B. Collard III graduated with honors in marine biology from the University of California at Berkeley. Afterward, he worked as a field biologist before earning a master's degree in scientific instrumentation from UC, Santa Barbara. Since the publication of his first two books in 1993, Sneed has written more than eighty books for young people.

To research his books, Sneed has traveled to Australia, Costa Rica, Southeast Asia, South America, and the deep-sea floor. His books have been featured on Junior Library Guild and NSTA-CBC Outstanding Science Trade Books lists and have won numerous awards. In 2006, he received the *Washington Post*–Children's Book Guild Award for Nonfiction for his body of work.

A popular, award-winning speaker, Sneed visits dozens of schools and conferences around the United States every year. He also teaches workshops for students, teachers, and other writers. Sneed is the author of nine novels.

When he is not writing, speaking, or teaching, Sneed enjoys bicycling with his daughter Tessa, traveling with his family, and, of course, birding. He and his son, Braden, write a weekly birding blog at www.fathersonbirding.com. Sneed lives in Missoula, Montana. Learn more about him at www.sneedbcollardiii.com and www.buckinghorsebooks.com.

recreation • lifestyle • conservation

MOUNTAINEERS BOOKS is a leading publisher of mountaineering literature and guides—including our flagship title, *Mountaineering: The Freedom of the Hills*—as well as adventure narratives, natural history, and general outdoor recreation. Through our two imprints, Skipstone and Braided River, we also publish titles on sustainability and conservation. We are committed to supporting the environmental and educational goals of our organization by providing expert information on human-powered adventure, sustainable practices at home and on the trail, and preservation of wilderness.

The Mountaineers, founded in 1906, is a 501(c)(3) nonprofit outdoor recreation and conservation organization whose mission is to enrich lives and communities by helping people "explore, conserve, learn about, and enjoy the lands and waters of the Pacific Northwest and beyond." One of the largest such organizations in the United States, it sponsors classes and year-round outdoor activities throughout the Pacific Northwest, including climbing, hiking, backcountry skiing, snowshoeing, camping, kayaking, sailing, and more. The Mountaineers also supports its mission through its publishing division, Mountaineers Books, and promotes environmental education and citizen engagement. For more information, visit The Mountaineers Program Center, 7700 Sand Point Way NE, Seattle, WA 98115-3996; phone 206-521-6001; www.mountaineers.org; or email info@mountaineers.org.

Our publications are made possible through the generosity of donors and through sales of more than 800 titles on outdoor recreation, sustainable lifestyle, and conservation. To donate, purchase books, or learn more, visit us online:

MOUNTAINEERS BOOKS
1001 SW Klickitat Way, Suite 201 • Seattle, WA 98134
800-553-4453 • mbooks@mountaineersbooks.org • www.mountaineersbooks.org

OTHER TITLES YOU MIGHT ENJOY FROM MOUNTAINEERS BOOKS

OWL
A Year in the Lives of North American Owls
Paul Bannick

THE LIVING BIRD
100 Years of
Listening to Nature
Cornell Lab of Ornithology
Photography by Gerrit Vyn
Foreword by Barbara Kingsolver

THE OWL AND THE WOODPECKER
Encounters with North America's
Most Iconic Birds
Paul Bannick
Foreword by Tony Angell
Audio recordings by Martyn Stewart

RARE BIRD
Pursuing the Mystery of
the Marbled Murrelet
Maria Mudd Ruth

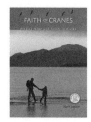

FAITH OF CRANES
Finding Hope and Family in Alaska
Hank Lentfer

www.mountaineersbooks.org